Representing Reason

Representing Reason

Feminist Theory and Formal Logic

Edited by
Rachel Joffe Falmagne
and Marjorie Hass

ROWMAN & LITTLEFIELD PUBLISHERS, INC.
Lanham • Boulder • New York • Oxford

ROWMAN & LITTLEFIELD PUBLISHERS, INC.

Published in the United States of America
by Rowman & Littlefield Publishers, Inc.
A Member of the Rowman & Littlefield Publishing Group
4720 Boston Way, Lanham, Maryland 20706
www.rowmanlittlefield.com

12 Hid's Copse Road
Cumnor Hill, Oxford OX2 9JJ, England

British Library Cataloguing in Publication Information Available

Library of Congress Cataloging-in-Publication Data

Representing reason : feminist theory and formal logic / edited by Rachel Joffe Falmagne and Marjorie Hass.
p. cm.
Includes bibliographical references and index.
ISBN 0-8476-9668-5 (alk. paper)—ISBN 0-8476-9669-3 (pbk. : alk. paper)
1. Logic. 2. Feminist theory. I. Falmagne, Rachel Joffe. II. Hass, Marjorie, 1965–
BC57 .R47 2002
160' .82—dc21

2002006968

Printed in the United States of America

∞™ The paper used in this publication meets the minimum requirements of American National Standard for Information Sciences—Permanence of Paper for Printed Library Materials, ANSI/NISO Z39.48-1992.

Contents

Acknowledgments

Many people helped to make this book possible. The editors would particularly like to thank Linda Nicholson and Sandra Harding for their enthusiastic encouragement and Jeff Della Rovere for his editorial assistance. Marjorie Hass appreciates the dialogues she has established with Lawrence Hass, Tim McCarthy, and Sally Tramel and thanks them for their ongoing intellectual and emotional encouragement. She also thanks Susan Seip for her many contributions to the production of the manuscript. Rachel wishes to thank the Five College Women's Studies Research Center for providing a stimulating interdisciplinary feminist context during the early years of this project, as well as Ann Ferguson, Kristin Waters, Linda Dusman, and Diane Bell for broad-ranging discussions across disciplines over the years and for their support of this work. Rachel also thanks the graduate participants in the informal feminist discussion group at Clark for their intellectually and personally valuable contributions to her thinking, in particular Emily Abbey, Christina Hatgis, Marie-Geneviève Iselin, Saeromi Kim, and Abigail Mansfield. Finally, we would like to thank our editors at Rowman and Littlefield: Maureen MacGrogan, who initially enthusiastically accepted the book; Eve DeVaro, who saw it through to the end; and Erin McKindley, who supervised the publishing process. A summer research grant from Muhlenberg College made it possible for Marjorie Hass to write her contribution to this volume. Rachel Joffe Falmagne's contribution and editorial work was supported by a three-year grant from the Spencer Foundation.

We acknowledge with thanks permission to reprint the following material:

"The Politics of Reason: Towards a Feminist Logic" by Val Plumwood. Reprinted with permission of the publisher from *Australasian Journal of Philosophy* 71, no. 4 (1993): 436–462.

"'Power in the Service of Love': John Dewey's *Logic* and the Dream of a Common Language" by Carroll Guen Hart. Reprinted with permission of the author and the publisher from *Hypatia* 8, no. 2 (Spring 1993): 190–214.

"Logic from a Quinean Perspective: An Empirical Enterprise" by Lynn Hankinson Nelson and Jack Nelson. Reprinted with permission of the author and publisher from *On Quine* (Belmont, Calif.: Wadsworth, 2000).

"'What Do Girls Know Anyway?' Rationality, Gender, and Social Control" by Pam Oliver. Reprinted with permission of the publisher from *Feminism and Psychology* 1, no. 3 (1991): 339–360.

INTRODUCTION

~

Representing Reason: Feminist Theory and Formal Logic

MARJORIE HASS AND RACHEL JOFFE FALMAGNE

This volume brings together recent essays addressing feminist issues in formal logic and logical issues in feminist theory. As the first volume with this specific focus, it places itself in a contested terrain. Among logicians, the thought that feminism might have something of value to say about formal logic is usually treated with skepticism if not dismissal. The convergence of feminism and logic may also be met with skepticism among some feminists who perceive the projects of feminism to be aimed at more pressing political concerns than the problematics of abstract theory.

It is our hope that this collection will dissipate those preconceptions. The chapters to follow reveal that many core concepts at issue in recent feminist theorizing and in philosophical logic overlap. The thematic center of the volume is the relationship between our informal assumptions about concepts such as difference, identity, and generality and our efforts to produce precise, formal representations of these concepts. It is here that feminist theory and philosophical logic engage most fruitfully.

Feminist theory has long argued that the exclusion of women from philosophical work was more than simply a matter of unfair treatment. When feminist activism made it possible for women to be "added" into theory, the full impact of their prior exclusion was finally revealed. This exclusion, in terms of the exclusion of both women thinkers from the academy and women's lives from philosophical consideration, was persuasively shown to undermine the presumed neutrality of many of philosophy's most cherished assumptions in areas ranging from political theory to ethics.

During the 1980s and 1990s, feminist philosophers extended their critiques of this traditional exclusion beyond the political sphere and into the bastions of science studies, informal logic, and epistemology. In a series of influential books and articles, the traditional stance of the man of reason (independent, neutral, and unemotional) was shown to be an illusory ideal, made possible only when fundamental features of human nature were bracketed and then dismissed as "womanly."[1] Far from identifying a special "feminine" way of knowing or a segregated woman-specific theoretic framework, this new work revealed the extent to which what philosophy had always attributed to women (particularly the specific limitations of embodiment) were in fact the property of every human being. Moreover, the traditional dichotomy between the man of reason and the emotional woman would need to be rethought in terms of a more complex single human subject, able to reason *and* feel, to exist independently *and* in relation. The scope of this work has revitalized epistemology, informal logic, and science studies, raising new and more complex questions about the nature of knowledge for these newly discovered embodied and perspectival knowers.

At the same time, the desegregation of the subject's attributes made possible a deeper analysis of the nature of sex and gender differences. Feminists were increasingly convinced that there were crucial differences between men and women and that these differences made a difference in the way that men and women theorized the world, albeit not in the ways that the philosophical tradition presumed. Two lines of work emerged. The first, grounded largely in Continental thought, suggested that the relevant differences between men and women emerged from the unconscious effects of their differing bodily configurations.[2] The second, drawing from an interdisciplinary body of feminist theorizing and, within philosophy, loosely associated with an analytic tradition, posited philosophical differences as emerging from the difference in perspective that accompanied positions of relative privilege or oppression.[3] Each of these traditions sought ways of understanding and modeling difference that exposed difference as potentially radical yet positive. Difference was to be theorized in a way that did not automatically demote one member of the differential pair while privileging the other. In a corresponding manner, new models of identity and generality began to emerge, also seeking to remedy limitations in traditional theories. Tensions between and within these emergent schools have produced a rich body of new feminist work that problematizes the very nature of difference and identity and its empirical foundation.

From this perspective, it is not surprising that feminists would turn their attention to formal logic. Logic reveals philosophy's most exact attempts to understand these concepts. Moreover, it serves a normative function as well, legislating the extension of these terms and holding up for us a model of how we *ought* to think. Andrea Nye's groundbreaking book *Words of Power: A Feminist Reading of the History of Logic* isolated this normative role, arguing that formal logic has historically functioned to legitimize the discursive patterns of the powerful and suppress the forms of speaking that might offer methods of resistance to exploitative power systems.[4] She indicted the very desire for a logical theory as an instantiation of the desire for power and control. The controversial nature of Nye's reading of the history of logic, and the consequent breadth of her charges against formal renderings of disputed concepts, inspired both thought-provoking and dismissive critiques. Although none of the authors in this volume (including Nye herself) echo Nye's early call for a dismantling of formal logic in favor of fully informal interpretations of inference, the influence of her book—the first to offer a specifically feminist critique of the desire for abstract logical representation—is still widely apparent.

The hope that informal logic would offer an unproblematic alternative to the perceived biases of formal logic has also been disrupted. As shown in a series of articles in *Informal Logic*, informal or critical thinking provides standards for reasoning that are open to biased application.[5] Trudy Govier has argued that even norms for reasoning that appear neutral and universal on the surface can be applied in ways that serve to silence those deemed to be outside the sphere of rhetorical credibility. If it is a mistake exclusively to single out abstraction or formalism per se as the instrument of epistemic oppression, then a deeper analysis of the language and structure of formal logic becomes necessary. More generally, we believe that internal critique is essential to the project of feminism and that criticism must inhabit the territory it critiques even as it presses urgently for a breach in the configuration of that territory.[6]

Logic is, most generally, the study of validity and the methods for determining whether a valid inference can be made from a given set of sentences to some other sentence. Broadly speaking, formal logic aims at providing an account of those validity relations that are established simply in virtue of the form or structure of the sentences. Logical theories typically identify a set of logical operations with which to represent the basic form of a sentence. It is, of course, important to recognize the great diversity of views about logic that exist among logicians themselves. There is no uniformly accepted thesis about the ultimate ground of validity or about the precedence that should be accorded syntactic versus semantic theories of validity. Nevertheless, the standard formal system yields an interpretation of such central logical concepts as negation, generality, and identity. These standard presentations depict these operations in ways that are taken as normative—that is, expressing the way that these concepts *ought* to be understood.

In part 1 of this collection, the authors respond to the role these formal concepts play in deliminating and representing the language of thought. A common theme is an insistence on differentiating between logic per se and particular logical systems. While the authors in this section are critical of specific concepts that emerge in standard formal logic, each is cognizant that alternative formalizations may provide more accurate or more useful conceptual frameworks. The first three chapters present efforts to theorize the differences between men and women in ways that do not presuppose an essential hierarchy or dependency. In each case, the authors expose the problematic effects of adopting the standard logic for negation as a model of difference. Val Plumwood, in a widely influential essay, argues that feminist philosophers must seek a logical language capable of accurately representing gender difference and differences among other human groups. She shows that the negation operator of standard formal logic models a dualistic and hierarchical form of difference and, as such, cannot be taken up by feminists as a paradigm for understanding the nature of otherness. Rather than indicting logic, Plumwood contrasts the standard negation operator with one embedded in relevance logic, an alternative formal system. Here, she argues, we may find a model of difference consistent with feminism. In contrast to this first project, Plumwood's second essay uses logical distinctions to map the difficult terrain of feminist theories of difference. By carefully distinguishing among forms of difference, Plumwood refutes attempts by some feminist theorists to identify dichotomous thinking with oppressive thinking.

Marjorie Hass addresses the limitations of logical concepts, including negation, by illuminating the ongoing critique of these terms in the work of Luce Irigaray. In Hass's view, Irigaray's work calls the neutrality of logic into question, suggesting that the standard formalism is capable of expressing only distorted and partial interpretations of negation, identity, and generality. More specifically, in Irigaray's work, standard symbolic logic is shown to be unable to represent the form of difference proper to sexual difference, the form of identity proper to feminine identity, and the form of generality proper to a feminine generic. Hass interprets and evaluates Irigaray's critique of logic, arguing that many of Irigaray's readers have misunderstood its nature and force.

Carroll Guen Hart's chapter aims at rehabilitating the logical conception of universality by reframing it in terms of a Deweyan logic. Feminist worries that universality is only maintained at the expense of an eradication of relevant differences or a marginalization of those perceived as different are shown to be less pressing when universality is conceived in Deweyan terms as functionalized and relativized. With this Deweyan understanding, Hart suggests that feminist action can be understood as aimed at furthering the well-being of women in general.

Concluding this section, Dorothea Olkowski's chapter offers an analysis of the need to develop a logic of sense. Drawing on the work of Gilles Deleuze, Olkowski defends formal logic against feminist theorists who have urged that we organize thinking around the principles of embodiment. She warns us against the complete merging of bodily functions and sense-making activities. In Olkowski's view, feminists need to acknowledge the usefulness of logical analyses at the same time that they must insist on formal systems that reflect and are tempered by human and humane values.

In part 2, the authors focus on the relationship between formal models of inference and empirical knowledge. A thematic thread through these analyses, which address knowledge of both the social and the natural world, concerns the nature of that relationship. Chapters in this section address various aspects of this problematic when considering the epistemic function of logic as one instrument of scientific knowledge, its objective to model thought, or the political ramifications of its normative status, yet the authors are in general agreement that an intrinsic relation exists between logic and the empirical world, whether on epistemic or political grounds. The first two chapters reinforce one another synergistically in arguing on their respective grounds that logic and, in particular, feminist logical models are part of an extended empirical enterprise.

Rachel Joffe Falmagne and Marie-Geneviève Iselin maintain that the critical and reconstructive project of developing feminist models of inference necessitates a transdisciplinary approach in which philosophically based modes of analysis and empirically based research inform one another dialectically and are integrated methodologically. They caution against the political danger of disciplinary isolationism, and they highlight the dialectic between empirical research on thinking and feminist theory construction. While the authors stress that empirical data grounded in the social world must inform feminist models of inference, they foreground the epistemological ambiguities concerning the nature of that relation.

Lynn Hankinson Nelson and Jack Nelson extend the work begun in the former's book *Who Knows: From Quine to a Feminist Empiricism*, by showing that a Quinean understanding of logic as an empirical field implies that logic remains open to revision in light of fundamental shifts in knowledge. Nelson and Nelson point to the revisions in scientific understandings made possible by the incorporation of women and women's lives as emblematic of the possible ways that feminist thought can provide a deep reworking of the structures of knowledge and thus potentially of logic. Although they are cautious of any conclusions that logic *must* change, their work offers a theoretical ground from which the effects of feminist theorizing on logic can be usefully explored.

From a different philosophical starting point but with an import converging with that of Nelson and Nelson, Andrea Nye is also concerned with the role of logic in science, linking the adequacy of logic with its applicability in a domain of scientific knowledge. Nye argues that the dominant predicate logic cannot adequately represent the issues surrounding attempts to divide organisms into species. Feminist critiques of the extensional theory of meaning lay the ground for alternative theories of categorization. Without renewed models of categorization, Nye submits, science is in danger of becoming a self-enclosed "logical" system, rather than an instrumental model of reality. This section ends with Pam Oliver's investigation of the political and epistemic consequences of associating rationality with the rules of formal logic. She argues that this association builds in a bias in favor of masculine dominance and that it is only when we acknowledge that rationality exceeds logic that women can equally serve as models of rational humanity.

One further purpose of this volume will, we hope, become clear. The chapters here cross over many of the traditional divides between continental and analytic philosophy, between philosophical reflection and empirical investigation, and between empirical investigations with an individual or a societal grain of analysis. The value of a multiplicity of approaches and perspectives is made possible by the framing of the relationship between logic and feminism in terms of issues rather than historical figures or methodologies. It is our hope that this collection will serve as a stimulus to further research on the underexplored intersection of logic and feminism and a model for the value of crossing these boundaries.

Notes

1. A very partial list of this body of work includes Sandra Harding and Merrill B. Hintikka, eds., *Discovering Reality: Feminist Perspectives on Epistemology, Metaphysics, Methodology, and Philosophy of Science* (Dordecht: Reidel, 1983); Alison Jaggar and Susan Bordo, eds., *Gender/Body/Knowledge: Feminist Reconstructions of Being and Knowing* (New Brunswick, N.J.: Rutgers University Press, 1989); Genevieve Lloyd, *The Man of Reason: "Male" and "Female" in Western Philosophy* (Minneapolis: University of Minnesota Press, 1984); Lorraine Code, *What Can She Know? Feminist*

Theory and the Construction of Knowledge (Ithaca, N.Y.: Cornell University Press, 1991); Louise M. Antony and Charlotte Witt, eds., *A Mind of One's Own: Feminist Essays on Reason and Objectivity* (Boulder, Colo.: Westview, 1993). Books that focus specifically on science include Ruth Hubbard, *The Politics of Women's Biology* (New Brunswick, N.J.: Rutgers University Press, 1990); Nancy Tuana, ed., *Feminism and Science* (Bloomington: Indiana University Press, 1989); Nancy Tuana, *The Less Noble Sex* (Bloomington: Indiana University Press, 1993).

2. Works in this tradition include Sandra Lee Bartky, *Femininity and Domination: Studies in the Phenomenology of Oppression* (New York: Routledge, 1990); Luce Irigaray, *An Ethics of Sexual Difference*, trans. Carolyn Burke and Gillian C. Gill (Ithaca, N.Y.: Cornell University Press, 1993); Elizabeth Grosz, *Volatile Bodies: Toward a Corporeal Feminism* (Bloomington: Indiana University Press, 1994); Naomi Schor and Elizabeth Weed, eds., *The Essential Difference* (Bloomington: Indiana University Press, 1994).

3. Works in this tradition include Marilyn Frye, *The Politics of Reality: Essays in Feminist Theory* (Freedom, Calif.: Crossing, 1983); Sara Ruddick, *Maternal Thinking: Towards a Politics of Peace* (Boston: Beacon, 1989); Sandra Harding, *Whose Science? Whose Knowledge?* (Ithaca, N.Y.: Cornell University Press, 1991).

4. Andrea Nye, *Words of Power: A Feminist Reading of the History of Logic* (New York: Routledge, 1990).

5. Including Karen Warren, "Critical Thinking and Feminism," *Informal Logic* 10, no. (Winter 1988); Trudy Govier, "When Logic Meets Politics: Testimony, Distrust, and Rhetorical Disadvantage," *Informal Logic* 15, no. 2 (Spring 1993); Sandra Menssen, "Do Women and Men Use Different Logics? A Reply to Carol Gilligan and Deborah Orr," *Informal Logic* 15, no. 2 (Spring 1993).

6. Elizabeth Wilson, *Neural Geographies: Feminism and the Microstructure of Cognition* (London: Routledge, 1998).

PART ONE

LOGIC AND THE STRUCTURE OF THOUGHT

CHAPTER ONE

~

The Politics of Reason: Toward a Feminist Logic

VAL PLUMWOOD

> For efficient subordination, what's wanted is that the structure not only not appear to be a cultural artifact kept in place by human decision or custom, but that it appear natural—that it appear to be a quite direct consequence of the facts about the beast which are beyond the scope of human manipulation or revision. It must seem natural that individuals of the one category are dominated by individuals of the other and that as groups, the one dominates the other. (13, p. 34)

The Possibility of a Feminist Logic

From Plato and Aristotle to Kant and beyond, the philosophical tradition of the West has delineated a concept of reason which is exclusive of women and other oppressed groups and is most fully represented by privileged social groups. For Plato, it is those who represent reason (the Guardians) who should rule over the other elements in the state, just as in the individual reason itself should rule over the body and the passions. Aristotle explicitly conceives the social and natural orders in terms of a rational meritocracy in which the rule of men over women, of masters over slaves, of Greek over barbarian, and of humans over animals is justified and naturalized by the supposed possession by the inferiorized side of each of these pairs of a lesser degree of reason (2, *Politics*, Book 1, chs. 4–5). For Kant, it is not only women who are excluded from reason by their possession of a gallantly presented but clearly inferiorized "beautiful understanding" (36), but also workers (36, p. 9), and blacks, the latter being ascribed an inferiority "as great in regard to mental capacities as in color" (35, p. 111). Modern social conceptions continue to treat reason as naturalizing the domination of ruling elites; thus the British colonial governor of Egypt, Lord Cromer, remarks about his Oriental subjects:

> The European is a close reasoner; his statements of fact are devoid of any ambiguity; he is a natural logician, albeit he may not have studied logic; he is by nature sceptical and requires proof before he can accept the truth of any proposition; his trained intelligence works like a piece of mechanism. The mind of the Oriental, on the other hand, like his picturesque streets, is eminently wanting in symmetry. His reasoning is of the most slipshod description. Although the ancient Arabs acquired in a somewhat higher degree the science of dialectics, their descendants are singularly deficient in the logical faculty. They are often incapable of drawing the most obvious conclusion from any simple premises of which they admit the truth. Endeavour to elicit a plain statement of facts from any ordinary Egyptian. His explanation will generally be lengthy and wanting in lucidity. He will probably contradict himself half-a-dozen times before he has finished his story. He will often break down under the mildest process of cross-examination. (Quoted in [68, p. 38])

It would be naive indeed to assume that these conceptions of ruling reason are merely "abuses" of a basically neutral concept, ideas about reason which have no impact on the construction of reason itself, but have been entirely accidental and extraneous to it. It has been the task of feminist philosophers particularly to show how the historical construction of reason as masculine has structured its dominant forms not only in an exclusive and oppositional relation to women, but to the characteristics and areas of life they have been taken to represent, such as emotionality, bodiliness, animality, and particularity (48; 46; 5; 25; 27). Other feminist philosophers have shown how conceptions of women and other oppressed groups as outside reason and as associated with the emotions, the body and animality are reflected in the dominant accounts of scientific objectivity and rationality (12; 5; 37; 26; 27; 23). The formal discipline of logic has been seen as the highest expression of reason; it is the form of reason whose practice has excluded and marginalized women to an even greater extent than science and philosophy (54). Although logic is usually assumed to be a paradigm of neutrality, the work of feminist philosophers has suggested that even logic has been shaped by these relations of domination (34; 28; 54; 61), a claim I will help to support here. Most feminist critics of reason have not argued for its complete rejection. Indeed many have explicitly argued against this strategy, and nearly all have opted for alternative development, the reconstruction or reworking of reason in less problematic and oppositional forms, as well as for a limitation of its role and a reduction of its traditional pretensions to constitute the ruling element in human identity and social relations (60; 61). It is only in the case of logic that feminist analyses (71; 54) have advocated complete rejection and abandonment, of formal and informal logic alike, as a sphere of unlimited abstraction and contest for mastery of the other (71, p. 199).

My argument in this chapter supports the contrary view that, as in the case of other areas of reason, feminists and others concerned to develop conceptual structures which can be tools of liberation need not abandon the field of logic entirely, and advocates the more moderate strategy of reworking, including critical scrutiny of dominant forms combined with awareness and development of alternatives based on engaged reason. As a preliminary to developing this argument, I shall examine more closely the basis for Nye's view that there can be no reform of logic, that logic can have no liberatory uses for feminists (54, pp. 175, 179) and is best expunged from human knowledge systems. Nye's condemnation of logic, which extends not only to the study of logic (both formal and informal) but to the disambiguation of concepts and the whole idea of logical fallacies, is part of the aggressive contemporary movement of the literary paradigm against other disciplines, especially philosophy. Thus Nye's concluding proposal for the development of a vaguely specified discipline of "reading" as an alternative to close philosophical reasoning (54, p. 183) appears to involve the elimination of much of what is distinctive about philosophy and its reduction to some form of literary studies. Nye's principal charges against logic are threefold:

1. The development of logic as a tool of social hierarchy and exclusion.
2. The abstract character of logic, the disengagement of the syllogism and the creation by logicians of artificial forms of language, which presuppose and create "relations between speakers which are alien to feminist aims" (54, p. 179).
3. The attempt to replace language by a unitary authority, its normative and "silencing" role in relation to other forms of speech, and its association with reductive programs such as logical positivism.

I shall consider these in turn.

Our understanding of the social context and construction of reason has been immeasurably advanced by the work of feminist scholars such as Lloyd and Nye. Nye's important book *Words of Power* contributes many insights about the social framework in which the classical concepts of reason and logic have developed. As Nye shows, in this context "the rationality of those who are natural rulers is continually defined in opposition to other unacceptable speech: the emotional expressions of women, the subrational words of slaves, the primitive political views of barbarians, the tainted opinions of anyone who does manual labour" (54, p. 50). However, most of these oppressive social relations attributed by Nye exclusively to logic, especially in the ancient context, can with greater justice be attributed to the broader concept of reason itself; the term "reason" would be the usual translation of many of the passages lauding logic Nye cites. It is ruling reason, and not just or even primarily logic, which is conceived in terms of opposition to a lower conceptual, material, and social order. Thus "the refusal of the physical world of generation and change" (54, p. 180), the desire for permanence and purity, is at least equally that of classical philosophy and classical conceptions of reason. It often seems as if Nye's use of the term "logic" over the alternative "reason" has an arbitrary component, and that "logic" is the term used for whatever is held to be objectionable in reason. But if the historical context of oppressive social relations which has also affected reason, does not entail abandoning, as opposed to reconstructing, reason (as Nye herself suggests in her conclusion it does not), why does it make a case for abandoning logic, as opposed to critically reconstructing it and making much more limited claims for it?

The answer must lie in the additional features of logic, its abstractness as well as its normative role. Both Nye and Walkerdine (71, p. 199) see logic as a sphere of unlimited abstraction and contest for mastery of the other. For Nye and Walkerdine, these features are inseparable from logic, so that logic can only coopt feminists: according to Nye "the feminist logician speaks from a script in which the master always wins" (54, p. 180). Nye makes the case against abstraction in strong terms, objecting to the social relations of disengagement and separation from experience she believes to be involved in any abstract or artificial language: "Desperate, lonely, cut off from the human community which in many cases has ceased to exist, under the sentence of violent death, wracked by desires for intimacy they do not know how to fulfil, at the same time tormented by the presence of women, men turn to logic" (54, p. 175)—a more suitable description, one might think, for the average alcoholic than the average logician. Certainly abstraction *can* be a retreat: the overriding value and role accorded abstraction and reason in classical philosophy reflects the devaluation of the sphere of the household, the domain of women, slaves and animals in an elite, male-dominated culture. But an analysis which makes an invariant claim of this kind about abstraction and then extends it to the motivation of each individual logician is both over-individualized and over-generalized. Although feminist worldviews have stressed the particular in contrast to the abstract (15; 16; 17) and feminists are, I believe, right to critique the dangers and high pretensions of abstraction and the inferiorization of particularity in philosophical traditions, can we really insist that *all* uses of language be grounded in personal experience, the testimony of the witness, and "the normality of human interchange that logic refuses" (54, p. 176)? Who, I begin to ask at this stage, is silencing whom? The area of intellectual activity potentially destroyed by such a program to eliminate abstraction and anything which departs from "normal" language begins to look alarmingly large—not only mathematics (which can be derived from logic and involves a similar level of abstraction) and large areas of science, but "computer programming, statistics, economic models . . ." (54, p. 181) and no doubt a great deal more we might not want to lose.[1] Such total rejection of abstraction would involve a program highly restrictive of thought.

A counterargument might be made that the inferiorization of the sphere of particularity and personal experience does not arise from the operations of abstraction and universalization in themselves, but from a particular set of philosophical and social doctrines *about* abstraction and universalization that those engaged in these operations can be encouraged to reject. If this is so, the rejection of abstract disciplines is unnecessary and does not address the real issues. The assumption that feminism can afford to jettison logical theories implicitly assumes that there is no problematic politics (other than the general politics attributed to logic and abstraction itself) involved in dominant logical theory and structures. If this hidden assumption of the political neutrality and unity of logic is incorrect, the most likely result of the suppression of critical logical discussion would be the implicit use of dominant accounts without critical examination. The failure to address the area could then leave significant aud influential sources of domination uncriticized and untheorized, and inhibit the development of alternative modes of thought. The most important objection to Nye's preoccupation with abstraction then is that it is a diversion, that while we are thus focused upon its supposed evils, the really damaging structures of thought the legacy of ruling reason has handed down to us—especially, as I will show next, those of instrumental and colonizing forms of rationality which dominate much modern thought in political and economic areas—get away unrecognized and unchallenged. These forms of rationality, which are both broader and narrower than logic and are not closely tied to abstraction, often seem to be the real target of Nye's attack on logic (e.g., 54, p. 181), but they are nowhere clearly identified in the text. In identifying them, as I shall also show next, some forms of logic can be of assistance.

Social Selection and the Diversity of Logic

The remaining part of the case against the possibility of a liberatory logic rests on the supposed claims of logic to authority over language, to the role of universal law, to be the monolithic core of language, and on the normative and silencing role it is allowed to play in relation to speakers and forms of speech judged less adequate. But are these really features of all possible forms of logic, or are they rather results of particular, perhaps dominant, conceptions of the role of logic? Certainly it is possible to do logic and to strongly reject the doctrines and aims of reductive philosophical programs such as logical positivism which Nye treats as the culmination of logical thought: logical positivism as a program involving logic bears approximately the same relation to logic as scientism does to science, and is actively in conflict with certain kinds of logic, such as modal and intensional logic. There are modern logicians who see logic as playing the role of follower rather than leader in relation to natural language, who reject the idea of logic as providing universal "laws of thought" (55), and who would see both logic and reason as playing a much more limited role than that ascribed to them in rationalist traditions of thought.

But it is the enormous diversity of modern logic, perhaps its most striking feature in comparison with the logic of the past, which does most to refute Nye's claims about the totalitarian politics inherent in logic and its inevitably normative and "silencing" role. If there is not one Logic, but in fact many different logics, if logics can be constructed which can tolerate even contradiction itself (63), logic itself can have no silencing role and no unitary authority over language. Nye's account itself *constructs* logic as a monolithic unity, not only by stopping the historical discussion at Frege[2] and ignoring the plurality of logics which is the most revolutionary feature of modern treatments, but by suppressing the existence of logical dissent and multiplicity in her account of the logical discussion of both the present and the past.[3] Thus the great debate around the issue of implication which has raged not only in contemporary logic but around the interpretation of the ideas of Boethius, Zeno, and Abelard (69; 65) does not rate a mention in her account of their work, or of logic generally. In these parts of her historical account, Nye follows the establishment histories of (64; 41; 47), histories which create an illusion of unity out a reality of diversity by reading the dominant contemporary accounts of implication back into the past (69) and discounting dissent in the present. But as in other areas of knowledge there are competing and contested accounts of reason, and correspondingly of logical systems. Given the actual diversity of logics, a key question in any political critique of logic is how and why this diversity has been obscured, but we cannot confront this crucial question within the framework of an indiscriminate rejection of logic.

Part of the answer to this key question, as I suggest below, lies in a set of social selection processes operating to favor dominant forms of logic, processes which reveal clearly the "fingerprints of the social" (in Sandra Harding's telling phrase) in logic and which give the lie to the widespread idea that logic occupies a pure realm beyond social engagement. The construction of logic as a monolith, in which undiscriminating types of feminist critique collude, is precisely what has permitted formal logical systems and principles to be considered value free and to escape serious social criticism or examination. In the context of the modern plurality of logics, a blanket rejection of logic on account of its abstraction and singularity removes the basis for any useful feminist critique, beyond these very problematic and general grounds of abstraction and singularity themselves. Once the plurality of logical systems has been acknowledged, feminist and other social critique can be more discriminating in its response to logics, and begin an exploration of the way in which different logical systems correspond to different forms of rationality. We can begin to understand systems of logic and their corresponding systems of rationality as *selected*, in much the same way that scientific theories are selected. I shall show that an understanding of the way selection has operated to privilege certain of these forms of rationality has much to contribute to an understanding of the deep roots of phallocentrism and other oppressive conceptual structures in Western thought, and that we can find in the selection of logical systems the same marks of elite perspectives which have been widely demonstrated elsewhere for supposedly neutral and universal forms of knowledge. These influences are to be found especially in the privileging and presentation as "intuitive" or "normal" of certain accounts of negation, especially the negation of classical logic.

The plurality of logics has made it possible for symbolic logic to provide and investigate not one but very many accounts of negation, of which certain ones (normally that negation which is derived from the system of classical logic) are selected by influential logical theorists as corresponding to what they take to be the standard, natural, and normal negation of ordinary speech and thought. But accounts of negation can be seen as providing, at a very abstract level, certain structures and principles for conceiving and treating otherness (34), the other which is not self, whatever self may be. Once this natural and obvious interpretation of negation is made, the illusion of the timelessness and political neutrality of logic vanishes, for as I shall show, even abstract accounts of otherness are far from being philosophically and politically neutral. The relationship of systems of logic to social structures may instead be seen as similar to the relationship of technology and of scientific theories to these structures. Many recent theorists have helped expose the social influences and social relations in the selection of technology and of scientific theories (42; 44; 22; 23; 24; 26; 37; 45; 51; 76; 77). Many mechanisms have been identified which can help account for the social construction of theory and the effect of social relations in technology selection. One basic mechanism involves a form of reciprocal selection in which those theories and technologies are selected from an adequate group which accord with and help to naturalize certain dominant social structures. These selected theories in turn help to fix, extend, and perpetuate social relations of domination (77).

The appearance of singularity and the dominance of classical logic may thus represent the results of theory selection and construction to validate, reflect and theoretically express certain worldviews implying principles of relationship to the other. I shall show that perspectives naturalizing an account of the other in terms of dualism and domination have had a great deal to do with which principles and accounts of negation have been viewed as "normal," "intuitive," and worthy of investigation and teaching, and which have been viewed as "deviant" and of formal or specialist interest only. I shall suggest that the structure of negation given by classical propositional logic—the dominant formal logical theory of our time—in particular has been privileged and selected over rivals on account of features which also make it appropriate to describe it as a logic of domination, features giving an account of the other in dualistic terms which naturalize their subordination. If theories of negation and of otherness are seen as linked to forms of rationality, this critique of dominant logics can be seen as extending and supporting the feminist and postmodernist critique of the phallocentrism of dominant forms of rationality (30; 46; 26).

An understanding of these areas can also extend and clarify feminist options for the deconstruction of dualized identity. In the following account I try to establish some of the abstract logical characteristics and principles of dualism, the structure of a general way of thinking about the other which expresses the perpective of a dominator or master identity, and thus might be called a logic of domination. This structure of thought is not just applicable to the domination of women, but applies to various groups of subordinated others. Feminism has had a good deal to say about the phallocentrism of Western thought, the way in which dominant conceptions of reason have excluded and denied dependency on the feminine and feminine-associated spheres of the body, nature, emotionality, reproduction, materiality and subsistence. But a broader concept than phallocentrism is needed because many of the key areas of exclusion are associated not only with women but with other subordinated groups such a slaves, the colonized, and with subordinated economic classes. Thus the exclusions of reason as conceived in the dominant traditions of Western thought express not a male but a master identity, and the ideology of the domination of nature by reason has been common to various forms of oppression. Women's oppression is not the only form of oppression to be reflected in this formation of reason, and feminist theorists have been joined by philosophers concerned with the black experience, racism, and colonialism in theorizing the principles for conceiving the other which arise from dualism.

Dualism, Difference, and Otherness

Both postmodernist philosophy and feminist philosophy have given a key role in their accounts of Western philosophy to the concept of binary opposition or dualism, the construction of a devalued and sharply demarcated sphere of otherness (67; 19; 18; 34; 9; 20; 31, p. 96; 30; 6; 70; 57; 58; 60; 21; 73; 74; 38; 39; 40; 28). Many feminists have pointed to the role of Western concepts of reason in excluding and inferiorizing the dualized contrast class of the feminine, nature, the emotions and various areas of human life counted as "irrational." The consideration of dualism and otherness in current concepts of reason has an important bearing on the feminist project of reconstructing reason in less oppositional ways. Accounts of the relation between self and other in terms of mutuality rather than in terms of dualism and domination have a key role in feminist ethics, political theory, and feminist psychology. However, this key concept for feminist thought stands in need of further investigation and clarification. A dualism, I argue, should be understood as a particular way of dividing the world which results from a certain kind of denied dependency on a subordinated other. This relationship of denied dependency determines a certain kind of logical structure, as one in which the denial and the relation of domination/subordination shapes the identity of both the relata. I use examples from a number of forms of oppression, especially gender, race, and class, to show what this structure is, and discuss its logical formulation.

Dualism can be seen as an alienated form of differentiation, in which power construes and constructs difference in terms of an inferior and alien realm. In random tyrannies, beings may be selected for oppression in arbitrary and random ways. But in systematized forms of power, power is normally institutionalized and "naturalized" by placing cultural constructions on existing forms of difference. Dualisms naturalize systems of domination and appropriation, and are their major cultural expressions and justifications.[4] Western thought and society has been characterized by a set of interrelated and mutually reinforcing dualisms which permeate culture, forming a fault line which runs through its entire conceptual system. Each of them has crucial connections to other elements, and has a common structure with other members of the set. The interrelationship of the elements of the structure means that the cultural meaning and characteristics of each of the elements of contrasting pairs is determined not in isolation but at least in part by the other members of the set. They should be seen as forming a system, an interlocking structure.

Key elements in the dualistic structure in Western thought are the contrasting pairs of culture/nature, reason/nature, male/female, mind/body, master/slave, reason/matter (physicality), rationality/animality, reason/emotion, mind (spirit)/nature, freedom/necessity, universal/particular, human/nature (non-human), civilized/primitive (nature), production/reproduction (nature), public/private, subject/object, self/other. I do not claim completeness for this list. Indeed, this is impossible, since any distinction can in principle be treated as having the structure which characterizes a dualism. But these dualisms are key ones for Western thought. The leading dualisms reflect the major forms of oppression in Western culture. Thus the dualisms of male/female, mental/manual (mind/body), civilized/primitive, human/nature correspond directly to and naturalize gender, class, race, and nature oppressions respectively, although a number of others are indirectly involved. Their development has been a historical process, following a historical sequence of evolution which is culturally specific. Thus dualisms such as reason/nature may be ancient, but others such as human/nature and subject/object are associated especially with modern, post-Enlightenment Western consciousness. But even the ancient forms do not necessarily fade away because their original content has changed, but are often preserved in our conceptual framework as residues, layers of sediment deposited by past oppressions. Culture thus accumulates a store of such conceptual weapons which can mined, refined, and redeployed for new uses. So old oppressions stored as dualisms facilitate and break the path for new.

Dualisms are not universal features of human thought, but conceptual responses to and foundations for social domination. An account of their development would also be an account of the development of institutionalized power, and for prehistory would necessarily be speculative. Consider Maria Mies's historical hypothesis concerning the origins of domination, according to which male hunting bands evolve into proto-military forces, living first off women's work as agricultural and subsistence laborers and then acquiring slaves from other tribes not thus militarily organized in a positive feedback process of accumulation (52, pp. 64–65). Such a process might give rise initially to such dualisms as sacred/profane (where male or chiefly power is religiously sanctioned), male/female, and master/slave. Later stages of the accumulation process would see the developmeat of new forms, often produced as nuances, new inflexions of older forms. Thus the period of colonial conquest in the West from the Fourteenth Century onwards brings to the fore civilized/primitive as a variant of reason/nature and of reason/animal and mind/body, and the rise of science brings to the fore subject/object dualism (5).

The exclusions of reason, as the principal concept representative of ruling elites in this process of forming dualisms, are thus multiple and not reducible to the exclusion of women. Nevertheless gender plays a key role, since gender ideals especially involve ideals of reason (46; 62), and women have often been the symbolic bearers of a wider class of exclusions. The supposedly universal ideals of reason invoke not only a male identity but the elite male identity of the master. Thus to read down the first side of the list of dualisms is to read a list of qualities traditionally appropriated to men and to the human, while the second side presents qualities traditionally excluded from male ideals and associated with women, the sex defined by exclusion, "made from the dross and refuse of a man" (53, p. 121). Women have been constructed and marginalized as nature, as body, as physicality, as animality (53, p. 187, 191).[5] Women have represented nature and emotion in contrast to male spirit or reason (53, p. 166; 46), and primitiveness in contrast to male civilization (Freud in 53, p. 80). Women have represented particularity in contrast to male universality (Hegel in 53, p. 62), and necessity in contrast to male freedom (Aquinas in 53, p. 183). The gendered nature of the contrasts emerges explicitly in Pythagoras' early set of contrasts, and in his comment "There is a good principle, which has created order, light and man; and a bad principle, which has created chaos, darkness, and woman" (53, p. 50; 46, p. 25). Despite changes in the conception of nature as a sphere of exclusion and the associations of femaleness over time (50), the linkage between women and nature as the sphere of exclusion from reason has been strongly and persistently made in Western frameworks. Nature can be thought of as a sphere of multiple exclusions of various areas of difference marginalized as other.

The structure of reason/nature dualism and its variants is the perspective of power; it represents as Nancy Hartsock notes, "a way of looking at the world characteristic of the dominant white, male Eurocentric ruling class, a way of dividing up the world that puts an omnipotent subject at the center and constructs marginal Others as sets of negative qualities" (28, p. 161). This perspective constructs these others by exclusion (or some degree of departure from the center) as some form of nature in contrast to the subject the master, who claims for himself the "norm" of full humanity and reason. The West's understanding of the key concepts through which it deals with the world, its understanding not only of reason and nature but of their specific dualistic forms, has been formed from such contrasts and exclusions.[6] I will now show how this has affected concepts of otherness, starting thought, as Harding (27) recommends, from women's lives.

Dualism and the Logic of Domination

There are a number of important characteristics of the relationship between members of contrasting pairs which make it appropriate to call it a dualism rather than just a distinction or a dichotomy. The critique of dualism in culture mounted by feminists is a powerful one. But its force has been considerably weakened by the vagueness and ambiguity of the concept of dualism and the presentation of dualism in ways which construe it as an all but inevitable feature of thought.[7] The term "dualism" is often used in ways which do not distinguish it from dichotomy.[8] But if we mean by "dichotomy" what is commonly meant, simply making a division or drawing a distinction, it is essential to distinguish between dualism and dichotomy. Equating them would either cripple all thought (if we were forced to abandon dichotomy along with dualism) or collapse the concept of dualism (if we were forced to retain dualism along with dichotomy). In either case escape from dualism becomes impossible. Both in terms of predicate logic and in terms of propositional logic, a dualism must be seen as a quite special kind of distinction or dichotomy, one involving particular features which result from domination. It is not just the fact that there is dichotomy, that distinctions are made between two kinds of things which is the key element in establishing a dualistic relation—indeed it is hard to imagine how anyone could get along without making at least some of the distinctions in the list of dualisms—it is rather the way the distinctions have been treated, the further assumptions made about them and the relationship imposed upon the relata which make the relationships in question dualistic ones. Thus by no means every dichotomy results in a dualism. In contrast, dualistic negations involve many further assumptions importing a special hierarchical structure to negation. Dualism should not be confused with dichotomy and seen as creating difference where none exists. Rather it capitalizes on existing patterns of difference, rendering these in ways which ground hierarchy. The point is important for several later conclusions. As I shall show, the way to escape this structure is to replace dualistic negations with others expressing a nonhierarchical concept of difference which does not import dualistic structures into thinking about the other.

A dualism then is more than a relation of dichotomy, difference or non-identity, and more than a simple hierarchical relationship. In dualistic construction, as in hierarchy, the qualities (actual or supposed), the culture, the values and the areas of life associated with the dualized other are systematically and pervasively construed and depicted as inferior. Hierarchies however can be seen as open to change, as contingent and shifting. But once the process of domination forms culture and constructs identity, the inferiorized group (unless it can marshal cultural resources for resistance) must internalize this inferiorization in its identity and collude in this low valuation, honouring the values of the center, which form the dominant social values. A dualism is an intense, established and developed cultural expression of such a hierarchical relationship, constructing central cultural concepts and identities so as to make equality and mutuality literally unthinkable. Dualism is a relation of separation and domination inscribed and naturalized in culture and characterized by radical exclusion, distancing and opposition between orders construed as systematically higher and lower, as inferior and superior, ruler and ruled, center and periphery. It treats the division as part of the natures of beings construed as not merely different but as belonging to radically different orders or kinds, and hence as not open to change. The following family of features is characteristic of dualism.

Backgrounding

This is a complex feature which results from the irresoluble conflicts the relationship of domination creates for the master, for he attempts both to make use of the other, to organize, rely on, and benefit from the other's services, and to deny the dependency which this creates. The master usually denies dependency through making the other inessential, denying the importance of the other's contribution or even his or her reality, and through mechanisms of focus and attention. One way to do this is to insist on a strong hierarchy of activities, so that the denied areas are simply not "worth" noticing. A related way to solve this problem is through treating the other as the background to his foreground. Marilyn Frye explains the essential features and tensions of this dynamic of denial:

> Women's existence is both absolutely necessary to and irresolubly problematic for the dominant reality and those committed to it, for our existence is

> presupposed by phallocratic reality, but it is not and cannot be encompassed by or countenanced by that reality. Women's existence is a background against which phallocratic reality is a foreground . . . I imagine phallocratic reality to be the space and figures and motion which constitute the foreground, and the constant repetitive uneventful activities of women to constitute and maintain the background against which this foreground plays. It is essential to the maintenance of the foreground reality that nothing within it refer in any way to anything in the background, and yet it depends absolutely upon the existence of the background. (14, p. 167)

The view of the other as inessential is the perspective of the master subject. The master's view is set up as universal, and it is part of the mechanism of backgrounding that it never occurs to him that there might be other perspectives from which he is background. Yet this inessentialness he believes the slave to have in relation to his own essentialness is an illusion. First, the master requires the other in order to define his own boundaries and identity, since these are defined against the other (see feature 4); it is the slave who makes the master a master, the colonized who make the coloniser, the periphery which makes the centre. Second, the master also requires the other materially, in order to survive, for the relation of complementation has made the master dependent on the slave for fulfilment of his needs. But this dependency is also hated and feared by the master, for it subtly challenges his dominance, and is denied in a variety of subtle and direct ways, with all the consequences of repression. The real role and contribution of the other is never recognized, the material order of which the slave is the representative is devalued or pronounced inessential, the economic relation is denied, mystified, or presented in paternalistic terms (49, p. 21; 72)

Radical Exclusion (Hyperseparation)

Because the other is to be treated as not merely different but as inferior, part of a lower, different order of being, differentiation from it demands not merely distinctness but radical exclusion, not merely separation but hyperseparation. Radical exclusion is a key indicator of of dualism.

The relation of radical exclusion is a nonidentity with special characteristics. For distinctness, for nonidentity or otherness, there need be only a single charasteristic which is different, possessed by the one but not the other, in order to guarantee distinctness according to the usual treatment of identity (e.g., in Leibniz's Law.) Where items are constructed or construed according to dualistic relationship however, the master tries to magnify, to emphasize, and to maximize the number and importance of differences and to eliminate or treat as inessential shared qualities, and hence to achieve maximum separation. "I am nothing at all like this inferior other" is the motto associated with radical exclusion. Denial of or minimization of continuity is important in eliminating identification and sympathy between members of the dominating class and the dominated, and in eliminating possible confusion between powerful and powerless. It also helps to establish discontinuous orders and separate "natures" which explain and justify widely differing privileges and fates. A major aim of dualistic construction is polarization, to maximize distance or separation between the dualized spheres and to prevent them being seen as continuous or contiguous. Separation may be established by denying or minimizing overlap qualities and activities. Conceptual structures stressing polarization allow the erection of rigid barriers to contact which protect and isolate dominant groups.[9]

Thus dualistic construal of difference usually treats it as providing not merely a difference of degree within a sphere of overall similarity, but as providing a major difference in kind, even a bifurcation or division in reality between utterly different orders of things. Dualism denies continuity, treating its pairs as comprising "two worlds between which there is a nothing in common," worlds between which there is a "vacuum" (34; 10, p. 39). Dualistic distinction aims to maximize the number, scope or significance of distinguishing characteristics and to disappear bridging characteristics. It does not do this in a random way, but usually by classifying characteristics as belonging exclusively, as far as possible, to one side or the other, thus setting up sets of complementary qualities formed through exclusion and denial of overlap. Thus the master claims for himself reason, contemplation, and higher pursuits, and disdains the slave's merely manual occupations, while the slave is forced to exclude from his or her makeup the characteristics of the master, to eschew intellect and become submissive and lacking in initiative. These very qualities then confirm the slave's different nature and fate, for she or he is "a slave by nature."

The polarizing treatment of gender characteristics in Western culture provides a good model of such dualistic construal, and of how common or bridging characteristics are ignored, discouraged, or actually eliminated by such conceptual/social construction. The division of gender characteristics as rigid complements eliminating overlap which is commonly noted by feminists (31, p. 316) illustrates such polarization. Thus men are defined as active, intellectual, egoistic, competitive, and dominant, while women are defined as possessing the complementary qualities, as passive, intuitive, altruistic, nurturant, and submissive. Because of radical exclusion, one member of a dualistic pair, that construed as superior, defines itself against or in opposition to the other, by exclusion of the latter's inferiorized characteristics. This leads to dualistically construed pairs being constructed as complementary, in that each has characteristics which exclude but logically require a corresponding and complementary set in the other. But because of the polarization and elimination of overlap such pairs normally present a false dichotomy, and in a different context it becomes possible to conceive the items distinguished in less oppositional terms.

Albert Memmi shows how similar distancing is used in colonization to create the image of separate, discontinuous natures and orders of being. Radical exclusion requires unbridgeable separation establishing different orders of being. It requires a separation not open to change, in extreme cases rendering continuity or proximity even unimaginable.

> The colonialist stresses those things which keep him separate, rather than emphasising that which might contribute to the foundation of a joint commnunity. In those differences, the colonised is always degraded and the colonialist finds justification for rejecting his subjects. But perhaps the most important thing is that once the behavioural feature, or historical or geographical factor which characterises the colonialist and contrasts him with the colonised, has been isolated, this gap must be kept from being filled. The colonialist removes the factor from history, time and therefore possible evolution. What is actually a sociological point comes to be labelled as being biological or, preferably. metaphysical. It is attached to the colonised's basic nature. Immediately the colonial relationship between the colonised and coloniser, founded on the essential outlook of the two protagonists, becomes a definitive category. It is what it is because they are what they are, and neither one nor the other will ever change. (49, pp. 71–72)

Such construction naturalizes domination, making it appear to be part of the nature of each and in the nature of things, and yields two hyperseparated orders of being. "Thus," concludes Memmi (49, p. 75) "due to a double reconstruction of the colonized and himself, he is able both to justify and reassure himself."[10]

Relational Definition (Incorporation)

A further important set of features of dualistically construed opposites discussed especially by a number of feminist writers is that the master defines himself by exclusion, against the other, and that the underside of a dualistically conceived pair is defined in relation to the upperside as a lack, a negativity. Simone de Beauvoir writes that "humanity is male and man defines woman not in herself but as relative to him; she is not regarded as an autonomous being . . . she is defined and differentiated with reference to man and not he with reference to her; she is the incidental, the inessential as opposed to the essential. He is the Subject, he is the Absolute—she is the Other" (8, p. 8). As Luce Irigaray notes, in phallocentric construals of otherness woman has not been considered as occupying a space on her own account, but as enclosing a space for another (29, p. 3).

Although each side of a dualistic pair is dependent on the other for identity and organization of material life this relation is not one of equal, mutual or symmetrical relational definition. The master's power is reflected in the fact that his qualities are taken as primary, and as defining social value, while those of the slave are defined or constrained in relation to them, as negations or lacks of the virtues of the center (28, p. 161). As Memmi writes, "The mechanism of this remolding of the colonised . . . consists, in the first place, in a series of negations. The colonised is not this, is not that. . . . He is never considered in a positive light; or if he is, the quality which is conceded is the result of a psychological or ethical failing" (49, pp. 83–84). Because the other is defined and perceived in relation to the center, he or she is not encountered fully as an independent other, and the qualities attributed or perceived are those which reflect the center's desires, needs, and lacks. Thus the role of the "noble savage" is to be a foil: he or she is seen as possessing all the good qualities thought to be missing in "civilization," when this is regarded negatively, and as lacking all the social virtues when it is regarded positively. Since qualities or activities which do not fit into the scheme are ignored or denied, an other so perceived cannot provide resistance or boundary for the self. Relational definition of identity has two important corollaries, instrumentalism, and homogenization.

Instrumentalism (Objectification)

Although the relationship is usually (as in Aristotle's case) presented as being in the interests of the dominated as well as the dominator, it is apparent that those on the lower side of the dualisms are obliged to put aside their own interests for those of the master or center, that they are conceived of as his instruments, a means to his ends. They are made part of a network of purposes which are defined in terms of or harnessed to the master's purposes and needs. The lower side is also objectified, treated as one without ends of its own which demand consideration on their own account, and defined as part of the sphere of the master's ends.

Since the relationship is seen as that of a superior to a separate inferior order, it is seen as fitting and natural that the lower side serves the upper as a means to his ends. The upperside is an end in itself, but the underside has no such intrinsic value, is not for-itself but merely useful, a resource. The identity of the underside is constructed instrumentally, and the canons of virtue for a good wife, a good colonized, or a good worker are written in terms of usefulness to the center. In the typical case this involves setting up a moral dualism, where the underside is not part of the sphere to be considered morally, but is either judged by a separate instrumental standard (as in the sexual double standard) or is seen as outside morality altogether, part of the realm of the "natural and expedient," of usefulness to the center.

Homogenization (Stereotyping)

More than polarization is needed for the relationship to be an appropriate one for domination. The dominated class must appear suitably homogeneous if it is to be able to conform to and confirm its "nature." In homogenisation, differences among the inferiorized group are disregarded (28, pp. 160–161). I well remember, as an Australian teenager of English-speaking background in the postwar years, homogenization as part of the contempt with which non-English "foreign" immigrants were treated. Their differences denied, they were all dismissed as "aliens," "wogs," or "reffos" (refugees); the multiplicity and dignity of their cultures and languages ignored, they were seen as "just jabbering away," much like animals. Why couldn't they speak English, a proper language, like us? And white Australians, like colonists everywhere, continue to ignore the multiplicity and diversity of indigenous culture and social organization. This disregard for or denial of the diversity of Aboriginal nations has inspired the forced congregation of Aboriginal people from different tribes together which has been a major mechanism of oppression, loss of identity and disruption of Aboriginal culture.

Homogenization supports both instrumentalism, relational definition and radical exclusion. As Hartsock (28) points out, homogenization is a feature of the master perspective. To the master subject, residing at what he takes to be the center, differences among those of lesser status at the periphery are of no interest or importance on their own account, and can be ignored unless they are relevant to his ends and desires; all the rest are just that, "the rest," the Others, background to his achievements and resources for his needs. They are conceived and defined in relation to him, to his desire, which is what matters. Diversity and multiplicity which are surplus to his desires need not be acknowledged. The other is not seen as a unique individual bound to the self by specific ties, and is related to as a universal rather than as a particular, as a member of a class of interchangeable items which can be used as resources to satisfy the master's needs. Elimination of reliance on any particular individual of the relevant kind also facilitates denial of dependency and backgrounding. Instrumentalization and commodification normally produce relations of this kind. Thus the claim "If you've seen one redwood, you've seen them all."

Homogenization in gender stereotyping is well-known, involving the appeal to homogeneous and eternal male and female "natures." The sage (e.g., Lucretius) and the popular maxim both appeal to the "eternal feminine" and assert that "women are all alike." The place of homogenization in the pattern of domination as a supplement to discontinuity is insightfully discussed by Marilyn Frye: to the extent that the demand for the dualism of just two sharply differentiated sexes is a social creation unsupported by any natural order (since sharp sexual dimorphism does not exist in newborn humans or elsewhere in nature) it requires constant vigilance and regimentation, the coercion of individuals in more or less subtle ways in order to maintain it. Radical exclusion and homogenization combine to naturalize domination:

> To make (domination) seem natural, it will help if it seems to all concerned that members of the two group are very different from each other, and this appearance is enhanced if it can be made to appear that within each group, the members are very like one another. In other words, the appearance of the naturalness of the dominance of men and the subordination of women is supported by anything which supports the appearance that men are very like other men and very unlike women, and that women are very like other women and very unlike men. (13, p. 34)

Homogenization as a feature of the colonial relationship is remarked upon by Memmi: the colonized are all alike, and are not considered in personal terms or as individuals. "The colonised is never characterised in an individual manner; he is entitled only to drown in an anonymous collectivity" (49, p. 25). Orientals, as Said remarks, are seen by Westerners as almost everywhere nearly the same (68, p. 38). Thus homogenization supports both instrumentalization and radical exclusion of the colonized. The colonized is reduced to a function, and the relationship of domination destroys the ability to perceive or appreciate characteristics of the other over and above those which serve this function. As Marilyn Frye argues, such dualistic structure becomes a matter not just of conception but also of construction, affecting the very constitution of identity and the construction of bodies. "Persons . . . with the power to do so actually construct a world in which men are men and women are women and there is nothing in between and nothing ambiguous; they do it by chemically and/or surgically altering people whose bodies are indeterminate or ambiguous with respect to sex" (13, p. 25).

Classical Logic as thc Logic of Domination

Dualism then imposes a conceptual framework which polarizes and splits apart into two orders of being what can be conceptualized and treated in more integrated and unified ways. These features of dualism provide a basis for various kinds of centeredness, the rendering of the world in terms of the views and interests of the upperside, the center. The master perspectives expressed in dualistic forms of rationality are systematically distorted in ways which make them unable to recognize the other, to acknowledge dependency on the contribution of the other, who is constructed as part of a lower order alien to the center. These forms of rationality are unable to acknowledge the other as one who is essential and unique, non-interchangeable and non-replaceable. The other cannot be recognized as an independent center of needs and ends, and therefore as a center of resistance and limitation which is not infinitely manipulable. This provides the cultural grounding for an ideological structure which justifies many different forms of oppression, including male-centeredness, Euro-centeredness, ethno-centeredness, human-centeredness, and many more.

This way of being constructed as other, which is shared by a number of marginalized groups, clearly has a formal logical pattern and corresponds to certain representations of otherness in formal logical theory. I shall argue that it corresponds closely to features of classical logic, but not to the principles of logic *per se*.[11] Logic offers alternative and contested accounts of concepts such as reason and otherness. Selection from among these accounts is made in accordance with the principles of theory selection used in other areas, and is influenced by the same sorts of social relations. Choices for the most part reflect the perspectives of those at the center, and theories which sit comfortably with this perspective are more likely to be successful than those which do not. Despite its notorious problems as an account of reasoning practice (irrelevance and the paradoxes of implication), classical logic is firmly entrenched as the Logic and still manages to get away with representing as "deviant" more implicationally adequate rivals such as relevant logic.[12] Thus Quine and others have vigorously defended classical logic as thc logic of "our ordinary" negation. There is, in Quine's view, no alternative to it, for any alternative would, in his revealing phrase, "change the subject" (64, p. 81). One reason for the entrenched character of classical logic, I shall argue, may be that "the subject" of classical logic is the master. At the level of propositional logic, classical logic is the closest approximation to the dualistic structure I have outlined.[13] The "naturalness" of classical logic is the "naturalness" of domination, of concepts of otherness framed in terms of the perspective of the master.

As work in relevant and paraconsistent logic (66) has shown, negation is the key axis of comparison among implicational systems. If negation is interpreted as otherness, then how negation is treated in a system, together with other features of the system, provides an account of how otherness is conceived in that system.[14] Classical logic provides an account of otherness which has key features of dualistic otherness. The negation of classical logic is a specific concept of negation which forces us to consider otherness in terms of a single universe consisting of everything. In classical logic, negation, (–p), is interpreted as the universe without p, everything in the universe other than what p covers, as represented in the usual Venn diagram representing p as a figure surrounded by a square which represents the universe, with –p as the difference. Such an account leads directly to the relevance paradoxes. But what is important for the issue we are considering here is that –p can then not be independently or positively identified, but is entirely dependent on p for its specification. Not-p has no independent role, but is introduced as merely alien to the primary notion p (56, p. 217).

This corresponds to the relational definition feature of dualism, to a logic of presence and absence in which the other is specified as the absence of the condition specified by p, rather than as an independent other. Such an account of –p specifies –p in relation to p conceived as the controlling center, and so is p-centered. The very features of simplicity which have helped to select classical logic over its rivals are implicated here. In the phallic drama of this p-centered account, there is really only one actor, p, and ~p is merely its receptacle. In the representation of the Venn diagram, p penetrates a passive, undifferentiated universal other which is specified as a lack, which offers no resistance, and whose behavior it controls completely. There is no room here for the complexities of the "dance of interaction" (4, p. 27) between the one and an independent other. These features also lead to the homogenization of the other, since the other of p, as receptacle, is indistinguishable from the rest of the universe (56). Homogenization involves binarism, interpreting the other as "the rest." These homogenizing properties of classical negation are associated with the failure of classical logic to make any finer discriminations in propositional identity than truth-functionality. These are precisely the features which help to make classical logic problematic as an account of reasoning practice.

The negation of classical logic (which is responsible for its paradoxical character), has features of radical exclusion of the alien other which lie behind distancing and discontinuity, as well as exhibiting other features which are characteristic of dualism. The radical exclusion aspects of classical otherness are evident in the classical treatment of contadictions as implying everything, for the effect of $p\&{-p} \rightarrow q$ is to keep p and its other or negation at a maximum distance, so that they can never be brought together (even in thought), on pain of the maximum penalty a logical system can provide, system collapse. It is the penalty of merger, of the loss of all boundaries, which threatens when p and its receptacle, –p, come together in the forbidden encounter of contradiction. Semantically, p and –p are treated classically as maximally distant in situational space. The extreme penalty classical logic provides for conjoining p and "its" other not-p, establishes a maximally strong relation of exclusion belween p and –p, in comparison to other systems of propositional logic which define much weaker exclusion relationships.

A further feature of classical logic which corresponds to the logic of dualism is its role as a truth-suppression implication, which permits the suppression of true premisses. (Simply, in the Aristotelian notion of suppression, a suppressed premise is an assumption used in arriving at the conclusion but not shown as among the premises.[15]) The suppression of premises on condition of their truth gives formal expression to the dualistic condition of backgrounding, in which the contribution of the other to the outcome is relied upon but denied or ignored.[16] If the major task of logic is about showing (showing everything that has been relied on), a logic allowing truth suppression is about hiding. Truth-suppression is closely related to another feature of classical logic, truth interchangeability, in which any truth can be substituted for any other truth while preserving implicational properties. It is also closely related to the feature that material equivalence as a criterion of propositional identity yields just one true and one false proposition. This interchangeability of truths can be alternatively viewed as indicating that material implication expresses instrumental or means-ends reasoning, in which conditions as means are interchangeable provided they equally produce equivalent effects or ends. The logic of dualism thus connects with the logic of instrumental reason, which is also expressive of the master identity, and is the dominant logic of the market and the public sphere (62).

Non-Hierarchical Concepts of Difference

I am not of course arguing that classical logic itself is the cause of women's oppression, and that if we just change the logical theory, all will be well.

Challenging dualistic otherness at the level of formal logical theory is only part of what needs to be done to problematize the naturalness of domination, and this conceptual and cultural challenge in turn is only part of a wider strategy for change. There are also quite specific strategies, both conceptual/cultural and social/material, which need to be adopted to overcome the forms of oppression this dualistic conception of otherness naturalizes and the forms of oppressed identity which this dualistic conception of otherness constructs. The general structural features of dualism expressed in dualistic otherness are shared by diverse groups whose specific forms of oppression are also diverse, but whose general form of identity has been constructed in terms of the canons of dualistic otherness as subordinated to a central master identity. (I have argued elsewhere that the construction of the human/nature relationship in the West has been shaped by this same structure of dualistic otherness [60; 61].) Examining this conceptual structure helps to clarify a general structure of identity that many oppressed groups have in common and to explain some of the steps oppressed groups take to overcome dualized identity. The transition however is not straightforward, and residues of dualism are often remarkably persistent. Dismantling a dualism based on difference requires the reconstruction of relationship, concepts of otherness and identity in terms of an appropriate non-hierarchical concept of difference. Such a relationship of non-hierarchical difference can be used to counter dualistic construction through the following specific features:

1: Backgrounding:
A non-hierarchical concept of difference requires a move to systems of thought, accounting, perception, decision making which recognize the contribution of what has been backgrounded, and which acknowledge the denied relationships of dependency.

2: Radical Exclusion:
A non-hierarchical concept of difference will affirm continuity (for example common humanity), reconceive relata in more integrated ways, and reclaim the denied area of overlap.

3: Relational Identity:
A non-hierarchical concept of difference must review the identities of both underside and upperside. It can aim to critically affirm the difference of the oppressed, to rediscover their language and story, and to reclaim positive independent sources of identity.

4: Instrumentalism:
A non-hierarchical concept of difference implies recognising the other as a center of needs, value and striving on its own account, a being whose ends and needs are independent of the center and to be respected in their own right.

5. Homogenization:
A non-hierarchical concept of difference involves recognizing the different concerns and diversity of the "other nations" which have been homogenized and marginalized in their constitution as excluded other, as "the rest."

It is some confirmation of the kind of account given here that these strategies do correspond to the central conceptual and cultural concerns of various liberation movements. Thus to set out clearly what is involved in dualism is already to have seen the signposts which point the ways toward escaping it. But the escape routes are mazes containing mirrors, traps, sidetracks, looped trails, and reversals. The two most common problems in reclaiming dualized identity are the denial of difference and the reversal syndrome.

The temptation to denial of difference sometimes comes from a partial understanding of the role of the role of dualism and radical exclusion in creating exaggerated distancing and hyperseparation between dualized orders. Failure to distinguish dualism and dichotomy particularly can suggest that the resolution of a dualism requires merger, or the elimination of all distinction and difference between these orders. This can result in the attempt to eliminate distinction between mind and body (via physicalism for example), between masculine and feminine (via androgyny), between sex and gender,[17] between humans and nature, and between self and other, and similarly for other pairs in the list of dualisms. But in general such a merger strategy is neither necessary nor desirable, because while dualism distorts difference and makes it the vehicle for hierarchy, it usually does so on the basis of already existing difference. And, as we have seen, the attempt to eliminate distinction along with dualism is misconceived.

The temptation to reversal can result from the attempt to treat dualism as a simple hierarchy, and to reverse value without attending to its identity forming and center-creating functions. Reversal maintains what Jessica Benjamin (4, p. 48) calls the "dual unity" and complementarity of the dominator/dominated pair, switching roles or reconceiving the underside as a new center. Reversal is a major conceptual problem for liberation movements. Thus one form of feminist reaction to devaluation has been the attempt to affirm a traditional identity for women without thoroughly reconceiving its dualistic construction. In feminist reversal, a new positively valued feminine identity comes to be specified in reaction to the old by exclusion of rationality and the qualities claimed for the masculine, thus conceding the male claim to these qualities, and indiscriminately affirming the feminine qualities or character acquired in subordination. But although some affirmation is called for, remedying the systematic inferiorization of thc underside of a dualism calls for critical affirmation of what has been devalued and critical reclamation of thc qualities and aspects of culture associated with it (33). Albert Memmi shows how the same dynamic of reversal of values appears for the colonized in his or her attempt at escape. The colonized now affirms his or her own culture's qualities as indiscriminately as the colonizer has despised them.

> Suddenly, exactly to the reverse of the colonialist accusation, the colonised, his culture, his country, everything that belongs to him, everything he represents, become perfectly positive elements. . . . We shall ultimately find ourselves before a countermythology. The negative myth thrust on him by the colonizer is succeeded by a positive myth about himself suggested by the colonized, just as there would seem to be a positive myth of the proletarian opposed to a negative one. To hear the colonized and often his friends, everything is good, everything must be retained among his customs and traditions, his actions and plans; even the anachronous or disorderly, the immoral or mistaken. . . . The colonized's self assertion, born out of a protest, continues to define itself in relation to it. In the midst of revolt, the colonized continues to think, feel and live against, and therefore in relation to the colonizer and colonisation. (49, p. 139)

Because the new identity is specified in reaction to the colonizer and still in relation to him, and has accepted the dualistic construction of identity, the appearance that the colonized has broken free of dualized identity is an illusion. The colonised who remains at this stage is tied by reaction to his or her original problematic of identity. An appreciation of this point has led postmodernists to the conclusion that the only escape route from binary oppositions is the dissolution of identity, despite the numerous problems for political expression and action this creates (1). The analysis I have presented points instead toward another solution, the critical reconstruction of dualized identity (61).

Toward a Liberatory Logic of Difference

None of the features of dualistic otherness or classical negation is an inevitable feature of logic, negation, otherness, or reasoning. Fully worked out logical systems which do not have these features are available and in use, and these can point in directions which might be promising for alternative conceptions of otherness and rationality. Some of these alternative systems, those of relevant logic for example, can also claim to be a more adequate expression of actual reasoning practice than classical logic (66). At the same time, the negation of relevant logic, relevant negation, can be interpreted as expressing a notion-of otherness as non-hierarchical difference. The resulting concept of relevant otherness avoids radical exclusion, for the conjunction of A and –A does not induce system collapse. Thus –A is not homogenised as simply part of "the rest," for an account of propositional identity based on relevant implicational equivalence can make fine discriminations among the elements of the propositional universe. Relevant negation considers exclusion not with respect to the universe, but with respect to a much more restricted state, so that the negation of A is not just to be specified in relation to A, but can be introduced as a relatively independent principle. The resulting concept of otherness can be modeled by a number of natural widely used otherness relations, such as "the other side," which lack hierarchical features (56, pp. 216–220). It is neither a cancellation of nor a lack or absence of a specified condition, but another and further condition—a difference—yielding the concept of an other which is not just specified negatively but is independently characterized and with an independent role on its own behalf.

These systems point toward alternative ways to think of otherness as non-hierarchical difference. In these alternative forms of rationality, which we might call the logic of mutuality (3; 4), the other can be conceived as one who is an independent center or self, who imposes constraints or limits on the initial centre or self. In the logic of mutuality, relationship between self and other can be mutual, interactive and a centred, rather than falling into the colonizing patterns of incorporation or elimination. Another so conceived is no mere reflection of self's needs and desires, nor is it merely a complementary appendage defined by elimination against the universe as a lack of the center's qualities. In the logic of domination, the instrumentalization of the other and the conception of the other as a resource defined in relation to the center is suggested by the weak replacement conditions which allow the other to be substituted for by anything else provided merely that it has equivalent truth value (as one conceived as a resource can be replaced by anything which equally meets the needs of the center). In these alternative systems, much stronger substitution principles allow the independence and uniqueness of the other to be recognized to a much greater degree. These forms of rationality thus challenge assumptions central to the logic of domination.

Logic is a prismatic glass that has the power to eliminate detail and particularity. This glass can, if we are not careful, cut us off from the world of life, but it can also enable certain general patterns to be better seen. Gazing into the prismatic glass can give us a candid glimpse of the master subject whose lineaments are usually lost in the flux of particularity, but the glass can also show us other more attractive forms and patterns of mutuality. For feminists and others to abandon selective engagement with logic would be to mount a very incomplete challenge to hierarchical thinking and oppressive forms of rationality, which, as I have shown, find their base less in the abstraction of logical thought itself than in the content of reigning logical theories and ruling structures of reason. It seems that a more complete feminist strategy would involve challenging these oppressive forms of rationality and working for their replacement. A strategy for changing conceptions of difference cannot of course just be one of investigating and teaching different logical systems it must primarily involve changing the practices associated with the oppressive forms of rationality built into key social and political structures, institutions, and forms of knowledge. But the critical consideration of logical theory and the development of alternative accounts of rationality, otherness, and difference does have something to contribute to many areas of radical and feminist thought, and to the development of a world which truly "changes the subject" so that modes of reasoning which treat the other in terms of domination can no longer pass without question as normal and natural.

Notes

1. The notion of abandoning the abstraction of logical theory faces the same problems as that of abandoning reason and scientific theory, discussed in (26).

2. Concluding the account with Frege makes it possible to ignore only the plurality of modern logics but also the existence of important socially progressive logicians such as John Stuart Mill and Bertrand Russell.

3. For detailed references to the extensive literature involved in this debate, especially around the issue of implicational logic, see (66; 63; 65).

4. On the importance of not locating explanation just in ideological systems see (78, pp. 36–62). On the false, dualistic choice posed by accounts which insist on either material or ideological primacy see (39).

5. "Woman is a violent and uncontrolled animal"—Cato (quoted in [53, p. 193]); "A woman is but an animal and an animal not of the highest order"—Burke (53, p. 187); "I cannot conceive of you to be human creatures, but a sort of species hardly a degree above a monkey"—Swift [53, p. 191]; "Howe'er man rules in science and in art. The sphere of women's glories is the heart"—Moore [53, p. 166]; "Women represent the interests of the family and sexual life; the work of civilisation has become more and more men's business"—Freud [53, p. 80]; "Women are certainly capable of learning, but they are not made for the highest forms of science, such as philosophy and certain types of creative activity; these require a universal ingredient"—Hegel

(53, p. 62); " A necessary object, woman, who is needed to preserve the species or to provide food and drink"—Aquinas (53, p. 183).

6. Those dualisms (such as particular/universal or public/private) which cannot immediately be seen as variants of a gendered reason/nature contrast can have their derivation from or connnection to this basic form revealed by making explicit further implicit assumptions which are used to connect them. These pairs are connected then by a series of *linking postulates*, and when so connected form a web. Linking postulates are assumptions normally made or implicit in the cultural background which create equivalences or mapping between the pairs. For example, the postulate that all and only humans possess culture maps the culture/nature pair onto the human/nature pair; the postulate that the sphere of reason is masculine maps the reason/body pair onto the masculine/feminine pair, and the assumption that the sphere of the human coincides with that of intellect or mentality maps the mind/body pair onto the human/nature pair, and, via transitivity, the human/nature pair onto the masculine/feminine pair. In the case of public/private the linking postulate connects the sphere of the public with reason via the qualities of freedom, universality and rationality which are supposedly constitutive of masculinity and the public sphere, and connects that of the private with nature via the qualities of dailiness, necessity, particularity and emotionality supposedly exemplified in and constitutive of the feminine and the private sphere (46, pp. 74–85). The civilized/primitive contrast maps all of the human/animal, mind/body reason/nature, freedom/necessity and subject/object contrasts.

The fact that different philosophers and different periods of philosophy have focussed on different pairs of these dualisms and have defended different linking postulates has obscured the pervasiveness of dualistic and rationalist influence in philosophy. Thus Hegel and Rousseau emphasize the postulates linking public/private, male/female, universal/particular, and reason/nature (46, pp. 80–85 and pp. 58–63). For Plato the emphasis is mainly on reason/body, reason/emotion, universal/particular; for Descartes it is on mind/body (physicality), subject/object, human/nature and human/animal; for Marx it is on freedom/necessity, culture (history)/nature, civilized/primitive, mental/manual (a variant on mind/body), and production/reproduction. But a philosopher's explicit focus on particular dualisms is often deceptive, for the gendered character of the dualisms for example may lurk in the background in unexamined and concealed form, as much feminist philosophy exposing phallocentrism has shown.

7. Thus de Beauvoir adds to her account of "the Other" the claim that "the category of the *Other* is as primodial as consciousness itself," treating the dualistic construal of otherness she goes on to outline as inevitable.

8. Dualism and dichotomy are not clearly separated in many decisions, for example the discussion of Jay (34) or that of Hartsock (28), and the terms "dualism" and "dichotomy" are used in the literature in manifold, unclear and ambiguous ways. Some writers seem to use the term "dichotomy" to indicate the structure I have characterised as "dualism," and dualism to mean "dichotomy" (see, for example, Warren's distinction between dualism and hierarchical dualism (73)). I do not claim to reflect

faithfully an ordinary or settled usage, and my proposal is essentially a recommendation or reform proposal aimed at clarifying the area. However, even if the terminology is variable, the distinction between the special structure of non-identity which constitutes a dualism and non-identity or distinction as such needs to be marked in some clear way. The problem with the use of the term "dichotomy" to mark the special structure I have characterized is that "dichotomy" already has a fairly settled meaning as division or distinction and hence facilitates confusion. The failure to mark the distinction has the disastrous result that all attempt to draw distinctions or to use negation comes under suspicion. In the case of Jay (34) however, a substantive rather than a terminological thesis is involved which convicts any distinction, based on the Law of Excluded Middle, of dualism, and proposes an alternative Aristotelian logical structure which abandons it. I offer a different analysis here of dualism which does not associate it with Excluded Middle. In terms of predicate logic I take dualism and radical exclusion to involve a maximization of non-shared characteristics, whereas the establishement of ordinary Leibnizian difference or non-identity requires only that a single characteristic be different. In terms of propositional logic, the dichotomizing functions of negations which simply divide the universe and recognise a boundary between self and other without importing a hierarchical structure are associated with the Law of Non-Contradiction (–(A & –A) and the Law of Excluded Middle (A v–A).

The Platonic and classical arguments using what Nye calls "logical division" (54, p. 30) and which she convicts of hierarchical thinking, involve much more than these principles, adding dualistic principles which systematically select one of the pair of disjuncts over the other and enable elimination. Their form could be better interpreted as that of the Disjunctive Syllogism were it not that in the Platonic arguments the disjuncts are usually not exhaustive. That is, most of the Platonic arguments are not formally valid, as Aristotle recognized.

9. As Jay (34) notes, certain ethnologists have seen this radical exclusion relation as important in religious thought in the distinction beween things sacred and things profane, and have also noted (although usually not with disapproval) one of its functions, namely, to mark out, protect and isolate a privileged group. Thus Emile Durkheim writes: "Sacred things are those which the interidctions *protect* and *isolate*; profane things those to which these interdictions are applied and which must remain *at a distance* from the first" (10, pp. 40–41, emphasis added). Profane things are thought of as threatening to sacred things, and the power they represent. Such a dualism of sacred and profane often occurs in the context of a powerful priesthood or religious ruler, or uses religious symbolism to protect the power of one group and intimidate and repress another.

10. Radical exclusion and other dualistic features appear in many aspects of relations between economic classes. Hyperseparation appears especially in the division of labor in production, which is often framed in terms of a rigid mind/body dualism in which mind people control body people. For example many tasks of decision making and various other intellectual tasks which can beneficially be amalgamated with the

practical or manual aspect of work are reserved for managers, with the purpose of setting them apart as a distanced and controlling elite. In culture radical exclusions appears in the division between high and low culture, as well as in cultural concepts and practices such as "quality" and conspicuous consumption which are designed to mark out higher classes by exclusion. Denials of dependency appear in many areas, especially in the foregrounding of the managerial or entrepreneurial contribution to the task and appropriation of the product, and in private property relations in the backgrounding of the social infrastructure and other social contributions which go to make entrepreneurial appropriation possible. For a discussion of some of the contemporary phenomena of class see (11, pp. 135–143). On the comparable mechanism of denial of dependency on the part of the colonizer see (49, pp. 54–55 and pp. 66–67).

11. The discussion in Hartsock (28, pp. 162–163) makes many of the important connections between the features of dualism and the perspective of power which I have amplified here, but seems to carry the implication that a dualistic account of otherness in an inherent feature of Logic.

12. See especially (66).

13. My argument in this paragraph draws especially on (56).

14. Nancy Jay (34, pp. 39–56) notes this feature in her discussion of dichotomy. However, Jay's discussion is problematic not only because of the failure to distinguish between dualism and dichotomy, but because of the attempt to theorise the area exclusively in terms of an Aristotelian logic which limits options and is a relatively insensitive tool for dealing with both negation and identity, the two central concepts for giving an account of dualism, difference and otherness.

15. For an account of suppression in terms of propositional logic, see (66, pp. 139–153).

16. Backgrounding as truth suppression is most clearly expressed in the principle (related to Exportation), $p \,\&\, ((p \& q) \rightarrow r) \rightarrow q \rightarrow r$, which accordingly might be called Exploitation.

17. For a critique of the treatment of gender in the dualistic terms found in "sex-role stereotyping" see (14); for a further critique of its treatment as indistinguishable from sex see (59) and (32). Gender has often been understood as pure culture, as if the body was irrelevant. But the alternative is not to treat it as indistinguishable from either nature (sex) or from culture. The distinction may still be useful and viable if treated in non-dualistic ways, and can be used to provide some sensitivity to social and cultural context, rather than used to treat gender as reducible to culture.

References

1. Alcoff, Linda, "Cultural Feminism Versus Post-structuralism: The Identity Crisis in Feminist Theory," *Signs* 13 (1988) pp. 405–436.
2. Aristotle, *The Basic Work of Aristotle* (ed.) R. McKeon (New York: Random House, 1941).

3. Benjamin, Jessica, "The Bonds of Love: Rational Violence and Erotic Domination" in *The Future of Difference* (eds) H. Eisenstein and A. Jardine (New Brunswick, NJ: Rutgers University Press, 1985).
4. Benjamin, Jessica, *The Bonds of Love: Psychoanalysis, feminism and the problem of domination* (London: Virago, 1988).
5. Bordo, Susan R., *The Flight to Objectivity: Essays on Cartesianism and Culture* (Albany: State University of New York Press, 1987).
6. Cixous, Helene and Clement Catherine, *The Newly Born Woman* (Manchester Manchester University Press, 1986).
7. Connell R. W., *Gender and Power* (Sydney: Allen and Unwin, 1988).
8. de Beauvoir, Simone, *The Second Sex* (Kettering, Northants: Foursquare Books, 1965).
9. Derrida, J., "Freud and the Scene of Writing" in *Writing and Difference*, trans. A. Bass. (London: Routledge, 1981) pp. 196–231.
10. Durkheim, Emile, *Thc Elemenrary Forms of the Religious Life* (London: Allen and Unwin, 1915).
11. Ehrenreich, Barbara. *Fear of Falling* (New York: Harper and Row, 1989).
12. Flax, Jane, "Political Philosophy and the Patriarchal Unconscious" in *Discovering Reality* (eds) M. Hintikka and S. Harding (Dordrecht: Reidel, 1983) pp. 245–281.
13. Frye, Marilyn, *The Politics of Reality* (New York: The Crossing Press 1983).
14. Gatens, Moira. "A *Critique of the Sex/Gender Distinction*," *Intervention* no. 17 (1983) pp. 143–160.
15. Gilligan, Carol, *In a Different Voice* (Cambridge, MA: Harvard University Press, 1982).
16. Gilligan, Carol, "Moral Orientation and Moral Development" in *Women and Moral Theory* (eds) E. Kittay and D. Meyers (Totowa, NJ: Rowman and Littlefield, 1987) pp. 19–33.
17. Gilligan, Carol, *Mapping the Moral Domain* (Cambridge, MA: Harvard University Press, 1988).
18. Gray, Elizabeth Dodson, *Green Paradise Lost: Remything Genesis* (Wellesley, MA: Roundtable Press, 1979).
19. Griffin, Susan, *Women and Nature: The Roaring Inside Her* (New York: Harper and Row, 1978).
20. Griscom, Joan L., "On Healing the Nature/History Split in Feminist Thought," *Heresies: Feminism and Ecology* 4 (1981) pp. 4–9.
21. Grosz, Elizabeth, *Sexual Subversions* (Sydney: Allen and Unwin, 1989).
22. Haraway, Donna, *Primate Visions* (London: Routledge, 1989).
23. Haraway, Donna, *Simians, Cyborgs and Women: Thc Reinvention of Nature* (London: Free Association Books, 1991).
24. Harding, Sandra and Hintikka, Merrill (eds), *Discovering Reality* (Dordrecht: Reidel, 1983).
25. Harding Sandra, "Is Gender a Variable in Conceptions of Rationality?" in *Beyond Domination* (ed.) C. Gould (Totowa, NJ: Rowman and Allanheld, 1984) pp. 43–63.

26. Harding, Sandra, *The Science Question in Feminism* (Ithaca, NY: Cornell University Press, 1986).
27. Harding, Sandra, *Whose Science? Whose Knowledge?* (Milton Keynes: Open University Press, 1991).
28. Hartsock, Nancy, "Foucault on Power A Theory for Women" in *Feminism/Postmodernism* (ed.) Linda J. Nicholson (New York: Routledge, 1990) pp. 157–175.
29. Irigaray, Luce, "The Ethics of Sexual Difference," trans. Carolyn Sheaffer Jones (unpublished ms, 1984).
30. Irigaray, Luce, *Speculum of the Other Woman*, trans. (Ithaca, NY: Cornell University Press 1985).
31. Jaggar, Alison, *Feminist Politics and Human Nature* (Brighton: Harvester, 1983).
32. Jaggar, Alison, "Human Biology in Feminist Theory: Sexual Equality Reconsidered" in *Beyond Domination* (ed.) Carol C. Gould (Totowa, NJ: Rowman and Allanheld, 1984).
33. Jaggar, Alison, "Feminist Ethics: Projects, Problems, Prospects" in *Feminist Ethics* (ed.) Claudia Card (Lawrence, KS: University of Kansas Press 1991).
34. Jay, Nancy, "Gender and Dichotomy," *Feminist Studies* 7 (1981) pp. 39–56.
35. Kant, Immanuel, *Fundamental Principles of the Metaphysics of Morals*, trans. James W. Ellington (Indianapolis, IN: Hackett Publishing, 1960).
36. Kant, Immanuel, *Observations on the Feeling of the Beautiful and Sublime*, trans. John T. Goldthwait (Berkeley, CA: University of California Press, 1981).
37. Keller, Evelyn Fox, *Reflections on Gender and Science* (New Haven, CN: Yale University Press, 1985).
38. King, Ynestra, "Feminism and Revolt," *Heresies: Feminism and Ecology* 4 (1981) pp. 12–16.
39. King, Ynestra, "The Ecology of Feminism and the Feminism of Ecology" in *Healing the Wounds* (ed.)J. Plant (Philadelphia: New Society Publishers, 1989) pp. 18–28.
40. King, Ynestra, "Healing the Wounds: Feminism, Ecology, and the Nature/Culture Dualism" in *Reweaving the World* (eds) Irene Diamond and Gloria Orenstein (San Francisco: Sierra Club Books, 1990) pp. 106–121.
41. Kneale M. and Kneale W., *The Development of Logic* (Oxford: Clarendon Press, 1962).
42. Latour, Bruno and Woolgar, Steve, *Laboratory Life: The Social Construction of Scientific Facts* (Beverly Hills, CA: Sage, 1979).
43. Latour, Bruno, *Science in Action* (Cambridge, MA: Harvard University Press, 1987).
44. Latour, Bruno, *The Pasteurisation of France: A Politico-Scientific Essay* (Cambridge, MA: Harvard University Press, 1988).
45. Lewontin, R. C., Rose, Steven, and Kamin, Leon J., *Not in Our Genes: Biology, Ideology and Human Nature* (New York: Pantheon, 1984).
46. Lloyd, Genevieve, *The Man of Reason* (London: Methuen, 1984).
47. Mates, Benson, *Stoic Logic* (Berkeley, CA: University of California Press, 1961).
48. McMillan, Carol, Women, *Reason and Nature* (Oxford: Blackwell, 1982).
49. Memmi, Albert, *The Colonizer and the Colonized* (New York: Orion Press, 1965).

50. Merchant, Carolyn, *The Death of Nature* (London: Wildwood House, 1981).
51. Midgley, Mary, *Evolution as a Religion* (London: Methuen, 1985).
52. Mies, Maria, *Patriarchy and Accumulation on a World Scale* (London: Zed Books, 1986).
53. Morgan, Fidelis, *A Misogynist's Source Book* (London: Jonathon Cape, 1989).
54. Nye, Andrea, *Words of Power* (London: Routledge, 1990).
55. Plumwood, Val and Routley, Richard, "The Semantics of Belief and the Laws of Thought Myth," *Journal of Symbolic Logic* 39 (1974) pp. 206–207.
56. Plumwood, Val and Routley, Richard, "Negation and Contradiction," *Revista Colombiana de Matematicas* 19 (1985) pp. 201–231.
57. Plumwood, Val, "Ecofeminism: An Overview and Discussion of Positions and Arguments" in *Women and Philosophy*, supplement to Australasian Journal of Philosophy 64 (1986) pp. 120–138.
58. Plumwood, Val, "Women, Humanity and Nature," Radical Philosophy 48 (1988) pp. 16–24, reprinted in S. Sayers and P. Osborne (eds), *Feminism, Socialism and Philosophy: A Radical Philosophy Reader* (London: Routledge, 1990).
59. Plumwood, Val, "Do We Need a Sex/Gender Distinction?" *Radical Philosophy* 51 (1989) pp. 2–11.
60. Plumwood, Val, "Nature, Self and Gender: feminism, environmental philosophy and the critique of rationalism," *Hypatia* 6 (1991) pp. 3–27.
61. Plumwood, Val, *Feminism and the Mastery of Nature* (London: Routledge, 1993).
62. Poole, Ross, *Morality and Modernity* (London: Routledge, 1992).
63. Priest, Graham and Sylvan, Richard (eds), *Paraconsistent Logic* (Munich: Philosophia Verlag, 1989).
64. Quine, W. V. O., *Philosophy of Logic* (Englewood Cliffs, NJ: Prentice-Hall, 1970).
65. Read, Stephen, *The Logic of Relevance* (Oxford: Blackwell, 1990).
66. Routley, Richard, Meyer, Robert K., Plumwood, Val and Brady, Ross T., *Relevant Logics and Their Rivals* (Atascadero, CA: Ridgeview Publishing, 1983).
67. Ruether, Rosemary Radford, *New Woman, New Earth: Sexist Ideologies and Human Liberation* (Minneapolis: Seabury Press, 1975).
68. Said, Edward, *Orientalism* (New York: Vintage, 1979).
69. Sylvan, Richard, *Bystanders' Guide to Sociative Logics* (Canberra: Research Series in Logic and Metaphysics, RSSS, ANU, 1989).
70. Trebilcot, Joyce, "Conceiving Women: Notes on the Logic of Feminism" in *Women and Values: Readings in Recent Feminist Philosophy* (ed.) Marilyn Pearsall (Belmont, CA: Wadsworth, 1986).
71. Walkerdine, Valerie, *The Mastery of Reason: Cognitive Development and the Production of Rationality* (London: Routledge, 1988).
72. Waring, Marilyn, *Counting for Nothing* (Auckland: Allen and Unwin, 1988).
73. Warren, Karen J., "Feminism and Ecology: Making Connections," *Environmental Ethics* 9 (1987) pp. 17–18.
74. Warren, Karen J., "The Power and Promise of Ecological Feminism," *Environmental Ethics* 12 (1990) pp. 121–146.

75. Washington, Booker T., *Up from Slavery* (Toronto: Airmont Publishing, 1967).
76. Wajcman, Judy, *Feminism Confronts Technology* (Cambridge: Polity Press, 1991).
77. Winner, Langdon, *The Whale and the Reactor* (Chicago: University of Chicago Press, 1986).
78. Young, Iris Marion, "Is Male Gender Identity the Cause of Male Domination?" in *Throwing Like a Girl and Other Essays in Feminist Philosophy and Social Theory* (Bloomington, IN: Indiana University Press, 1990).

CHAPTER TWO

~

Feminism and the Logic of Alterity

VAL PLUMWOOD

Liberation and Otherness: The Need for Theory

Much recent feminist thought has placed the logic of alterity at the top of the feminist philosophicological agenda. Feminist philosopher Rosi Braidotti provides an excellent articulation of the leading questions feminists ask about otherness and logic: "Can we formulate otherness/difference without devaluing it? Can we think of the other as not other-than, but as a positively other entity? Can we utter a non-hierarchical truth, a non-hegemonic reason? Can we extricate reason from domination and the belligerent ways which guide it?"[1] In this chapter, I take up some of these questions in relation to the conception of otherness. Feminism seems to require a concept of women's difference and women's presence as positively-other-than rather than as other-than-the-male. Recent feminist philosophers have argued that one of the key feminist tasks is constituting ourselves as women as "positively-other-than" beings rather than as the Others of men, as other-than-the-male, or as the absence-of-it (the phallus) (Braidotti 1991; Frye 1996; Irigaray 1985). Dominant hegemonic and patriarchal forms of thought deny or make unavailable such a concept and replace it by the concept of other-than that thinks difference as lesser, the sort of "wife" term who is conceived as secondary, inessential, and hierarchically dependent on a "husband" term, treated as the center or supposedly primary form. But in feminist contexts woman is not defined in such a secondary or negative way; rather, as Marilyn Frye puts it, "women's collective projects are bringing the category of women into concrete social reality . . . positively constituted by who we are to each other, informations of our own making that give rise to meanings, including meanings of our bodies" (1996, 1009).

That woman has not been treated as positively-other-than but has been given a secondary and dependent status as Other, especially as an absence or deficiency of the male, is one of the fundamental theses of the second wave of feminism. This is well illustrated in the work of Simone de Beauvoir who, in the *locus classicus* for many of these fundamental logical ideas, *The Second Sex*, appears to identify assignment to the logical category of Otherness as at the heart of women's subjugation. In a passage early in this major feminist text, de Beauvoir states that "humanity is male and man defines woman not in herself but as relative to him; she is not regarded as an autonomous being . . . she is defined and differentiated with reference to man and not he with reference to her; she is the incidental, the inessential as opposed to the essential. He is the Subject [or One], he is the Absolute, she is the Other" (1989, 11). The asymmetries of power, the conception of woman as lesser, as receptacle or residue, as an absence of male qualities rather than as a positively specified and independent being, the subordinate position of those who "come second," the later patriarchal-Aristotelian theory of reproduction that held that women supplied only the matter that gave bodily expression to the male "rational" contribution of form, the view that women were only the "nurses" for the children that were really the accomplishment of the male, the story of Adam and the rib—all are expressions of this concept of woman as the Other. Humanity is seen in terms of a male norm; man is the primary concept that subsumes that of woman, who is defined, in Braidotti's terms, as an other-than-the-male rather than as a positively-other-than being.[2] The challenge to the hegemonic definition of woman constructed as an Other, and the attempt to counter it by discovering a positively-other-than identity (or positive difference) for woman, lies at the heart of feminist struggle. It is reflected in such consciousness change as the refusal to be identified as Mrs. or Miss—that is, defined in relation to father or husband.

Both feminist and postcolonial thought stress that their respective conceptual fields of gender and colonization or race have been divided in problematic and oppressive ways between a privileged, dominant One and a devalued or subordinated Other and that there are other ways to make this conceptual division that provides the basic logical framework underlying genderized and racialized identities. Whiteness, for example, as many thinkers have pointed out, is treated in dominant contexts as a privileged One or norm, which is assumed to be not itself a "color" and does not require "marking" (it is "unmarked"); in contrast with whiteness, "color" is defined as deviant, requiring remark or identification (it is "marked") and bringing the status of Otherness-to-the-norm. The field of race like that of gender is thus divided between a powerful unmarked norm or center and an Other who is marked or defined as relative to that center (Friedman 1995; Collins 1990; hooks 1984). Theorists of colonization such as Edward Said have explained how hegemonic otherness functions in a similar way in Western frameworks of colonization to construct the colonized other as "an inferior foil to self."

Concepts of dichotomy, dualism, and binary opposition have provided alternative routes into investigating problematic concepts of otherness that allow a more general focus on the larger context of alterity, the mode of division of a field. These concepts are used in various and often ill-considered and conflicting ways in contemporary discourses. Sometimes "dichotomy" is used in ways that make it equivalent to or synonymous with the concept of dualism many feminists have employed to indicate a polarized, oppositional, and oppressive form of differentiation (discussed later). I see this identification of "dichotomy" with "dualism" or "binary opposition" as problematic, for it obscures the crucial distinction between the operation of distinction or differentiation itself and oppressive forms of this operation. According to the *Oxford English Dictionary*, the basic meaning of *dichotomy* is simply cutting, splitting, or division—"division into two" (as in "false dichotomy") or "repeated bifurcation" (as in botanical or zoological classification). Dichotomy in this sense of "division into two" can be contrasted with trichotomy, or division into three, and with other more multiple-term modes of division. That is, the classical meaning of the term *dichotomy*, well established in some two thousand years of logical usage, indicates no more than separation—therefore, distinction, difference, division, or nonidentity on a binary base. This meaning of dichotomy as binary division is well established in current usage in phrases such as "false dichotomy" to indicate an incorrect binary division and resulting false choice. Since we do need a way to mark such concepts of division simpliciter, and since those who condemn a vaguely specified "dichotomy" only rarely wish to make a considered and unqualified condemnation of operations of division or distinction, the usage of *dichotomy* as equivalent to *dualism* or the idea of polarity and opposition invites major miscommunication. I will therefore stick to using the term *dichotomy* in that well-established sense in this chapter.

Concepts of dualism, on the other hand, have been less fixed, more open in usage, and thus require a greater degree of theorization and decision. Within feminism, the concept of dualism has played a fundamental role in second-wave theory and activism, going back to early to mid-1970s feminism.[3] Taking its lead from philosophers' concepts of mind/body dualism—the concept of dualism was used especially to problematize the polarizing aspects of oppressed/oppressor types of identity construction—seen, for example, in the regimentation of people to fit the rigid and radically separate male and female natures that women's liberation challenged (often under the rubric of "sex-role stereotyping"). These are symmetrical polarizing and oppositional features of the sort that are not necessarily part of dichotomy as separation or division per se. But the concept of dualism has often been understood to take in also asymmetrical hegemonic or hierarchical features, and both aspects of dualism have been crucial for women's activism. The polarizing aspects of dualism involve sorting a field into two homogenized and radically separated or highly distanced classes, typically constructing a false choice between contrasting polarities in a truncated field that can be (re)conceived in much more continuous and overlapping ways.

For example, in a polarized, dualistic structure, the attributes of real men are taken to overlap as little as possible with the attributes of real women, and normalized male and female natures are contrasted in homogeneous ways. "Male-dominant culture, as all feminists have observed, defines masculinity and femininity as contrasting forms. In contemporary society, men are defined as active, women as passive; men are intellectual, women are intuitive; men are inexpressive, women are emotional; men are strong, women weak; men are dominant, women submissive, etc; ad nauseam" (Jaggar 1983, 316). Feminism urged women and men to reclaim their possibilities for continuity and to break down to the polarities, so that women could take on attributes and roles previously held to be reserved for males (e.g., agency and rationality) and men could rebel against the exclusion from the "real man" stereotype of characteristics associated with women (e.g., care for children, emotionality). The challenge to the polarities posed by challenging dualistic gender construction was important for gay as well as women's liberation because it opened up the space for the formation of third or multiple terms in place of a polarized binary gender structure.

The asymmetric and hegemonic features of a dualistic division of a field tended to be theorized in terms of the concept of the Other: that woman "is not regarded as an autonomous being . . . she is defined and differentiated with reference to man and not he with reference to her" (de Beauvoir 1986, xix). Hegemonic features of a dualistic division involve the subsuming of the Other under, in relation to or by the One. This can take many forms: in terms of agency it could mean backgrounding the Other in relation to the One as foreground, devaluing or denying their contribution to joint or complex undertakings in the construction of what Lorraine Code (2000) calls a "hyperbolized autonomy" for the dominant party. In terms of value it could mean valuing or recognizing the Other just to the extent that the Other could be made to reflect or serve the primary term—for example, to resemble the colonizing self or One, as in assimilation of the colonized Other or as instrumental for the One. In terms of identity, it can mean taking woman and her essential nature to be centrally defined by her relationship to man but not vice versa. Women's identity, agency, and value in work and other aspects of life have been treated this way in many societies. Hegemonic features of dualism were especially problematized in the postcolonial context, and challenges to both polarizing and hegemonic aspects of dualistic gender construction were central parts of both early 1970s and later feminist activism.

Some feminist theorists, however, have challenged the usages of *dichotomy* and *dualism* suggested by these roles. Thus, Raia Prokhovnik (2000) in *Rational Woman: A Feminist Critique of Dichotomy* uses and explicitly argues for terminology that runs counter to that adopted here, treating dichotomy as meaning a polarizing form of distinction and assuming that dualism and dichotomy can be employed as more or less equivalent terms. But in the established dictionary sense of the term *dichotomy*, the assumption that dichotomy is automatically a polarizing function is fallacious. A separation is not the same as a polarization. Polarization (which involves what I would term "hyperseparation," in contrast to separation) as a radical form of separation or distancing is expressed differently in different kinds of logics: at the level of predicate logic, it can be expressed as the construction of a minimum overlap of properties held by nonidentical subjects that might otherwise, in a nonpolarizing context and in accordance with Leibniz's law, have a very high degree of intersection and similarity. At the level of propositional logic, polarity can be expressed in terms of various special features of certain negation operators, but it is not correct to interpret any negation, any division or separation, as polarizing. This is to confuse the operation of dividing or separating (which is compatible with high degrees of intersection) with the minimizing of intersection or overlap that characterizes sorting a field into two poles, highly or extremely distanced or separated from one another.[4] However, since the terms *dichotomy* and *dualism* are now used in multiple and conflicting ways within feminism, it may be helpful to mark the relevant distinction in alternative terms as that between separation, otherness, or alterity in the generic sense and hegemonic otherness, the latter yielding the concept of the Other.

Despite the widespread use of these frameworks of analysis and their vital importance for feminist and other liberation thought, there are substantial unclarities about how these categories of otherness and division are to be theoretically expressed and treated, and resulting differences and conflicts between feminist theorists. These differences can have major implications not only for theoretical programs but also for the basic direction of feminism. The area requires careful theorization also because the consequences of failing to distinguish adequately between division simpliciter and oppressive forms of division can be serious. In the absence of a clear distinction, unclarity and conflict about these theoretical concepts can make their appearance in the most basic places in which the concepts originate in feminist theory, giving rise to inconsistencies in the work of foundational feminist thinkers.

De Beauvoir's further comments in *The Second Sex* on the condition of being Other illustrate this. Although de Beauvoir identifies assignment to the logical category of Otherness as at the heart of women's subjugation, she does little to identify this crucial logical category clearly, and her statements about it are confusing. To be Other is to be defined through a division of the field based on privileging men as the holders of power, her statement in *The Second Sex* suggests (11). If women's oppression is contingent and removable, though, which is the main thesis of *The Second Sex*, the assignment to the category of Other must be able to be changed. De Beauvoir goes on however, almost immediately after her classic statement quoted earlier, to undermine the connection between Otherness (or dualistic division) and power, suggesting that the category of Other is "primordial" and inevitable and that it is to be explained and illustrated by such relatively innocent constructions as being faintly suspicious of other passengers in a train. These suggestions of de Beauvoir are in many ways mystifying and inconsistent. They immediately give rise to two serious problems. First, de Beauvoir's thesis that the category of the Other is inevitable undermines her main claim that "woman" is made rather than born. Second, the innocence of the train passengers example that immediately follows her major statement on Otherness undermines her case for considering the category of Otherness to give an account of or some explanation of an important form of oppression.

This unclarity about the category of the Other and how to escape it seems to be one of the factors that pushed de Beauvoir's thought into the "liberal feminist" form in which it is often criticized today by a wide variety of feminists, since it appears that the only real way to escape the category of the Other is to join that of the One, or to extend the category of the male—hence de Beauvoir's extraordinary conclusion about the "brotherhood" women had to be allowed to join in order to become fully human and her well-known overvaluation of male-coded traits and life areas relative to female-coded ones.

We can see two related problems emerging here. First, in taking the category of the Other to be inevitable, de Beauvoir seems to have conflated dualism and dichotomy—that is, forms of division that inscribe oppressive power relations with division per se—assumed that division itself was inevitable, and therefore concluded (against the direction of her own analysis) that the dualistic Otherness concept she problematized was likewise inevitable. As we will see, many others have followed her down this same path, which illustrates why the distinction between dualism and dichotomy or between alterity as such and hegemonic otherness needs to be marked clearly. The conflation of dualism and dichotomy also lies behind certain kinds of "backlash" positions and is used to throw doubt on the soundness of these basic tools of feminist analysis. Thus, Jean Curthoys (1997) employs the identification of dichotomy as the problem category for feminists to argue that since dichotomy is basic to rationality, such forms of feminist theory are "surrational" (which she glosses as "combin[ing] quite appalling methods of reasoning with a sophisticated, scholarly appearance" [62]).

There are not only theoretical gains for feminism in clarifying and refining these key concepts of analysis but also many practical, strategic, and political ones. Conceptual difficulties in redistributing power and value between a pair of terms provide an important test for the presence of hegemonic otherness, indicating that the terms of a division are not independent (but are "binaries" in the astronomical sense, requiring each other or defined in relation to each other). Thus, issues of reversal (reallocating value and agency so that roles or values between dominant and subordinate parties are reversed) are of great practical as well as of theoretical significance. Whereas identities have been conceived in terms of hegemonic otherness, liberation movements aiming at reallocating power cannot avoid addressing the issue of reversal, because such divisions conceptually block a satisfactory reallocation of power that removes the domination/subordination aspect built into those terms or identities. Without the ability to question such hegemonic constructions of alterity, opposition is locked into strategies of reverse centrism or reversal of power or value—the according of positive value to the traditionally subordinated side and of lesser value to dominant side—since this maintains the same kind of logical relationship and merely replaces one oppressed party by another. Reversal is thus the easy, beckoning way, the way most traveled, but also the one most commonly doomed to failure.

Typically reversal strategies are failures from a liberation perspective, first, because they tend to retain similar power relations to the ones they replaced and, second, because they run afoul of the paradoxes of power—for example, valuing or making powerful those aspects of the oppressed associated with their powerlessness, which of course are unlikely to survive translation into contexts where women are powerful. An example of this, in the case of women, is appeal to their more "peaceful" nature. The political significance of this is that in such dualistic contexts we cannot move forward without some reconceptualization of the terms or parties to the division; in other words, some logicophilosophical therapy is usually necessary for oppressed groups to unravel the conceptual knots of Otherness. Mainstream philosophy has given little attention to this problematic, to refining the concepts involved or unraveling certain prevalent confusions about Otherness that are tending to bring these basic concepts for liberation movements into some disrepute. A specifically feminist approach to these issues of logic is therefore a necessary and urgent development. Some clarification of multiplicity and careful consideration of available alternatives is a priority program for feminist logic. But the debate so far has been far from systematic, leaving the range of possible answers uninvestigated and untested.

Are Negative Categories Oppressive?

A tempting and often-encountered approach to the problem of the Other arises from the idea that Otherness is the product of dichotomy and goes on to identify Otherness with the conception of woman as a so-called negative category, one that is "constituted by the-absence-of-it (maleness or the phallus) via dichotomy" (Frye 1996). If dichotomy is cast as the first problem, negation must become the next problem (and associated with this, of the law of excluded middle [LEM], *p* versus not-*p*). Negative categories can come to be seen as the source of oppressive constructions of Otherness, in the way several feminist positions suggest (Jay 1981; Frye 1996; Grosz 1989; Prokhovnik 2000). This position is sometimes buttressed by a metaphysical one holding that everything that exists exists positively (Jay 1981; Prokhovnik 2000). This kind of analysis suggests a counterstrategy of converting all categories to "positive categories," substituting this apparently more Aristotelian approach for negation based on "universal exclusive dichotomy" of the sort found in modern logic (Jay 1981; Frye 1996). I want to argue that despite its superficial plausibility, this approach, which I call *negationism*, is based on a mistaken analysis of where the problem lies, as well as a mistaken analysis of Aristotelian logic as "positive," and it ultimately bogs feminists down in a morass of difficulties, arbitrary prohibitions, and unnecessary limitations on expression.

Eurocentric and androcentric thinking often pictures its Others as deficient versions of the center, defining them as lacking the center's virtues. The Other is said to be distinguished by its lacks—of the wheel (in the case of indigenous Australians), of a well-controlled and distanced rationality (in the case of women). The Other's achievements and excellences are not mentioned—that they had the aerofoil in the boomerang, that a blend of reason and care has an essential role in maintaining the conditions for life. The Others of Eurocentrism and androcentrism are pictured in terms of negative otherness, as other-than-the center rather than in terms of nonhierarchical difference, as positively-other than. Positive otherness is crucial for their liberation. However, this should not lead us to support negationism, for at least two reasons. First, we should not interpret positive otherness as involving a ban on negative descriptions; second, we would have to overcome the problem of finding a way to distinguish negative from positive properties.

The idea that negative characterizations are automatically oppressive and must be avoided at all costs if we are to attain liberated discourse is widespread among intellectuals of various kinds. It can seriously distort and limit expression in a variety of movement contexts, not just in feminism. At a recent conference I attended on postcolonial issues in Australia, for example, several speakers who wished to raise questions about the relationship between indigenous identity and the identity of other Australians encountered conceptual and terminological problems in expressing their ideas because they did not feel able to use the term *nonindigenous*. Most could not articulate good reasons for their unease. Some of those who could thought that *nonindigenous* suggested a form of reversal in which indigenous identity was treated as central and other identities defined in relation to it, in much the same way as *white* had been treated for so long as central and had defined others in relation to that identity, as "nonwhite." Others (such as myself) felt that this was a possibility, perhaps a risk in some contexts, but by no means a certainty just on the basis of the use of a negative term.

Discussion of the original issue was hamstrung because there was no general agreement on a suitable replacement term for the subject of the thesis, the contrast class to "indigenous." Some favored the locution "settler" identity, since this expression was felt to be positive, but others pointed out that it made the fact of migration and settlement central to most Australian lives and identities in ways that did not reflect orientation or consciousness for contemporary people whose ancestors may have been in Australia for four or five generations, and thus it did not seem to identify many of the relevant group in a way they would accept or recognize. Others noticed that "settler" was problematic because those who were now thought of as indigenous had, according to scientific opinion, at one stage been migrants and settlers themselves, but a long way back; this group inclined to the terminology "first settler" and "second settler." But according to yet another group, this terminology invited the story that everyone moved in on everyone else and that the injustices of colonization were a natural and inevitable part of human life. Also, it characterized indigenous people in terms of a narrative of themselves as "settlers" they mostly did not accept.

It seemed that, despite its positive appearance, the term *settler* was able to escape these ambiguities only to the extent that it relied implicitly, for a clear-cut identification of the proper group, on being surreptitiously treated as equivalent to the contrast class to the indigenous, identified as those who had been there from the beginning. That is, it relied implicitly on identifying the settler group with those who were *not* "there from the beginning" and hence on an implicitly assumed equivalence to the negative term *non-indigenous*. The appearance of avoiding the negative term was just that—an appearance, one that did not hold up when the usage was scrutinized carefully. What is clear from this experience is that the distinction between positive and negative categories is far from straightforward and that the insistence that in liberated discourse all categories must be positive categories is seriously distorting and limiting.

I shall argue that we should think carefully before interpreting positive otherness, in the way some theorists have assumed, as proscribing negative characterization. The ban on so-called negative characterizations or categories has the potential to carry feminists far from their basic agenda and has sweeping implications, casting suspicion on conceptual division in a rather indiscriminate way. Negationism sees the treatment of woman as a negative category as the problem indicated by the concept of woman as the Other. To the extent that any form of separation or distinction opens up the possibility for negative characterization, and the problem of Otherness is identified with eliminating the possibility for negative characterization, dichotomy as separation and distinction must also be seen as problematic. Since distinction and difference are as basic to feminist thought as the operation of all other thought, a program to eliminate them is self-destructive.

Under these analyses in their more extreme forms, the feminist commitment to critique the construction of woman as Other can balloon into a very drastic reduction and translation program to eliminate forms of speech perceived to be negative. Such a program is reminiscent of logical atomism and of twentieth-century logic's programs of reduction and persecution of intentional discourse in support of extensionalist science. We should think hard about the wisdom of trying to reconstitute Western thought from the bottom up in order to overcome some rather vaguely specified ideas supposedly associated with the concept of dichotomy, a concept that, as we have seen, involves a high level of ambiguity and potential for miscommunication.[5] At the extreme, this revolution of thought is imagined to be so radical in its break with traditional thought as to be virtually unspeakable (except for the efforts of the vanguard practitioners of *écriture feminin*); that is, we cannot now even imagine the form postpatriarchal thought will take after it is accomplished (Braidotti 1991; Cixous and Clement 1986). There are more moderate forms of negationism (Frye 1996; Jay 1981) in which LEM and "universal exclusive dichotomy" are rejected, but there is a specific and relatively clear proposed "reform" solution involving an Aristotelian-type reformulation of all categories as positive categories. But even in this case there are serious problems and costs in proscribing all negative characterizations.

Centrism, Not Negation, Is the Problem

What is often not realized is that the negationist strategy that brings on these and other difficulties is neither the only possible interpretation of the concept of Otherness nor the most plausible interpretation when a fuller range of options are considered, and that it is possible to honor basic feminist insights on woman as Other in much less costly ways. I will advocate here as a rival to negationism a counterhegemonic conceptual strategy in which Otherness is analyzed as a problem not of dichotomous negation or conceptual division as such but of *centrism*, a primary-secondary pattern of attribution that sets up one term as primary or as center and defines the Other as secondary in relation to it.[6] The difference between negationism and centric analysis can be expressed as follows: for negationism, to think of the other as "positively-other-than," we have to avoid all negative characterizations; for the counterhegemonic analysis focusing on centrism, what is necessary is to avoid certain (asymmetrical) patterns of distribution of *all* attributions (whether positive or negative) that set up a centrism or a reverse centrism. We can make good logical and feminist sense of the concept of positive otherness without rejecting dichotomy, without needing to proscribe either negative categories or exclusive/exhaustive dichotomies in any general way. To be positively-other-than is to be characterizable as other in ways that allow a high degree of independence and that avoid these centric forms of construction. Centric forms exhibit hegemonic and asymmetrical patterns of relationship that can sometimes involve certain kinds of negatively specified qualities but are neither confined to these kinds of negativity nor exhausted by them.

Since there are different analyses of and ways of dealing with the problem of Otherness, it seems like a good idea to look at each of these alternatives and make comparisons of the costs and benefits of each before opting for one of them. I consider four positions here: negationism, centrism, and two more minor positions, relationism, and externalism. Negationism, I shall argue, although the currently popular analysis, is a poorly directed scattershot approach that rules out far too much and does not accurately identify the oppressive elements in the construction of Otherness. The centric analysis not only involves more careful consideration of where the oppressive elements in the construction of Otherness lie but does not require the very problematic distinction between positive and negative qualities or categories on which the negationist position relies so crucially. These rival analyses are correspondingly associated with contrasting positions on the concepts of dualism and dichotomy. For negationism, all forms of dichotomy are problematic, and the act of division that marks off a term from an infinite plenum is itself oppressive (Jay 1981; Frye 1996). For the centric analysis, the main problem does not lie in dichotomy (meaning conceptual division) at all but in those forms of conceptual division that inscribe relations of power in their mode of division—that is, in those subsets of dichotomies we can term dualisms or binary oppositions.

Where such oppressive dualistically constituted categories of Otherness are not clearly distinguished from those created by dichotomy (where dichotomy involves "the cut," the use of negation or distinction), the rejection of dualistic constructions of otherness can throw suspicion on the law of excluded middle and on all dichotomous uses of negation to draw distinctions between a category or proposition and what it excludes. Frye (1996), for example, has identified such oppressive dualistic constructions with "universal exclusive dichotomy," which is often thought of as the heart of negation. Frye contrasts this with an apparently Aristotelian construction of the other as a positive category (the resort to this allegedly Aristotelian positive logic being somewhat paradoxical in this context, given Aristotle's explicit identification of women as deficient males). I agree with Frye that the feminist project involves moving from the "deficient male" concept of woman to the idea of woman as positively-other-than, but I disagree with her identification of this oppressive concept of Otherness with negation or with universal exclusive dichotomy.[7]

The negationist strategy of identifying oppressive Otherizing attributions with negative characterizations is both too wide and too narrow, indicating that necessary and sufficient conditions for oppressiveness have not been properly identified in negationism. It is too wide because it disallows a range of nonproblematic negative categories and thus generates excessive logical fallout in problematizing conceptual division in an overly general way. At first, there is nothing inherently or obviously oppressive in merely being attributed characteristics that invoke an absence or involve a negation. What's oppressive about "Whatever else we know of Jane, we know that she is not the kind of person to let others down" or "You are not among those selected for this round of conscription"? What's oppressive about "I am not (identical with) ice cream"? Surely we stretch the concept of oppression if we apply it here beyond the point of usefulness or comprehension. Are botany and zoology advanced forms of oppression because their distinctions are based on repeated dichotomous cuts or divisions? It is hard to argue convincingly that it is automatically oppressive to make divisions or cuts in the world. Certainly a logical framework that allowed us only to make cuts and never allowed us to represent the flow of the world would be one of severe limitation, but limitation is not the same as oppressiveness. And a satisfactory logical vocabulary would allow us to represent both divisions and flows, since there is no reason why we cannot choose both or why one way of viewing the world must completely exclude the other.

If, on the one hand, the negationist diagnosis that the problem of Otherness is one of negative characterization is far too wide and takes in a variety of nonproblematic cases, it is also too narrow because it fails to address an important range of relationships feminists have found oppressive that do not turn on being characterized negatively. In feminist thought a very different range of relations seem to be problematized in gender relations of Otherness than negative characterizations of women. Often the construction of Otherness involves a primary/secondary type of relationship, like that of Eve to Adam, where she comes temporally later and is constructed (from his rib) as a helpmate and companion. That is, woman is Other because she is defined in both secondary and instrumental terms in relation to man. As Luce Irigaray (1985) points out, modern androcentrism has conceived woman, perhaps with slightly more subtlety than classical androcentrism, according to the housewife model, not as occupying a space herself in her own right but as *enclosing a space for another* (who is thus treated as primary).

There are many notorious difficulties about what gets to count as a negative/positive characterization, and there is a large gray area where decision is difficult, to say the least. For this reason, many deny that the concept is viable at all. I do not need to go this far and am willing to allow that there may be some intuitive legitimacy to the concept. But assuming we do accept the distinction, it is hard to see why we should not allow the characteristic Irigaray points to—the enclosure of space for another—to be a positive characteristic. A house or shelter can be seen as enclosing space in a positive and active way, surely. On whatever ground this feminine role of enclosing space for a male other is problematic for feminists, then, this ground cannot be simply that it is a negative quality or one that specifies woman as an absence of maleness. Rather, what is objectionable about the concept of woman as enclosing a space for a (male) other rather than occupying a space in her own right is that, *where this kind of role is attributed asymmetrically to just one gender,* woman, it clearly treats the male as the primary term and attributes a secondary and instrumental role to woman in contrast. Asymmetry is important here; if the enclosure is mutual—that is, if each encloses a space for the other—it is unclear why we should as feminists see such a relationship as oppressive. Asymmetry, a major feature of de Beauvoir's account, is a mark of a power relationship, especially of a primary/secondary type of power relationship.

Thus, feminists, too, have found highly problematic the traditional idea, expressed in conventional Western female titles, that a woman is properly to be identified in relation to a husband or another subsuming male as center—for example, as someone's wife (Mrs. John Doe), daughter (Miss Ro Doe), or "relict" or widow. In insisting on "Ms" and in challenging the custom of taking the male name, feminists are insisting on being identified as "positively-other-than," but this does not seem to involve any change from a negative to a positive category. What is problematic about "Mrs. John Doe" is surely not that she is identified as "NOT"-something, and certainly not that she is identified as NOT-Mr. John Doe (for as Mrs. John Doe, she is not identified in this way at all), but rather that she is identified crucially and asymmetrically in relation to him and not he in relation to her.[8] De Beauvoir's phraseology emphasizing the asymmetry of the One (or Absolute) and the Other was well chosen.

As these points indicate, not only is negation or absence itself in a description not inherently oppressive, but there is much more than characterizing one thing as the absence-of-the-other that is oppressive in the hegemonic category of the Other. In centric conceptions of otherness, for example, the center is the source of value or meaning, and all others derive their value or disvalue ultimately from their relationship or lack of relationship to the center. Such hegemonic constructions function to "naturalize" colonizing distributions that make the Other into a way to enlarge or strengthen the One.[9] These ways to define the Other in terms of the One may not involve negation or absence at all. Further hegemonic features not involving absence include incorporation (colonization or assimilation) and instrumentalization—the reduction and absorption of the Other to the status of an inferiorized version of the self; foil to self or to that of mere means or resource for the self or center, and the Other's reductive redefinition entirely or largely in terms of its relationship to the center; and the center's needs. Incorporation entails a failure to come to terms with what Iris Young (1990) calls "unassimilated otherness"—otherness that is reduced, assimilated, or incorporated.

Alternative nonoppressive constructions of otherness can involve reconception of the other as a positively-other-than center of needs and "independent" or intrinsic (not purely instrumental-to-the-center) value and nonhierarchically conceived difference that do not have to be brought back conceptually to the center as the source of value or meaning. The case in which the Other is defined as the absence or lack of the One or Center is thus a special case of a larger set of hegemonic relations of alterity that need not involve negation or absence at all.

We can mount a similar argument against the related idea that the problem of Otherness lies in woman being characterized *in relation to man (relationism)*. If oppressiveness does not lie in being characterized negatively, neither does it lie in being characterized relationally. If both parties are identified equally in relation to the other—for example, as "husband of Mrs. Doe" and "wife of Mr. Doe"—then there is no indication of a problem of crucial concern to feminists in the use of such mutual relational identifications. If he holds his name in his own right, but she holds her name because of her relationship to him, then there is a problem for feminists, but it is not relationality or the use of relational characteristics as identifying features that is the problem. If all individuals are formed in relation to and in interaction with others, as so many feminists have insisted, only an overatomized or overindividualized worldview that denied this could see relationality as unhealthy dependency or as problematic in itself. No, these concepts involve hegemonic centrism not because they involve relationality per se but *because they systematically recognize and distribute this relationality in asymmetrical and hegemonic ways*, treating one party as background or support for the other as foreground, or in the "relict" or "virgin" case, as what the center leaves behind or omits to vanquish. In these examples, the wider problem behind this type of definition is the oppressive pattern of relationships I have called "centrism," involving the asymmetrical identification of woman *in terms of her relationship to man*, and not he in relation to her, rather than any form of negative or relational characterization itself.

Does feminism require negationism? I think the answer must be no. When we look carefully, say, at de Beauvoir's classic statement quoted earlier, we can see several elements that enable us to locate her fundamental analysis as one of centrism rather than negationism or relationism. She states first that "humanity is male and man defines woman not in herself but as relative to him." The problem is identified in this passage as one of taking the male as primary, as the norm or center and defining woman in secondary terms in relation to this center. To say that woman is *defined* as being not "in herself" but as "relative to him," or "with reference to him and not he with reference to her," is not to locate oppressiveness in relational terms or descriptions generally but to point to a pattern of distribution of relational and other descriptions that is asymmetrical and centric. This pattern is also indicated by the term *defined,* since to be so defined and differentiated in relation to man is also to be summed up by this relationship, to be *reduced* to being a "helpmate" or secondary being in relation to man—hence the title *The Second Sex.* That is, it is not just the odd attribution of a relational property that is problematized in the use of the phrase "defined and differentiated" but the idea that what is central to and defining of woman's nature is to be found in this relationship to man. This makes it an asymmetrical relationship, since what is taken as defining of woman's relationship is her relation to man, but what is taken as defining of man's nature is not his relationship to woman. In this pattern of relationship, man occupies the position of primary term, thus reducing woman to a secondary form of being. What is required to detect such oppressive definitions is pattern recognition, not a witch-hunt for odd or isolated negative descriptions.

When we examine carefully the analyses of feminists who have essayed an explanation of the phallocentric or androcentric structure that feminists have found problematic, we can usually see similar evidence that indicates an implicit appeal to a centric type of analysis.[10] The belief that feminist analysis requires negationism or relationism and that what is therefore indicted is dichotomy, division, or negation itself is a fallacy.

Is Logical Negation Centrist?

A general proscription of dichotomy or negative description is then inaccurate, unnecessary, and unhelpful. Nevertheless, it is true that some kinds and uses of negation and dichotomy exhibit, entrench, and naturalize centric patterns of thought. Thus certain *kinds* of negative characterizations that conceive the Other asymmetrically as absence, lack, residue, or deficiency[11] of the One are plainly centric, exhibiting that pattern of distribution that places one term at the center and treats the other as derived or secondary. Centric uses of negation include those of classical androcentric frameworks expressed in the work of Aristotle and others that explicitly conceive woman as a deficient man, as a lack of the fully human qualities of the male. Similarly, the idea of the other as a *terra nullius,* as a vacuum, an absence of self, a space inviting occupation, is the other side of the dualistic formation of a colonizing self primed to fill that vacuum with itself and its works. The eurocentric colonizer defines the other as background to his foreground, as deficiency of reason or civilization, as inessential in contrast to himself as essential. Defined thus in relation to the norm or center as a lack or deficiency, the Other is seen as having a secondary form of existence, in contrast to a center conceived as primary, subsuming, and self-sufficient (or, as de Beauvoir put it, as Absolute). When the qualities of one item are specified negatively in relation to another item conceived as norm or center, what is oppressive is not negation as such but the power relation, the hegemonic centrism that distributes both positive and negative attributions in ways that privilege the center.

The conception of the Other as an absence of or as a deficient version of self is a common strategy of colonizing frameworks. If in these frameworks woman is conceived as the same but lesser, inferior, or those respects in which she is not the same are seen as contributing to her supposed inferiority, no positive mode of being other is available to her. Modern androcentric frameworks often continue to represent the feminized other as an absence of or deficiency in relation to the male. Germaine Greer (1998), for example, has argued that the tendency to classify as women those males regarded as defective or dubious is one of a number of features that confirms the continued treatment of the category woman as the mere remainder of the primary category of man rather than as an independently identifiable positive category. But in these cases, it is not negation as such that is the problem but the insertion of negative qualities such as absence into a centric pattern in which one term is privileged and the other defined as its absence or lack. Concepts of absence or lack themselves are not automatically to blame for this pattern of usage that places one term at the center and defines the other in relation to it as a lack of it or its qualities (real or supposed). In fact, this is just a special case of defining one term as secondary in relation to another taken as center, as discussed earlier.

To say this, however, is not to endorse the idea that centrism and phallocentrism are always external to logic itself, just a matter of informal assumptions and usage. This idea—externalism—is in conflict with the central and fundamentally correct insight of the theory of Other, that oppressive assumptions can become naturalized as part of the logical structure of concepts of otherness, where they are very difficult, without employing considerable logical and philosophical skill, to detect, expose, and discard. The opposite extreme from taking logic (Nye 1990) and/or negation (Jay 1981; Frye 1996) to be automatically oppressive is treating them as above contest and irrelevant to issues of oppression, which are treated as always external to the logic and as never calling logic into question (as in the work of Curthoys [1997] and Haack [1996]). Curthoys (1997) reacts to the overkill of negationism by defending both logic and the law of excluded middle in such generalized terms, articulating an externalism that holds that assumptions of the inferiority of one term in a dualism or binary opposition can never be "part of the logic," since logic is neutral and unquestionable but must always be located as separate assumptions that are external to the logical structure concerned (74). Although I share her concern about negationism, I believe externalism to be quite inadequate as an account of what can be expressed via logic and to underestimate the potential forms and modes of inferiorization that are available through logical frameworks. The assumption that the Other belongs to an inferior order sometimes appears as a separate explicit assumption, but more often the assignment of the Other to a lower, secondary order appears in a more subtle and insidious form as embedded in the logic, or in the choice of logical framework.[12] There are multiple ways the inferiorization and subsumption of one term in a two-term construction can be expressed directly in the logical structure of certain otherness and negation operators without appearing in terms of separate identifiable assumptions. So it is not true that questions of centrism are not a matter for or of logic, although centrism itself is part of a larger pattern of relationships that is much bigger than logic.[13]

Centrism can be reflected in the formal structure of negations, even if it cannot be reduced to a matter of negation. Negationists and externalists, although strongly opposed, have in common the failure to appreciate the multiplicity of logics and negations (also fatally obscured by a singularizing and homogenizing term like *dichotomy*). Modern symbolic logic presents us with a multiplicity of significantly different negations, only some of which are plausible candidates for oppressive otherness interpretations. Clearly, if a multiplicity of otherness concepts are expressible in terms of negation, we must be cautious in making any simple identification of negation per se with either oppressive or nonoppressive constructions of otherness. Some negations are much more centric than others, the extreme case being classical negation, where *p* completely controls its other not-*p*, as I have argued (Plumwood 1993a, 1993b). The negation of classical propositional logic treats difference as a sort of "deviance."[14] It takes *p* as primary and treats its negation as having a secondary role, as delineating what is left over after the primary term "*p*" has finished taking up its slice of the universe. Classical not-*p* cannot be independently identified and homogenizes the Other as an oppositional remainder. Although classical logic has symmetrical negation features such as double negation, a proposition and its negation are not really treated as on an equal footing, in classical terms; although any proposition can occupy the primary role, once this is set the behavior of its negation is completely determined (i.e., it is entirely a residue or remainder). If we think of *p* and its negation as debate partners, what emerges from a debate between *p* and its classically conceived negative partner is a kind of monologue, because a classical proposition completely controls and determines its negation or other, delineating a monological logic that allows a proposition to swallow up the difference its negation represents and push it into the role of being background to its foreground.[15] Classical "not-*p*" does not have the sort of independence of movement a debate or dialogical partner has; it is identified as and reduced to being just a foil to *p*. Although simplicity is often advanced as a reason for favoring classical logic, this is problematic because it is always simpler to represent a monological system in comparison to a dialogical one. I have conjectured that the dominance of such a logic in the formal thinking of the West may reflect the dominance of a "logic of colonization" in its history and culture (Plumwood 1993a).

Classical negation, then, is a centrist negation, but not all dichotomous negations are centrist. The idea that all dichotomous negations are like classical negation is one of the misconceptions underlying the objections that negationists Nancy Jay and Marilyn Frye make to "dichotomy." Jay (1981) objects that because two terms in a dichotomous structure are contradictory, they are mutually exclusive and discontinuous, and there is no possible meeting point between them. Similarly, says Jay, they are mutually exhaustive, and there is no middle ground between them. The two terms between them cover every situation and possibility (exhaustive) and can never both be present in any situation (exclusive). This is true of classical logic (taking terms as propositions), but it is not true of certain nonclassical logics that are dichotomous (in the sense that they do not abandon the principle of division, the law of excluded middle). It is notorious (and has been the subject of much discussion in paraconsistent and relevance logic circles) that in the case of certain relevant ("deviant") logics, for instance, the associated formal semantics includes situations that are both incomplete and inconsistent.[16] That is, they do not fit the description of dichotomy Jay gives, which is assimilated to classical logic.

What needs to be acknowledged here is that "dichotomy" like negation can take multiple forms or grades. The truth-functional negation of classical logic represents a very strong grade of dichotomy that polarizes truth and falsity, and it insists that the only rules for negation we can use are the exclusive and exhaustive ones appropriate for consistent and complete situations or worlds. This form of dichotomy is exclusive and exhaustive everywhere.

Classical logic assumes that the rules of dichotomy appropriate for consistent and complete situations are the only ones we can ever have. In contrast, the form of dichotomy expressed in certain nonclassical "deviant" negations like relevant negation (in some of its forms) is exclusive and exhaustive only in some places (truth-functional places). Instead of working with a highly polarized account of truth and falsity, it allows us to take account of intentionality and of different ways of constructing and (mis)understanding the world. This type of negation allows that we will need rules of dichotomy for many situations (e.g., the "intentional worlds" of knowledge, belief, fiction, and fantasy) we will encounter or can construct, where neither a proposition nor its negation belongs and where both may belong. This is a less polarizing and more widely applicable form of dichotomy, but one that still allows a form of exclusive and exhaustive dichotomy to be expressed in suitable contexts.

But even if Jay's argument did not fail to make this distinction, it faces another problem. Jay does not explain clearly where the problem for feminists is supposed to lie in the exclusive and exhaustive division feature, and the argument she gives for objecting to it appears to conflate the polarization characteristic of dualistic structures with something quite different, the separation or division that is part of dichotomy. Gender dualisms set up opposed hyperseparated or polarized gender categories, complementary normative natures for men and women that tend to emphasize or even to maximize the distance between them and to minimize the overlap between the characteristics of "real men" and "real women" (Plumwood 1993a; Frye 1983). Such dualistic polarities are among the main ways their binary and oppositional character is expressed in logical terms. Polarized or radically dichotomous gender structures exclude middle ground as far as possible, leave few characteristics open or ungendered, and aim to prevent the realization of gender ambiguity or commonality. But these oppositional and distance-maximizing features are certainly not part of dichotomous division simpliciter, since nonidentity and division (and exclusion) between terms can be achieved if they differ only minimally—for example, by a single characteristic according to Liebniz's law. In short, dichotomy, separation, or division, even exclusive and exhaustive division, is not at all the same as opposition or polarity, in the way Jay's objections seem to assume. The confusion in this argument between dichotomy as a conceptual division, cut, split, separation, distinction, or difference on the one hand, and division based on polarity and opposition on the other, shows once again why we need to distinguish more clearly between dualisms (binarisms) and dichotomies.

The second and major feature of Jay's objection is elaborated by Frye (1996): a dichotomous structure must establish a primary/secondary relationship between a term and its other, since the second term is defined through the "infinitation of the negative" as the universe minus the first term. In short, a dichotomous structure is automatically a centric structure. Thus, according to Frye, "when woman is defined as not-man, she is cast into the infinite undifferentiated plenum." Although Frye may be right to identify the consigning of the Other to an infinite, unqualified, and homogenized plenum as a hegemonic feature,[17] her association between dichotomy, LEM, and such a consignment is mistaken, depending, once again, on the importation of features of classical logic and classical negation to all logics and negations. Not all dichotomous negations consign the other to an infinite undifferentiated plenum in the way Frye assumes. Thus, some of the dichotomous negations of so-called deviant logic (known to their supporters as relevant or paraconsistent logics), for example, treat division and otherness in terms of a structured and relevantly qualified plenum, not one that is specified only as excluded by the primary term, and is otherwise chaotic or totally formless, as Frye claims. In relevant logics not-*p* is not completely controlled by *p* as in classical logic; not-*p* is independently identifiable and operates more like an equal presence or dialogical partner as constituting an equal but different debating presence. Such negations do allow us to formulate concepts of positive otherness.[18]

Proponents of the negationist perspective go on to reformulate logic and negation as an Aristotelian logic of terms in which all categories are, in effect, positive categories, to express the concept of positively-other-than (Frye 1996; Jay 1981). But categories emerge as positive in this kind of logic because it contains a very weak theory of negation, which does not permit us to make compound terms through negation and other logical operators; what would otherwise be expressed in terms of negation simply appears as a further independent term. It is rather misleading to describe such independent terms as "positive," since negative terms can still be used provided they are not analyzed. However, such a logic of categories not only lacks the means to express an important range of ideas (as in the nonindigenous example I discussed in the second section) but also cannot adequately express the contrast between the two kinds of otherness, and it cannot adequately serve the purposes of feminists and other liberation theorists who wish to study and teach about this contrast. In a sense such a theory also cannot give an adequate account of positive otherness, since there is no contrast class. If all forms of otherness are expressible in a logical framework only as positive or else as negative, we cannot formulate the distinction between oppressive and nonoppressive constructions of otherness. The advocacy by some theorists of an Aristotelian framework of A/B terms in place of dichotomy proposes to solve the problem of dualisms in the ostrichlike way of refusing to allow us to represent them. But if we can represent both oppressive and nonoppressive forms of otherness (e.g., as different concepts of negation) in terms of symbolic logic, that is a superior solution, since it enables us to compare and contrast them and discuss their relationship. As Hass (1998) argues, Aristotelian contrariety does not have the sorts of properties feminists are seeking.

The overall implications for the status of Western reason of the rival positions of negationism and centrism are as different as could be expected, following a similar pattern to those discussed earlier. Negationism tends to condemn Western reason as committed to oppressive forms in a highly generalized way. For the centric analysis, Western reason, which is multiple and not politically neutral, requires some major modification and the exercise of theory choice to select liberatory forms, but fortunately this not does not imply the total rejection of principles that seem as fundamental to thought as dichotomous division. The Western tradition does not emerge unscathed from the centric analysis, although it does not need to be and should not be rejected in its entirety or in as extreme a way as negationism suggests. Armed with these distinctions, not only are we better equipped to validate feminist claims that in important respects the dominant tradition has been dualistic and phallocentric, but also we can formulate an intelligible alternative.

Here I have argued that since not all forms of dichotomy inscribe relations of power in their mode of division, not all forms of dichotomy need to be rejected. To avoid confusion, the problematic forms of conceptual division should be clearly distinguished terminologically—for example, as dualisms, binary oppositions, or hegemonic centrisms, none of which should be equated with dichotomy as such. It is a challenge for feminist theory to delineate the characteristics of that subset of dichotomies that are oppressive and can properly be termed dualisms or binarisms, and for feminist logic to investigate the logical expression of oppressive and oppositional forms of division.

The debate between negationist and centrist analyses raises some brave and broad philosophical and logical questions for feminists. Is the logical capacity for negation and division the fundamental source of oppression and opposition, of an obsessively and egocentrically divided view of the world? Or is it, as I am inclined to think, as basic to the functioning of life and thought as the making of distinctions, the ability to discriminate one thing from another, as telling you from me, your place from my place? What is the role of negation and negations in human culture, in particular cultures? Is a form of life replacing contradiction by contrariety and using exclusively positive categories imaginable, and what could it look like? How would it rework botany and zoology? How much would we lose? These questions cannot be settled by an appeal to tradition, as in externalism (Curthoys 1997), or foreclosed by ambiguous and conflating terminology or simple assumption, as in negationism. They need real investigation, which must form part of the future philosophical agenda for feminist logic.

Notes

1. Braidotti (1991, 177).
2. The terminology "positively-other-than" is used by Braidotti (1991).
3. For example, 1970s feminist theologians and writers such as Rosemary Ruether, Mary Daly, and Susan Griffin investigated the development of mind/body and spirit/matter dualism as linked to male/female dualism.
4. Prokhovnik (2000) advances various specific arguments for identifying the important problems she addresses with the term *dichotomy* (172). She argues that "dualism implies the oppositional but not necessarily the hierarchical component at issue." This is true, as I have noted earlier, but exactly the same can be said of the term *dichotomy*, which in its established dictionary sense carries no general hierarchical implications. The concept of dualism can readily be extended beyond the polarization feature to include the fuller case of hegemonic otherness, since there is no conflict with well-established usage, as there is in the case of dichotomy. A further unfortunate effect of addressing these issues of alterity in terms of "dichotomy" is to place excessive emphasis on the binary aspect of a separation as the source of oppressiveness. But binariness itself is neither necessary nor sufficient for oppressiveness. There can surely be oppressive trichotomous divisions, so it is not necessary, and it is quite unclear, that we should consider the dichotomous forms of classification widely used in biology to be problematic. Prokhovnik argues secondly that feminist usage treats the terms as interchangeable; this approach is highly problematic, since at least some feminists have objected to such assumptions of equivalence, but in any case such usage would remain problematic to the extent that it entrenched the confusions and miscommunications identified earlier. Interchangeable usage of the terms in feminism could reflect the small overlap between feminism and logical theory. In any case, feminist usage and communication are not the only matters to be considered here, since feminist theory is not an island but needs to make connection where possible with other relevant theoretical discourses. Finally, Prokhovnik argues, "Dichotomy suggests a radical, extreme and fixed form of distinction, whereas dualism can imply no more than a pair of alternatives." It seems to me that, in terms of both the *Oxford English Dictionary* entries and of established usage in logic, precisely the opposite is the case; it is dichotomy that may imply no more than a pair of alternatives and dualism that suggests a radical, extreme, and fixed form of distinction. However, I do not really care how the distinction is marked terminologically as long as it *is* marked somehow in a nonconfusing way. For example, it can be marked as a distinction between separation and hegemonic otherness. That is, the issue is primarily one not about preferred terminology but about the crucial character of the distinction.

5. Thus, Prokhovnik's condemnation of dichotomy is directed against a large range of vaguely specified "tendencies" such as adversarial thinking and intolerance of ambiguity. To the extent that a real problem exists here, it seems to lie in the dominance of these modes in certain contexts, but the nature of the contexts in which they are problematic is not specified. Ambiguity is therefore problematic in some contexts but not in others. Some of the problems Prokhovnik points to may be thought of as a special case of a dualistic form—namely, the dualistic construction of argument and truth—but these are not part of dichotomy as such and are not the same as the problem of hegemonic otherness.

6. I use the general term *centrism* rather than *phallocentrism* because the relevant pattern identified is not limited to gender or genderized relationships, although dominant gender relations in many societies are prime examples of centric patterning. See Plumwood (1993b).

7. Frye rejects the term *dualism* on the grounds that it involves no genuine recognition of the items as two independent items, since one controls the other. She is right in this point, I believe, but I would take the term *dualism* not as indicating that two independent items are recognized but rather in the sense she mentions of "two together," where two terms are constituted in relation to one another—for example, oppositionally in relation to one another with one as center to periphery, sometimes also described as a binary opposition. Although these formations certainly have an underlying monological aspect, as Frye notes, they also have characteristic features ascribed to dualism—namely, hyperseparation and polarization of categories. A two-term construction in which one term dominates is only doubtfully captured in the term *monism* that Frye recommends, since this recognizes only one term or element.

8. Choice of surnames can carry this primary/secondary structure even in the absence of the titles feminists have problematized.

9. For more details on this centric structure and its use to naturalize oppression, see Plumwood (1993b).

10. What feminists usually indict, even where the rubric "dichotomy" is invoked, is the pattern of relationship characteristic of centrism. Thus, Moira Gatens (1991), in her textbook on feminist theory, identifies phallocentric thought as occurring "where one central term defines all others only in terms relative to itself" (92). Terry Threadgold (1990) takes phallocentrism as involving "a construction of [the] world in binary terms such that one term is always regarded as the norm and highly valorised, while the other is defined only ever in relation to it and devalorised" (1). Many more examples could be supplied.

11. Residue and deficiency concepts are already assymmetrical, whereas absence itself is not clearly or always so.

12. There are multiple ways the inferiorization of one term in a two-term construction can be expressed directly in the logical structure of certain otherness and negation operators without appearing as a set of separate identifiable assumptions or meanings (i.e., as "content"). There are structural reasons why this kind of subtlety is especially important in modernist liberal democracy. To the extent that a polity justifies its rule by presenting its provision of justice in a universalized form, as liberal

democracy especially does (Walzer 1983), built-in exclusions have to be hidden or presented in a nonexplicit form on pain of contradiction. Burying them in identity constructions or in the logical structure itself can be the best ways of hiding them and making them inaccessible for critical examination, achieving exclusion without directly contradicting the apparent universality and inclusiveness of its claims to justice.

13. Important questions persist about whether all centrisms are hegemonic. I think that although centrisms may share a common logical structure (a conjecture that remains to be closely investigated), only a certain class is hegemonic; that is, questions of oppression cannot be reduced to a matter of logical structure. Thus, some concepts in some contexts can get to be treated as the norm or as privileged in terms of expectations of occurrence, and their contrasts as exceptions, without our being able to say that the outcome is "oppressive" or involves power (e.g., "clear" in contrast to "cloudy" for those living in the desert). A hegemonic centrism would involve a larger range of contexts than normalcy of occurrence, privileging one term over the other—for example, as a source of value, meaning, agency, identity, and so forth. To allow for this, I prefer the terminology "hegemonic centrism" (see, e.g., Plumwood 1998).

14. Ironically, this is just the opposite way around from what is suggested by the scornful term "deviant logic" applied to relevant and paraconsistent logics by defenders of classical logic (Quine 1970; Haack 1974). It is classical logic that treats otherness as deviance and alternative forms of logic that have the potential for avoiding this through a more independent role for negation.

15. We can, as I have argued in Plumwood (1993a), relate these features to the paradoxes of material implication that relevant and paraconsistent logics are designed to counter.

16. See Routley and Plumwood (1972).

17. This feature of classical logic also can be linked to its production of the paradoxes of material implication.

18. As I argue in Plumwood (1993b).

References

Braidotti, Rosi. *Patterns of Dissonance*. London: Routledge, 1991.

Code, Lorraine. "The Perversion of Autonomy and the Subjection of Women." In *Relational Autonomy: Feminist Perspectives on Autonomy, Agency, and the Social Self*, ed. Catriona Mackenzie and Natalie Stoljar. Oxford: Oxford University Press, 2000.

Collins, Patricia Hill. *Black Feminist Thought*. London: Routledge, 1990.

Curthoys, Jean. *Feminist Amnesia: The Wake of Women's Liberation*. London: Routledge, 1997.

Cixous, Helene, and Catherine Clement. *The Newly Born Woman*. Manchester: Manchester University Press, 1986.

de Beauvoir, Simone. *The Second Sex*. New York: Vintage, 1989.

Friedman, Susan Stanford. "Beyond White and Other: Relationality and Narratives of Race in Feminist Discourse." *Signs* (Autumn 1995): 1–49.

Frye, Marilyn. *The Politics of Reality*. New York: Crossing, 1983.

———. "The Necessity of Differences: Constructing a Positive Category of Women." *Signs* (Summer 1996): 991–1010.

Gatens, Moira. *Feminism and Philosophy: Perspectives on Difference and Equality*. Cambridge: Polity, 1991.

Greer, Germaine. *The Whole Woman*. London: Doubleday, 1998.

Grosz, Elizabeth. *Sexual Subversions*. Sydney: Allen & Unwin, 1989.

Haack, Susan. *Deviant Logic, Fuzzy Logic*. Chicago: University of Chicago Press, 1974. (New edition 1996.)

———. "Preposterism and Its Consequences." *Social Philosophy and Policy* 13, no. 2 (1996): 296–315.

Hass, Marjorie. "Feminist Readings of Aristotelian Logic." In *Feminist Interpretations of Aristotle*, ed. Cynthia A. Freeland. University Park: Pennsylvania State University Press, 1998.

hooks, bell. *Feminist Theory: From Margin to Centre*. Boston: South End, 1984.

Irigaray, Luce. *Speculum of the Other Woman*. Ithaca, N.Y.: Cornell University Press, 1985.

Jaggar, Alison. *Feminist Politics and Human Nature*. Brighton: Harvester, 1983.

Jay, Nancy. "Gender and Dichotomy." *Feminist Studies* 7, no. 1 (1981): 38–56.

le Doeuff, Michele. *Hipparchia's Choice*. Oxford: Blackwell, 1989.

Nye, Andrea. *Words of Power*. London: Routledge, 1990.

Plumwood, Val. *Feminism and the Mastery of Nature*. London: Routledge, 1993a.

———. "The Politics of Reason: Towards a Feminist Logic." *Australasian Journal of Philosophy* 71, no. 4 (December 1993b): 436–462.

———. "Paths beyond Human-centredness: Lessons from Liberation Struggles." In *An Invitation to Environmental Philosophy*, ed. Anthony Weston. Oxford: Oxford University Press, 1998.

Prokhovnik, Raia. *Rational Woman: A Feminist Critique of Dichotomy*. New York: Routledge, 2000.

Quine, W. V. *Philosophy of Logic*. Englewood Cliffs, N.J.: Prentice Hall, 1970.

Routley, R., and Val Plumwood. "The Semantics of First Degree Entailment," *Nous* 6 (1972): 335–359.

Threadgold, Terry, and Anne Cranny-Francis, eds. *Feminine/Masculine and Representation*. Sydney: Allen & Unwin, 1990.

Walzer, Michael. *Spheres of Justice*. Princeton, N.J.: Princeton University Press, 1983.

Young, Iris. *Justice and the Politics of Difference*. Princeton, N.J.: Princeton University Press, 1990.

CHAPTER THREE

~

Fluid Thinking: Irigaray's Critique of Formal Logic

MARJORIE HASS

Luce Irigaray is often read, by both her critics and her defenders as advocating a rejection of logical discourse in favor of a retreat to an irrational, but more authentic *parler femme*. Although this is one of the most celebrated (and condemned) aspects of her work, her critique of formal logic and its relation to *parler femme* remains largely unexplored and, I think, misunderstood. Far from a retreat to irrationality, Irigaray's critique of logic is reminiscent of her critique of other representational structures constitutive of Western culture, such as law and language. In each case she argues that the supposedly neutral symbolic mechanism conceals a hidden isomorphism with our cultural structuration of masculinity. And as in these other cases, Irigaray's response is not to try to "neutralize" the system in question. Instead, she gestures toward an alternative representational structure that can serve as a counterpoint by symbolizing that which remains necessarily unsymbolized in the system.

Irigaray's critique of logic has received less attention than the challenges she makes to law and language. Yet it is in many ways her most important. Logic is the symbolic structure that we hold up as the most neutral of all, as essentially, definitionally neutral. It serves as the exemplar of neutrality itself. For Irigaray to unmask logic is to call the very possibility of neutrality into question. But for this very reason, the case against logic is also the hardest to make plausible. When she turns to language, Irigaray has empirical evidence to support her conjecture that language is never sexually neutral.[1] When addressing law, she can point to a specific history in which women are explicitly excluded.[2] The case of logic, however, is different, in kind. As we shall see, Irigaray's approach to logic is the most theoretical and associative of her treatments of formal systems, requiring her to use her full range of philosophical techniques. In this chapter, I interpret and evaluate Irigaray's critique of formal logic as it is revealed in her analyses of three key logical concepts: negation, identity, and generality.

Before turning to her specific critique, I want to situate Irigaray's approach to logic within her overall philosophical project. Irigaray has identified her work as comprising three phases. The first, including *Speculum of the Other Woman*, *This Sex Which Is Not One*, and *An Ethics of Sexual Difference*, showed how the masculine subject had interpreted the world; the second phase explored the possibility of defining a second subject; the third shows how to define a relationship between two subjects.[3] As this episodic presentation of her intellectual work indicates, Irigaray's work rests on the premise that the generative, sense-giving structures of Western culture (e.g., law, language, logic, and economy) provide no representation of feminine existence, except insofar as it is commensurable with masculinity. More problematically, these structures are such that it is impossible to fully represent feminine otherness within them. All that is available is the small space of representation assigned to women's bodies: the symbolic images of flow, fluidity, indefiniteness. In her work, Irigaray uses these images as a lever, encouraging us to push our thinking and speaking in new directions and bring about a transformation in consciousness. She acts as both prophet and muse urging us to a land just slightly out of reach, just beyond the next horizon. And it is in just this mode that Irigaray returns again and again to the logic of negation, identity, and generality to illustrate the monosexuality of our theoretical paradigms, to gesture toward new paradigms, and to reconstruct relationships.

This description of Irigaray's philosophical perspective discloses two features of her work that are central to her critique of formal logic. The first is her insistence on the fundamentality of difference, particularly sexual difference, and her parallel insistence that genuine difference is ignored even when we think we are focusing on it. Irigaray acknowledges sexual difference at the level of bare physiognomy: "nature has a sex, always and everywhere."[4] But, as Rosi Braidotti has shown, there is a second register in which difference unfolds: "Irigaray defends the notion of 'difference' in a conditional mode. This means that woman does not yet exist and that she will be unable to come into being without women's collective efforts. . . . Sexual difference as the difference that women make has to be constructed, and, for Irigaray, it is the task of the women's movement to set the conditions of possibility for this becoming."[5] For Irigaray, sexual difference—indeed, difference itself—has yet to be thought at the deepest and fullest sense in Western culture; it has yet to enter into the symbolic constructions that constitute our culture. Moreover, thinking sexual difference is not simply a matter of adding women into the existing constructions. The structures themselves resist these additions since they are in fact constituted to resist difference.

Indicting the structures themselves points us beyond the particular content of an expression within a system and toward the assumptions and practices that constitute the structure. Irigaray insists, for example, that grammar itself sustains the monosexuality of language; in a parallel case, it is the "neutrality" built into democratic law that hides its monosexual character. And, as we shall see, we are directed to the definitions of the logical operations to see the way in which they eliminate the possibility of representing sexual difference as a form of difference. In Irigaray's work, a variety of supposedly neutral structures, then, are revealed as expressions of a cultural desire for sameness. A desire that must be revealed and interpreted before difference can be thought.

Approaching formal logic through this lens is unusual and, from the perspective of traditional philosophy of logic, perhaps impossible. One of Irigaray's unique contributions to philosophy has been to bring the techniques of analytic listening to bear on philosophical writing. Her well-known reading of Freud's essay "Femininity," for example, is titled "The Blind Spot of an Old Dream of Symmetry."[6] In it she argues that while Freud claims to have discovered a reductive and symmetrical relationship between the sexes, what his text reveals is a *desire* for symmetry, a desire expressed in Freud's theoretical "dream" in which the "little girl is really just a little boy."[7] It is a dream in which the feminine Other is understood only in relation to the masculine self, replacing the fundamentality of sexual difference with a more limited representation of "less than." More broadly, Irigaray finds this "dream of symmetry" to be a nearly universal component in Western theorizing. In close readings of the master works of Western philosophy, Irigaray continually reveals elements of difference, excess, and disorder that are ignored and marginalized by the theoretical apparatus intended to explain the total of reality. She interprets this as a refusal to recognize genuine difference and to represent sexual difference adequately in our symbolic frameworks. Furthermore, as Irigaray continually reminds us, these marginalized elements of experience are closely identified with femininity and serve as the very metaphors by which Western theorizing has sought to characterize femininity itself. Margaret Whitford sums up one aspect of Irigaray's complex use of psychoanalytic insights: "the problem as defined by Irigaray is that the female has a particular function in symbolic processes: to subtend them, to represent that which is outside discourse."[8]

When Irigaray confronts logical theory, then, she is looking for at least two things: the elements of logical reality that exceed formal logic's representational capacity and the desires revealed by the marginalization of these elements. While logicians focus their attention exclusively on the formal properties of logical concepts, Irigaray's psychoanalytic perspective includes the Imaginary meaning of logical connectives. In other words, while she is interested in the literal meaning of, for example, the negation symbol, she is also attentive to the associative, symbolic function of contradiction and, at a deeper level, the way that negation functions in the cultural Imaginary.

Irigaray's writings on logic are developed throughout her corpus. She addresses formal logic most directly in two essays: "The 'Mechanics' of Fluids" and "Is the Subject of Science Sexed?"[9] In each of these instances, and in several of her other references to formal logic, the context is the same: Irigaray is concerned with scientific theorizing and practice and uses her exploration of "fluidity" to reveal the sexed nature of the scientific enterprise. Formal logic is presented not as representing scientific thinking but as providing the underlying language of science. A third essay, "Le Langage de l'homme," also directly problematizes formal logic but in a slightly different context.[10] Here, Irigaray identifies the implications of what she calls the "masculine sexuation of discourse," arguing that reason is structured on a masculine model of singularity and solidity. In addition to theses focal essays, Irigaray's references to negation, identity, and generality are integral to the core elements of her work on feminine subjectivity. Any interpretation of her critique of logic must reconcile her writing on logic with her more general accounts of these phenomena.

Negation

The treatment negation receives in classical formal logic can be summed up in a single slogan: negation is contradiction. The only negative operation available in the standard formalism is the unary "~" that maps a given proposition onto its contradictory proposition. As with all logical operations, ~ has a standard syntactic and semantic interpretation, which are meant to be isomorphic. The characteristic truth table for negation and the introduction and elimination rules associated with it yield an understanding of negation such that:

1. Every proposition has one and only one negation, although several equivalent forms may express it.

2. A proposition and its negation are never both true (law of noncontradiction).
3. At least one of a proposition and its negation are true (law of excluded middle).
4. Negation is a formal property (i.e., the negation of *p* can be represented as a truth function of *p*).

To say, however, that this is the standard treatment of negation does not mean that it stands immune from criticism. A strong current within the field of formal logic insists on retrieving a formal representation of a second form of negation: contrariety, often symbolized as "¬."[11] Whereas ~ is intended to characterize the relationship between, for example, "This is red" and "This is not red," ¬ is intended to characterize the relationship between, for example, "This is red" and "This is nonred." A key difference is that the law of excluded middle does not hold for contraries—there is always a third (or more) possibility such that both the original proposition and its (contrary) negation can be false. Other differences emerge as well. A proposition can have many nonequivalent contraries and contrariety is not truth-functional. In fact, of the characteristics listed earlier, only the law of noncontradiction holds for contrariety.

Irigaray's critique of logical negation is often understood as though she were arguing in favor of contrariety. And there are places in her writing that give rise to this interpretation. She is, for example, critical of the focus on bivalent rather than on multivalent logical theories.[12] She points to vocal pitch and to the sexed divisions of colors as two markers of sexual difference that are not binary: "voices and colors cannot be reduced to bipolar couples. Obviously there is a potential bipolarity: blue/red, high/deep . . . but there are many nuances, variants, and scales of values that move uninterruptedly from one extreme to the other."[13] This criticism of logical negation has been made by a number of theorists who insist on the multiplicity of sexual identities.[14] If the binary conception of sexuality is constructed over a more diffuse and complex field of bodily configurations as some psychological and empirical research suggests, then sexual difference might be better described by a contrary form of negation rather than a contradictory form.[15]

But when we see that the preference for understanding sexual difference as contrariety is based on a conviction that there are (or ought to be) more than two sexes, it seems unlikely that Irigaray's worries about logical negation can be cashed out simply as a preference for contrariety. Irigaray's theoretical emphasis on the "couple" and her conviction that "human nature is two" point us in a very different direction.[16] I read in Irigaray's work a suggestion of something more complicated than the proposal that sexual difference is a contrary relation. What I find is a critique of contradiction that refuses to bypass the couple, which refuses to concede that every binary opposition must be contradiction. Rather than simply multiplying the poles of difference, Irigaray encourages us to think fully through the relationship of one sex to one other and to reconceive it in a nonhierarchical, nonreductive, way. This, she suggests, is the project that has never begun.

For Irigaray, the difference that is sexual difference is the *limit*: "the negative in sexual difference means an acceptance of the limits of my gender and a recognition of the irreducibility of the other."[17] A limit is a boundary, an end, and an edge. It is a direct consequence of the denial of universality, and, in the case of sexual difference, it is the end of the universality of "man." As Irigaray insists, "if this *one* does not exist, limit is therefore inscribed in nature itself."[18] While limitations may obtain within a multiplicity, as I emphasized earlier, Irigaray's work unveils the consequences of the limit set by a single other. It is this primary limitation, the thinking of sexual difference, that will, she insists, "be our salvation."[19]

Why must duality be rethought? The logical negation operator presents dichotomy along a single trajectory. The characteristics so neutrally expressed earlier reveal a form of difference that would be totally unacceptable (yet all too familiar) as a model of sexual difference. On a symbolic level, contradiction is a structural relation of dominance and erasure. The hierarchical "meaning" of negation has been well noted by Val Plumwood, who argues that logical negation constructs difference in terms of "exclusion" (a proposition and its negation are maximally distinct) and "backgrounding" (the negated proposition is defined in terms of the original proposition).[20] When sexual difference is conceived of as corresponding to logical negation in this way, a "dualistic" pair male/female is constructed. For Plumwood, dualism is "an alienated form of differentiation, in which power construes and constructs difference in terms of an inferior and alien realm."[21] In practical terms, this means that women come to be understood in terms of the ways they differ from, and fail to measure up to, a masculine standard.

Many feminist theorists assume that the trouble is with the binary relationship itself. For these thinkers, the law of the excluded middle, the assumption that there are only two possibilities, two poles of difference, is the very source of domination.[22] They see, in other words, only danger in modeling sexual difference on the basis of the "couple." Two is rejected in favor of three (or more). But Irigaray's work reminds us that the relationship of the couple cannot be passed over. Sexual difference cannot be neutralized, she argues, for "this neutralization would mean an end of the human species. The human species is divided into two genders which ensure its production and reproduction."[23] The (so far) inescapable dimorphism of human reproduction (no matter the socially mediated method by which sperm and egg meet) makes the couple inescapable: "A social thinking which gives no thought to the couple is abstract, cut off from the matter that nourishes it, and perverted by its abstractness from addressing the passage from the individual to the race."[24] If we attempt to move beyond the binary without rethinking it in a nonhierarchical way, we can never rescue the couple from its present condition as a site of hierarchy.

In the place, then, of contradiction, Irigaray offers us "limit," a new representation of negation intended to model the nonhierarchical duality of sexual difference. Limit differs from contradiction in two key ways. In the first place, a limit, as Irigaray understands it, is not *reversible*. In the logical treatment of contradiction, the pole that counts as the negative is determined by its structural position rather than its content. In other words, which proposition is the negative one is an arbitrary determination. p can equally represent "The ball is red" and "The ball is nonred." In either case, p identifies the negative proposition. But for Irigaray, sexual difference is not reversible in that the two poles of difference are not interchangeable. "Woman" and "man" are not merely structural positions for her.[25] One's sexual limits cannot be overcome even if one adopts the structural position of the other sex.

Crucially, limit marks a form of difference in which the terms are not interdefinable. In the case of contradiction, the specification of one of a pair of contradictories determines the specification of the other. A limit, on the other hand, requires the independent determination of the poles of difference. Disclosing the way that the independent specificity of femininity has been occluded is, for Irigaray, a key feminist task: "[Women] should not put it, then, in the form 'What is woman?' but rather, repeating/interpreting the way in which, within discourse, the feminine finds itself defined as lack, deficiency, or as imitation and negative image of the subject, they should signify that with respect to this logic a *disruptive excess* is possible on the feminine side."[26] The key here, however, is that neither of these poles of difference are meant to overpower the other. They can coexist and be in relation even though they differ. Irigaray's critique of the logical laws governing contradiction, insofar as they are taken to model sexual difference, makes way for the possibility of this new relationship.

The conception of limit that Irigaray formulates cannot be directly articulated in the language of formal logic. There is no standard symbology capable of expressing a relationship between exactly two terms such that they never coincide but are not interdefinable. When we come close—for example, ~(p & q)—the formula carries no axiomatic force. In one sense then, the relationship that Irigaray describes is *nonlogical.* But this is not to say that it is unreasonable or irrational. At the center of Irigaray's work is the task of drawing our attention to an as yet unsymbolized possibility. She uses a variety of techniques for expanding our thinking, for drawing us just enough beyond our current representations that we can begin to create a new representational possibility. Of these, the most widely discussed is her use of mimesis. In the case of "limit," we find another of her strategic techniques: association.[27] As I suggested earlier, Irigaray is interested in the symbolic associations binding culturally significant concepts. In the case of negation, for example, the logical rules that, given the negation operator, carry with them a force that goes beyond the framework of formal logic per se. Logic and its operations come to represent rationality, meaning, and sense of themselves.

It is in her subsequent critique of the law of noncontradiction that we find Irigaray at her most provocative: "Sexed identity does not obey the logic of contradiction. It bends and folds to accommodate that logic but it does not conform."[28] The problem with using the law of noncontradiction to understand sexual difference is that it presupposes that difference can always be overcome. One of the differends must overpower and eradicate the other—only one pole can be true, for example. Since our experience of difference is only sometimes as simple, concrete, and definite as the laws of logic, Irigaray raises the question of why these become the privileged features of reality in Western conceptuality. It indicates, she suggests, a preoccupation with definiteness that parallels the masculine Imaginary. Irigaray points out that women are never associated with this kind of definiteness but always represent a "disruptive excess."[29]

When Irigaray identifies the associations between the law of noncontradiction and masculine identity, she need not be read as claiming that women cannot do logic or think as logically as men or as claiming that formal logic is men's intellectual provenance. We can better hear this as a suggestion that culturally we have modeled our theorizing on the properties we associate with masculinity. Those associated with femininity lack even a proper acknowledgment or representation in our theoretical models of reality. While some theorists respond by attempting to reassociate femininity with the culturally validated properties, Irigaray urges us to begin to think through the "feminine" properties and attempt for the first time to symbolize them.[30]

"Limit" names a relation between the couple that is grounded in their specificity. In *Être Deux* she expresses this in a poetic vision of what one might say to a beloved Other: "'You who are not and never will be me or mine,' you are and you remain a you (tu) because I cannot know you, understand you, possess, you. You escape from all capture, from all mastery on my part if I respect you as transcendent not over your own body but over me."[31] The picture that emerges is not the yin-yang in which the dark and light shapes are a perfect, reversible mirror image of each other, forming a pattern in which one half can be deduced from the negative hole left by the other half. Irigaray's picture is rather that of two incommensurable figures meeting and bounding each other. Even this image is somewhat distorted. For it still calls to mind two closed figures. But as I have indicated, and will now explore, Irigaray's critique of the logical interpretation of identity and her construction of feminine (non)identity as open and fluid makes the incommensurability of the figures even more profound.

Identity

Whereas the logical treatment of negation remains contested within the institution of logic itself, the logical law of identity, $\forall x(x = x)$, has no official rival. So while the history of logical negation can be understood as a debate over the logical fundamentality of contrariety, the correct representation of identity claims to be firmly settled within the field of logic.[32] The indescernibility of identicals or, as it is sometimes known, the substitutability of identicals, remains the official ground of logical identity.

Widely recognized critiques of logical identity have not been absorbed into the field of formal logic. These critiques (and I am thinking most specifically of those produced by Martin Heidegger and Gilles Deleuze) argue that the formulation of the law reveals an inescapable dependence on difference. Heidegger interprets the law as yielding an understanding of identity as "the belonging together of the same," showing that the very togetherness mandated by the law is made possible by the differentiation inherent in the specification of the law itself. Two tokens (two instances of x) are necessary to represent the identity of the object.[33] In a similar vein, Deleuze shows that the repetition required for the statement of the law is the mark of difference not of identity.[34] For both Heidegger and Deleuze, the truth of identity is that it never is total; the residue of difference persists.

Irigaray's approach to identity is perhaps the element of her work that has received most critical attention from her readers. Her provocative claim that the law of identity does not "apply" to women, coupled with her mythological allusions to the identificatory substratum of women's bodies, makes for a complicated stance. With Heidegger and Deleuze, Irigaray affirms the ubiquity of a residual difference exceeding the law of identity. But unlike these other thinkers, Irigaray's analysis is sex based. Irigaray repeatedly emphasizes the association between this residue and femininity. As in the case of the law of identity, in which the diversity necessary for the statement of the law is both displayed and ignored, femininity is also that which exceeds any attempt at specification. What Irigaray reveals through her critical readings of the masters of Western rationality is equally well revealed in our ordinary encounters with popular representations of femininity: the feminine symbolizes excess. Whatever danger or pleasure is associated with femininity, the emotive basis is the excessive and irrepressible nature attributed to femininity. One of Irigaray's most definitive statements of this association is expressed in "This Sex Which Is Not One" in which she illustrates the overflowing and fluid aspects of femininity by depicting feminine sexuality as overflowing any attempt to unify or fix it.[35] In a similar vein, Irigaray often alludes to the fluid character of feminine sexuality, recalling for us the problems that fluids pose for solid mechanics. The associative relations between femininity and fluidity on the one hand, and masculinity and solidity on the other, are established in our culture through a series of conscious and unconscious maneuvers. For Irigaray, woman is "the sex which is not one," a designation that she expresses in a variety of ways: "she is neither open nor closed. She is indefinite. . . . She is neither one nor two."[36] In Irigaray's work, fluidity belongs on the woman's side.

Irigaray's refusal to acknowledge the law of identity as constitutive of feminine identity appears, then, as a dual critique. On the one hand, Irigaray is describing the symbolic associations that attach to feminine identity. In speaking of Irigaray's critique of identity and negation, Margaret Whitford writes, "the practical value of these principles, without which rationality would be inconceivable, is so evident that it appears unquestionable. The logic of identity is the prerequisite of any language or society at all. However, the point is that there will always be a residue which exceeds the categories, and this excess is conceptualized as female."[37] But Irigaray's critique extends along a second path as well. She is equally critical of attempts to reconstitute feminine identity along lines of solidity and definiteness. Rather than remake feminine identity so that it is subject to the *intention* of the law of identity, Irigaray opts to create a new possibility: a feminine identity that is loyal to the *substance* of the law of identity—that is, that respects the multiplicity inherent in any attempt to state the law of identity.

To inaugurate this new representational possibility, Irigaray develops a metaphorics of fluidity within which feminine subjectivity can be expressed. She attempts what from the perspective of the law of identity is impossible: to find symbols for this "sex which is not one," to defend its goals, and to lay claim to its rewards.[38] It is toward this end that she presents her infamous evocative associations among fluidity, excess, and elements of the female body.

The character of Irigaray's reconstruction of identity has been the subject of intense debate among her readers. While early critics saw any association between the female body and feminine identity as evidence of a regressive biological essentialism, recent interpreters have given more nuanced readings, seeing the associations as strategic or metaphorical.[39] But even if we read Irigaray's celebratory images of fluidity as metaphors for femininity, problems remain. Patricia Huntington aptly characterizes the risk that Irigaray runs: "If feminists offer an alternative metaphorization of the feminine instead of a pure metonymic exposure, then they reassert a masculine strategy of identity which ties woman to a single, unitary, homogeneous, and exclusionary notion of womanhood."[40] In other words, even an explicitly metaphorical depiction of fluid feminine identity is in danger of reverting back to the solidity of the law of identity by claiming to unveil the singular truth of feminine identity. For Huntington, Irigaray is willing to risk this reversal in order to allow for a fuller, more potent critique of the solidity of the masculine conception of identity. As she says, "For Irigaray, we do not circumscribe the real simply by showing the logic of the symbolic to rest upon a male imaginary. Instead we generate the possibility of a new poetic-erotic form of life through fantasizing a positive alternative."[41]

In contrast to Huntington's defense of Irigaray's depiction of a fluid feminine subjectivity, Alison Weir argues that in her effort to reject the enclosed solidity of masculine subjectivity, Irigaray eliminates feminine identity altogether: "Irigaray moves from the insight that individuation in our culture too often entails a fetization of separation and a denial of relationship to the claim that individuation and relationship are necessarily, logically, mutually exclusive. Thus the logic of identity must be replaced with a logic of non-identity, a relational logic which resists identity."[42] For Weir, Irigaray is led to refuse feminine identity because she equates difference with domination: "Irigaray can come up with no other way to eliminate domination than the elimination of distinction."[43]

As should be clear from my discussion of Irigaray's theory of the limit, it is my view that Irigaray does suggest a way to eliminate domination while retaining distinction. While I agree with Weir's insightful defense of the importance of affirming feminine identity, I would argue that Weir has ignored Irigaray's efforts to creatively imagine a new form of binary difference, one in which distinctness does not give rise to domination. *Limit* marks a form of relatedness that originates in the specificity of the related terms. As such, the domination made possible by the logical interpretation of negation does not appear. Irigaray has gone beyond the equation "binary relation = domination" and so can imagine a form of feminine identity that is both distinct and "in relation." More strongly, it is only the possibility of sexed identity that can save us from the totalizing effects of domination. As Irigaray argues, "Sexed identity rules out all forms of totality as well as the self-substituting subject . . . the *mine* of the subject is always already marked by a disappropriation: gender. Being a man or a woman already means not being the whole of the subject or of the community or of the spirit, as well as not being entirely one's self."[44] Yet, although sexed identity frees us from the self-substituting model of identity characterized by the logical law of identity, it is also what makes individual identity possible: "becoming one's gender also constitutes the means for returning to the self. . . . I am born a woman, but I still must become this woman that I am by nature."[45]

Irigaray has identified a sense, then, in which the law of identity does not "apply" to women. Femininity represents the excess that surrounds the very possibility of self-substituting identity. Rather than reshape femininity to match the solidity of the original model, Irigaray creatively imagines a fluid form of identity. This is a sexed identity that is substantive enough to mark a specific "spot" from which women can be in relation but one that refuses to give up the elements of itself that transcend full fixity. Irigaray does not deny—in fact, she affirms—the importance of mythologizing a specifically feminine form of identity. Without their own specific form of identity, women cannot function as a limit to the male sex, they cannot resist the totalizing impulse of the logical structure of negation and identity. A specific form of identity carries with it, however, a need for representation that goes beyond the bodily existence of each particular woman. For this, we must look to a theory of generality.

Generality

Frege's treatment of generality was perhaps the most revolutionary aspect of his *Begriffschrift*. In insisting that generality follow a mathematical model of incomplete functions, he freed logic from its dependence on substance and transformed it into a pure "concept-script." In Frege's view, generality is achieved by abstraction from any part of a thought. It is expressible thanks to the notational properties of the variable that allow representation of the deficiency in the function and its, perhaps infinite, potential completions. Dorothea Olkowski has argued that Irigaray is sympathetic to Frege's achievement, appreciating the importance of the emphasis on concepts rather than substance.[46] Irigaray's critique of generality does not engage the standard logical representation, $\forall x$. Instead, she repeatedly refers to an alternative representation, a representation found in the work of Ferdinand de Saussure and Jacques Lacan. Saussure exemplifies the key distinction between language (langue) and speech (parole) in relation to their differential relation to multiplicity. Language, he says, "exists in the individual, yet is common to all. . . . Its mode of existence is expressed by the formula: 1 + 1 + 1 + 1 . . . = *I* (collective pattern)."[47] Saussure contrasts this with the additive nature of speech: "In speaking there is only the sum of particular acts, as in the formula: (1 + 1' + 1" + 1'''. . .)."[48] The distinction then is between generality and summation. In the case of language, the specific instances give rise to something that is *qualitatively* more general; in the case of speech, only quantitative expansion is achieved. Irigaray's critique of the logic of generality engages this first, "one plus one" model. In the course of her work, she exposes it as a model of pseudogenerality, of singularity masquerading as plurality. The "one plus one" as it is applied to women reinforces singularity rather than plurality. It represents an attempt to reduce women to a single function. In replacing the specificity of the individual with a collective pattern, the importance of multiplicity is overlooked. In the case of femininity, maternity has served as the "collective pattern."

Irigaray calls for the origination of a representation of feminine multiplicity. The pseudogenerality of the "one plus one" notation reminds us of the difficulty of making conceptual or representational space for more than one woman at a time. Mythic and theatrical space often includes only a single female in a "cast" of male figures. Even when it seems that more than one woman is present, it is often the result of femininity being divided up into its parts and those parts distributed to a few different characters (e.g., the good mother and the bad whore). Irigaray centralizes this problem of the lone woman in her critique of Freud. For Freud, she points out, there is only ever one woman in the unconscious, one feminine symbol.[49] The singularity of this symbol has the effect of limiting the possibilities for relationships between women to one of two types: identity or rivalry. In other words, if the unary nature of the feminine symbol is to be maintained, women must be imagined as the same, threatened by and threatening any difference between themselves. Or, alternatively, women must be in competition, each seeking to replace the other in order to function as *the* woman. The first is the horizontal model of utopian sisterhood, the second, the vertical, competitive mother–daughter model.

In place of these limited models, Irigaray articulates two mythic visions for feminine multiplicity, two symbolic representations of women "in the plural." On the one hand, she makes use of the imagery of *parler femme* or "women among themselves" (i.e., women in conversation with and about each other). It is a vision that includes both conflict and camaraderie, a vision enacted by feminist dialogue and political action. A second strategy is to reconstruct models of feminine genealogy, emphasizing the mother–daughter and its history. These strategies disrupt, respectively, the functioning of the vertical and horizontal axes of feminine relationship since they are each symbolic structures that require the presence of more than one woman at a time. The pseudogenerality of the "one plus one" is replaced by representations of women in relation to other women.

When she does apply this to the standard formalism, $\forall x$, Irigarary points out the connections between identity and generality. In formal logic, the function of identity and generality are to sanction certain substitutions. But if differences between women are to be acknowledged, the generality of the term *woman* has to be such that substitutions are recognized as restricted. Surprisingly, *woman* can achieve generality, only by a refusal to substitute one woman for another and so to allow for the possibility of a plurality of women.

A New Logic or Logic's End?

Irigaray's work calls the neutrality of logic into question, arguing that the standard formalism is capable of expressing only distorted and partial interpretations of negation, identity, and generality. More specifically, her work suggests that symbolic logic fails to represent the form of difference exhibited by genuine sexual difference, the form of identity proper to feminine identity, and the form of generality required to express a feminine generic. Each of these relationships remains outside logic, remains "illogical." Thinking of difference, identity, and generality in the new ways that Irigaray asks of us requires that we expand on the representational possibilities offered to us by the standard formalism.

To what extent is this a criticism of logic and its practices? On one level, Irigaray's critique can be legitimately ignored by the logician. Insofar as logic is the study of inferential structures, Irigaray can make no objection to the continued study of the standard formalism. It is only insofar as this formalism is used as a model for sexual difference that Irigaray's critique gets its purchase. In this sense, Irigaray's claims about formal logic are analogous to those offered by quantum or intuitionist logicians. In each case, a situation is uncovered that is claimed to have a structure that is not isomorphic to the structure of the standard symbolic logic. According to the quantum theorist, quantum reality cannot be accurately modeled by classical logic. For the intuitionist, it is constructivist mathematics that resists the classical model. For Irigaray, the structure of sex and sexual difference is not adequately described by the classical model. But the analogy between Irigaray's critique and these others quickly breaks down. In other cases, the recognition of a limitation has led to the development of new syntactic structures. Irigaray, however, insists that there can be no new formalism, that the problems she has identified are problems *with formalism itself*.

In closing, then, I want to suggest two further lines of exploration, those that I take to be the fundamental evaluative questions raised by my interpretation of Irigaray's work. In the first place, this mistrust of formalism per se refers us back to the question of desire. Irigaray asks the logician to interrogate his own desire for a closed logical system. Given that language and experience overflow the boundaries of logic, what pleasures are found in the narrowing and restricting of attention that formal logic demands? Asking into this level of desire is fundamentally foreign to the logician who focuses on instrumental ends and deemphasizes even the aesthetic pleasures associated with an elegant proof or a spectacular technical solution. The relationship between desire and logic has already been opened by Wittgenstein in his *Investigations*. One open question, then, is the extent to which Irigaray has provided a sexed basis for this relationship, showing that the deep pleasures, desires, and frustrations that give rise to our pursuit of formal logic are the same ones that structure our sense of masculinity: closure, unity, and solidity.

A second line of debate is opened by the radical nature of "difference feminism" itself. Irigaray's presentations of difference, identity, and generality are known to be widely controversial among feminists. As I emphasized earlier, Irigaray insists on duality, presenting an account of sexual *difference*. This is rejected by feminists who would emphasize sameness and equality and who can find no specifically feminine pleasures worth recuperating or inventing. Moreover, Irigaray's work tends to deemphasize the underlying principle that difference takes place within similarity. The maximal difference that serves as the genesis point for wonder or desire occurs only within a framework of overarching similarity. So, for example, the difference between two human beings similar in almost every respect except sexual identity is more salient than the difference between a human being and a frog. It is, it would seem, the play of sameness and difference, rather than difference in itself that gives rise to desire. The extent to which the importance of sameness can be recognized within Irigaray's paradigm and the effect such a recognition would have on her central insights remains a second open question.

Notes

1. I address Irigaray's critique of language in Hass (2000).

2. For discussions of Irigaray and law, see Schwab (1996) and Deutscher (1997). For an analysis of Irigarary and economy, see Colebrook (1997).

3. Hirsh and Olson (1996).

4. Irigaray (1993b, 108).

5. Braidotti (1994, 250).

6. Irigaray (1985b).

7. Irigarary (1985b, 26).

8. Whitford (1991, 66).

9. Irigaray (1985c, 108–118).

10. In Irigaray (1985a, 281–292).

11. See Sommers and Englebretsen (2000).

12. Irigaray (1987, 315).

13. Irigaray (1993b, 157).

14. Nye (1990); Butler (1990).

15. Alice Domurat Dreger describes the medical interventions practiced on intersexed individuals. She argues that dimorphic sexuality is a *result* of medical invention. See "Ambiguous Sex" (1998a) and *Hermaphrodites and the Medical Invention of Sex* (1998b). See also Herdt (1994).

16. *Être Deux* (Irigaray, 1997) takes this as its theme.

17. Irigaray (1996, 13).

18. Irigaray (1996, 35).

19. Irigaray (1993a, 5).

20. Plumwood (this volume, 23–25).

21. Plumwood (this volume, 19).

22. For examples of arguments that link binary conceptual frameworks with domination, see Nye (1990). For examples of arguments in favor of a feminist disruption of binary sexuality, see Connell (1987, 290) or Butler (1990).

23. Irigaray (1993b, 12).

24. Irigaray (1987, 153).

25. This is a key point at which Irigaray's distance from Marxism is exhibited. Although she has written of woman as a commodity, in the final analysis, the commodification of women is not defined in terms of a structural economic role that happens to be occupied by women. Economy is another structure that Irigaray offers up for analysis. Although not as fully developed as her critiques of language, logic, and law, the outline of the critique is much the same.

26. Irigaray (1985b, 78).

27. Patricia J. Huntington (1998) offers a sophisticated and important account of Irigaray's use of the techniques of metonymy, association, and metaphor.

28. Irigaray (1993b, 139).

29. Irigaray (1985b, "Volume-Fluidity," 227–240).

30. For an example of this type of criticism, see Le Doeuff (1998).

31. Irigaray (1997, 39).
32. Horn (1989, chap. 2).
33. Heidegger (1969).
34. Deleuze (1994, 49–50).
35. Irigaray (1985c).
36. Irigaray (1985b, 229; 1985c, 26).
37. Whitford (1991, 67).
38. Whitford (1991, 49).
39. See, for example, the essays in Burke, Schor, and Whitford (1994) and Braidotti (1994).
40. Huntington (1998, 126).
41. Huntington (1998, 131).
42. Weir (1996, 102).
43. Weir (1996, 102).
44. Irigaray (1996, 106).
45. Irigaray (1996, 106–107).
46. Olkowski (1999, xxx).
47. Saussure (1959, 19).
48. Saussure (1959, 19).
49. Irigaray (1985b, 80).

References

Braidotti, Rosi. *Nomadic Subjects*. New York: Columbia University Press, 1994.

Burke, Carolyn, Naomi Schor, and Margaret Whitford. *Engaging with Irigaray*. New York: Columbia University Press, 1994.

Butler, Judith. *Gender Trouble: Feminism and the Subversion of Identity*. New York: Routledge, 1990.

Colebrook, Claire. "The Trope of Economy and Representational Thinking: Heidegger, Derrida and Irigaray." *Journal of the British Society for Phenomenology* 28, no. 2 (May 1997): 178–191.

Connell, R. W. *Gender and Power*. Stanford, Calif.: Stanford University Press, 1987.

Deleuze, Gilles. *Difference and Repetition*, trans. Paul Patton. New York: Columbia University Press, 1994.

Deutscher, Penelope. "French Feminist Philosophers on Law and Public Policy: Michèle Le Doeuff and Luce Irigaray." *Australian Journal of French Studies* 34, no. 1 (1997): 24–44.

Dreger, Alice Domurat. "Ambiguous Sex—or Ambivalent Medicine?" *The Hastings Center Report* 28, no. 3 (May/June 1998a): 24–35.

———. *Hermaphrodites and the Medical Invention of Sex*. Boston: Harvard University Press, 1998b.

Hass, Marjorie. "The Style of the Speaking Subject: Irigaray's Empirical Studies of Language Production." *Hypatia* (Winter 2000): 64–89.

Heidegger, Martin. "The Principle of Identity." In *Identity and Difference*, trans. Joan Stambaugh. New York: Harper & Row, 1969.

Herdt, Gilbert, ed. *Third Sex, Third Gender: Beyond Sexual Dimorphism in Culture and History*. N.p.: Zone, 1994.

Hirsh, Elizabeth, and Gary Olson. 1996. "Je Luce Irigaray": A Meeting with Luce Irigaray, trans. Elizabeth Hirsh and Gaetan Brulotte. *Jac: A Journal of Composition Theory* 16 (3): 341–361.

Horn, Laurence R. A *Natural History of Negation*. Chicago: University of Chicago Press, 1989.

Huntington, Patricia J. *Ecstatic Subjects, Utopia, and Recognition*. Albany: State University of New York Press, 1998.

Irigaray, Luce. *Parler n'est jamais neutre*. Paris: Minuit, 1985a.

———. *Speculum of the Other Woman*, trans. Gillian C. Gill. Ithaca, N.Y.: Cornell University Press, 1985b.

———. *This Sex Which Is Not One*, trans. Catherine Porter and Carolyn Burke. Ithaca, N.Y.: Cornell University Press, 1985c.

———. "Is the Subject of Science Sexed?" trans. Carol Mastrangelo Bové. *Hypatia* 2 (Fall 1987): 65–87.

———. *An Ethics of Sexual Difference*, trans. Carolyn Burke and Gillian C. Gill. Ithaca, N.Y.: Cornell University Press, 1993a.

———. *Sexes and Genealogies*, trans. Gillian C. Gill. New York: Columbia University Press, 1993b.

———. *I Love to You*, trans. Alison Martin. New York: Routledge, 1996.

———. *Être Deux*. Paris: Grasset & Fasquelle, 1997.

Le Doeuff, Michèle. *Le Sexe du savoir*. Paris: Flammarion, 1998.

Nye, Andrea. *Words of Power: A Feminist Reading of the History of Logic*. New York: Routledge, 1990.

Olkowski, Dorothea. *Gilles Deleuze and the Ruin of Representation*. Berkeley: University of California Press, 1999.

Plumwood, Val. *Feminism and the Mastery of Nature*. New York: Routledge, 1993.

Saussure, Ferdinand de. *Course in General Linguistics*, trans. Wade Baskin. New York: McGraw-Hill, 1959.

Schwab, Gail. "Women and the Law in Irigarayan Theory." *Metaphilosophy* 27, nos. 1 & 2 (January/April 1996): 146–177.

Sommers, Fred. *The Logic of Natural Language*. New York: Oxford University Press, 1984.

Sommers, Fred, and George Englebretsen. *An Invitation to Formal Reasoning: The Logic of Terms*. Aldershot, England: Ashgate, 2000.

Weir, Alison. *Sacrificial Logics: Feminist Theory and the Critique of Identity*. New York: Routledge, 1996.

Whitford, Margaret. *Luce Irigaray: Philosophy in the Feminine*. London: Routledge, 1991.

CHAPTER FOUR

~

"Power in the Service of Love": John Dewey's *Logic* and the Dream of a Common Language

CARROLL GUEN HART

Like many women in philosophy, I did not begin there as an undergraduate, mostly because of logic. I majored in English literature precisely because I would have to take symbolic logic if I majored in philosophy. I had enjoyed courses in informal logic and the history and philosophy of science, as well as other assorted subjects, but I had taken a look at the logic textbooks, glimpsed the "alphabet soup" of symbolic logic, and knew I could never grasp all of this. This intuition was confirmed for me as a graduate student when I was told by my mentor, in the course of a trying seminar on ontology, that I had no gift for high abstraction. I remember going home and crying for three days about that remark—with this crucial disability, obviously, I did not have what it took to be a philosopher.

Several years later I am still in philosophy, but I continue to have deep insecurities about my inability to do logic. For logic still seems like "real" philosophy, and the ability to do it still seems to be that which makes one a "real" philosopher. My discovery of feminist philosophy has helped in some ways but not in others. Feminists speak my language—that is, not the language of high abstraction. But feminists by and large don't do symbolic logic. And this suggests to me the common stereotype of the women in the kitchen talking psychotherapy and relationships while the men are in the living room talking "real" philosophy—logic and epistemology.

Recently I discovered John Dewey's theory of logic. His major work, *Logic: The Theory of Inquiry*, published in 1938, is intended to be a critical reconstruction and reformulation of the tradition of formal logic from a pragmatist perspective. I was shocked to find a logic text without a single page of alphabet soup—one that works primarily with images of roots, seeds, matrices, flourishing, and cultivation. I have found this logic readable and even exciting. However, this very readability has managed to reinforce my insecurities about logic, because Dewey's cannot be real, hard-core *logic*. Since it was written, *Logic* has never been accepted by the arbiters of logic; it has never found its way into the textbooks on logic, and by those in the know it has never been thought really to deal with logic. Through all of this I have been longing to believe that at least part of the problem lies with logic, but I have not been able to convince myself fully of this.

Until, that is, I discovered Andrea Nye's book, *Words of Power*. This book, demonstrates convincingly that there are very good objective reasons why women in general feel put off by logic. For logic as Nye has described it is a distinctively male way of escaping from and controlling those areas of life that threaten some men—and these areas include, predominantly, those areas of life associated with women. For example, the nuanced and multivalent quality of ordinary language, traditionally associated with women's frivolity and trickiness, is part of the "problem" that logic was invented to "solve." Reading Nye made me feel immediately better, even possibly superior, about my inability to do logic. Perhaps as a woman, and as a feminist, I am constitutionally unable to buy into the life-denying power-mania of logic. However, unsettling questions remain. For I have a sense that there is a kernel of truth to any aspect of life that has been lionized in this way. Rather than just throwing out the whole thing, my instinct is to try to pick out that kernel of truth, find out what need it was meant to fill, and see if it can be developed for good rather than for evil.

In this context, then, I find that Dewey's logic is increasingly interesting. For it now clearly seems to be a minority voice in the tradition of logic and, as such, warrants further investigation. At the very least, it will provide another voice in the conversation and may even increase women's options in dealing with the problem of logic. As my contribution to this conversation, I shall try in my own way to add Dewey to the conversation begun by Nye's fine analysis of the history of logic.

John Dewey and Feminist Suspicions about Pragmatism

Feminists have largely shared the continental suspicion of pragmatism. Most would accept Heidegger's analysis of pragmatism as a "power-mania," pointing out the Baconian motifs of power and control that are evident in pragmatism and identify it as a successor to Enlightenment scientism. As Richard Rorty has pointed out, Heidegger would insist that pragmatism is the ultimate version of the Platonic desire for power and certainty. Its only virtue is in bringing out this motif so strongly and so nakedly that we see how unattractive it is and are no longer tempted by it (Rorty, 1991a). Readers who are critical of Dewey can easily find passages in which he talks about "control" and "engineering" and "scientific method." Here is one very revolting Baconian image:

> Active experimentation must force the apparent facts of nature into forms different to those in which they familiarly present themselves; and thus make them tell the truth about themselves, as torture may compel an unwilling witness to reveal what he has been concealing. (Quoted in Dewey [1920] 1982, 32)

Feminists experience the Platonic power-mania in a very pointed way. For women, like nature itself, have been colonized and controlled by theory in a way that has legitimated not only the suppression of women's experience but also a totalitarian power that ranges from control over reproductive choice to rape and physical abuse. With this history of suppression and control, largely carried by theory, feminists are justly concerned that feminist theory not perpetuate the same sort of abuse. Feminists of different sorts legitimately emphasize "difference" as a way of challenging the totalizing pretensions of theory and of logic. In this context it is understandable that a philosopher who talks about logic, metaphysics, and scientific method would, if he is thought about at all, be considered unambiguously one of the enemy.

In order to challenge this Deweyan stereotype, I will borrow a phrase from Rorty. Although Rorty himself would never use this phrase of Dewey's *Logic*—he thinks the work an embarrassing but minor glitch in Dewey's *oeuvre*—I think it applies as well to the *Logic* as it does to its original context. Rorty says that Dewey's pragmatism "puts power in the service of love" (Rorty 1991d, 48). I suggest that Dewey's logic puts power in the service of love. I mean that logic is no longer the master but the servant of primary experience. Its power lies in its ability to elicit and articulate the connections between apparently unrelated things, so that when we act, we may do so with ecological sensitivity, "in deference to the connections of events" (Dewey [1925] 1981, 143). Like other tools, says Dewey, logic is a good servant but a bad master. Its pulling back from primary experience is extremely valuable when relativized as a tool but becomes damaging and oppressive when pulled out of its proper context, hypostatized, and absolutized.

The Inquiry into Logic

For Dewey "logic" has two different but related senses, both of which are tied to the fundamental meaning of rationale or systematic ordering. Logic in its narrower, more "proximate" sense is the systematic interrelation of logical universals that we find in any logic text. Dewey notes:

> Proximate subject-matter is the domain of the relations of propositions to one another, such as affirmation-negation, inclusion-exclusion, particular-general, etc. No one doubts that the relations expressed by such words as is, is-not, if-then, only (none but), and, or, some-all, belong to the subject-matter of logic in a way so distinctive as to mark off a special field. (Dewey [1938] 1986, 9)

These logical universals are called "logic" because they are quite uniquely constituted by systematic ordering and the having of a rationale. They simply are a systematic ordering and nothing else; this is the condition of their existence. In this sense they form a distinctively logical subject matter. However, "the more developed this field becomes, the more pressing is the question as to what it is all about" (Dewey [1938] 1986, 9). And, as Dewey points out, there is no consensus about this ultimate subject matter—except that logic in some way goes beyond ordinary experience and constitutes a realm of "pure possibility," the "order of nature," the "rational structure of the universe," or, on a different level, the "formal structure of language as a system of symbols," providing us with a "universal algebra of existence" ([1938] 1986, 10). Dewey points out that logical universals in the proximate sense are used to greatest effect in experimental science; but our logical theory of their working remains mired in classical Greek metaphysics. The troubling implications of this state of affairs leads Dewey into an inquiry into the nature and function of logic in contemporary experience.

Hence, whereas logic as it functions in science has only a relative or functional universality as an articulation of the self-regulation of experience, logical theory conceives of logical forms as "antecedent fixities" that have absolute authority over chaotic, disorderly experience. In these terms, anything that participates in the normative function of experience is split off and hypostatized, located in an idealized world all its own and separate from experience. Ideals that should guide experimentation, and be themselves modified in the process, are split off from experience and become absolutized ideals that then make experience look inadequate by comparison. Relations and connections, which should remain a functional division of labor, are plucked out and become the whole nature of reality, thereby throwing most of primary experience into question. Refined sensory impressions, created for the purpose of establishing evidence, are absolutized and become the nature of reality. It seems that normativity can be truly normative only on its own, cut off from genuine relation with experience.

Now ideality and reality, of course, originally belong to each other as reciprocal parts of a functional coordination. Ideals are not finished objects but visions that are to be realized. When they are split apart, ideals no longer guide our shaping of reality but take on their own independent existence in another ideal world. Such an ideal world is simply "the hypostatizing in a wholesale way of the fact that actual existence has its own possibilities." When we split them off, we contemplate such "remote and unattached possibilities" (Dewey [1929] 1988, 244), worshiping them rather than using them to transform reality. Rather than contributing to the "common experience" of mankind, such ideals become "curiosities to be deposited, with appropriate labels, in a metaphysical museum" ([1925] 1981, 26).

This fixed, hypostatized normativity is not functional or open to the test of consequences. As Dewey says:

> A thing "absolutely" stable and unchangeable would be out of the range of the principle of action and reaction, of resistance and leverage as well as of friction. Here it would have no applicability, no potentiality of use as measure and control of other events. (Dewey [1925] 1981, 64)

However, such absolute fixities are supposedly all the better for not being functional. Cataleptic rigidity and isolation become signs of superiority; to be in relation, to be flexible and growing are signs of inferiority. Such normativity exists in and for itself, utterly complete and independent. It is absolute and relates to existence only as an unchanging absolute, as a king or emperor. It idealizes isolation, squashing and devaluing mutuality and relationality. It reflects pessimism as to any inherent normativity of experience. Philosophy, mesmerized by antecedent fixities, has denied "that common experience is capable of developing from within itself methods which will secure direction for itself and will create inherent standards of judgment and value" (Dewey [1925] 1981, 41). Foundations and antecedent fixities are an alien and external form of normativity, needing to be "shoved under" experience because experience on its own has no normativity.

Almost from the beginning, philosophy has been closely involved with traditional institutions. They need philosophy to rationalize their power and defend it from contemporary challenges, and philosophy needs their support to maintain its own power to regulate culture. Hence philosophy continues to operate "with effective support only from old institutions whose prestige, influence and emoluments of power depend upon the preservation of the old order" at the very time when review and change are most needed (Dewey [1948] 1982, 261–262). The result is that,

> to the vested interests, maintenance of belief in the transcendence of space and time, and hence the derogation of what is "merely" human, is an indispensable prerequisite of their retention of an authority which in practice is translated into power to regulate human affairs throughout—from top to bottom. (Dewey [1948] 1982, 261–262)

In order to maintain and solidify its cultural power, philosophy, like the other traditional institutions, has *had* to denigrate experience. For experience is a threat and must be put down if a normativity based on old institutions and power structures is to maintain supremacy.

The tragedy is, of course, that once we have committed ourselves to antecedent fixities and their form of normativity, it is inevitable that experience will actually *become* chaotic and disordered. We could bear with the pretensions of philosophy if it did not actually destroy the integrity of experience in this way. But antecedent fixities set up an impossible standard of absolute certainty, isolation, and fixity, and on this basis the flow of experience will always appear deficient and antinormative. With this in mind, "men have not been able to trust either the world or themselves to realize the values and qualities which are the possibilities of nature" (Dewey [1929] 1988, 240). Furthermore, when we have diverted our attention to nonexistential realities, we will begin to lose our sensitivity to experience. Dewey says that "no one knows how many of the evils and deficiencies that are pointed to as reasons for flight from experience are themselves due to the disregard of experience shown by those peculiarly reflective" ([1925] 1981, 41). For experience split off from value is assumed to be barren, and it becomes so if so treated. And split-off value cannot guide action in any significant and orderly way. Then, if engaged in without care, sensitivity, and intelligence, experience does take on a haphazard quality; we reap the consequences of ill-directed and careless action. Actions and consequences cross each other, and nothing can reliably be understood or anticipated. Foundations and antecedent fixities cause us to act on automatic pilot, with cataleptic rigidity, without thinking, and this way of acting typically emphasizes the problematic and the discontinuous in experience as hindrances rather than as opportunities.

Moreover, the intellectualization of Reality has put all nonintellectual qualities into metaphysical limbo. As a result, the world itself is reduced to mechanism and "the self becomes not merely a pilgrim but an unnaturalized and unnaturalizable alien in the world" (Dewey [1925] 1981, 30). Viewing this reality as antecedently fixed then requires us to call "subjective and phenomenal all objects of experience that cannot be reduced to properties of objects of knowledge" ([1929] 1988, 175). On this assumption, we are guaranteed to find our primary experience wanting—both irrational and antinormative. As Dewey says, "the quality of irrationality is imputed only because of conflict with a prior definition of rationality" ([1929] 1988, 168). This alienation from primary experience consisting of a "sense of incompetency" and a "sloth born of desire for irresponsibility" ([1929] 1988, 240)—then becomes the best possible reason for retreating once again into a secure ideal world; and the pernicious spiral goes on.

Dewey sets out to construct a theory of logic which must meet his own requirements of theory—it must come from somewhere rather than being "drawn from the void and proffered simply *ad hoc*"; it must be able to account for the proximate subject matter of logic; it must be able to account for the arguments that are advanced in support of other theories. Dewey's theory, in short form, is that "all logical forms (with their characteristic properties) arise within the operation of inquiry and are concerned with the control of inquiry so that it may yield warranted assertions" (Dewey [1938] 1986, 11). This is not a dogmatic statement but a hypothetical one, subject to the test of existential consequences.

Existential Ground: Human Problems, Human Flourishing

The theory of logic that Dewey presents focuses on logic as functional or instrumental rather than as a picture of a higher, perfect Reality. What traditional logic has most lost sight of, in Dewey's view, is the functional *office* of logic in human experience. "Office" means that logic has a definite task set for it by experience and that it is responsible to experience to fulfill this task.

In order to understand the office of logic in experience, we first need to grasp Dewey's conception of experience. "Experience" is the self-conserving, expanding spiral of human life as it has developed onto the levels of body-mind. I call this conception an "ecology of human experience" because Dewey structures it around organic images like heliotropism, interaction, and emergence. (For more on Deweyan ecology, see Chaloupka 1987). He uses these images, he says, to point out that experience is not private or mentalistic but active and that it is not inherently "cognitional" but multifaceted (Dewey [1939] 1988, 11). Such "experience" is the ultimate normative context for human life, because its pattern of interaction and emergence underlies and shapes our development and our experience. This process is larger than any one person, larger than humanity in general. It happens primarily apart from human consciousness and choice. We are part of this process and are fundamentally subject to it. We cannot decide to change the fact that we function only in strict correlation with our environment nor that community is a necessary condition for the development of subjectivity. Although we can disrupt the process through neglect and interference, we cannot change the fact that this process is a condition of our existence. We interfere in or ignore these conditions at our own peril. But fortunately for ourselves as organisms, we never deal with experience as a whole, "all at once," only with individual "experiences"; Dewey's term for these individual experiences is "situations" ([1939] 1988, 28).

The individual situation as an experience has all the ecological dynamics of experience. Hence a situation "contains in a fused union some *what* experienced and some processes of experiencing. In its identity with a life-function, it is temporally and spatially more extensive and more internally complex than is a single thing like a stone, or a single quality like red." The ecological structure of the situation avoids both atomism, which denies connections, and "absolutistic block monism which, in behalf of the reality of relations, leaves no place for the discrete, for plurality, and for individuals." Further, the ecological situation provides an alternative to empiricism, for "no living creature could survive, save by sheer accident, if its experiences had no more reach, scope or content, than traditional particularistic empiricism provides for" (Dewey [1939] 1988, 29). Thus the situation begins not with disconnected entities, then trying to connect them, but with interconnections, in the midst of which we can distinguish relatively separate entities. Hence the situation, not a discrete entity or person, is the "individual" that acts and grows. Within this context, an "object" is some aspect of a situation that "stands out conspicuously because of its especially focal and crucial position at a given time in determination of some problem . . . which the *total* complex environment presents." The situation is the "contextual whole" that gives meaning to the objects, persons, and interactions which belong to it ([1938] 1986, 72). Dewey says that "failure to acknowledge the situation leaves, in the end; the logical force of objects and their relations inexplicable" ([1930] 1984, 246).

Although the fundamental organic pattern of interaction provides the basic dynamic shape of the situation, the particular energies and their interrelations are historically specific and therefore also unique; every situation has its own "intimately individual" form (Dewey [1934] 1987, 142). Cultural "mind," consisting of historically specific institutions, expectations, and assumptions, enters into the situation. For the environment, like the organism, is "never twice alike" ([1922] 1988, 105). And once subjective individuality has emerged, with individual persons bearing the subjective functions of consciousness, imagination, and deliberation, they become constitutive parts of the situation; individual human impulses and desires, as well as human capacities for choice and deliberation, shape the situation. Dewey says that "an individual . . . participates in the genesis of every experienced situation" and that "the way in which it is engaged affects the quality of the situation experienced" ([1925] 1981, 189). This means that the woven pattern of the self, with its distinctive disposition and character, becomes a significant energy in the development of the situation. Because it is genuinely individual and specific, it is essential for us to be open to the situation. Although we may assume some basic things about its generic structure, we can never simply function on automatic pilot.

Fortunately, although the situation is extremely complex and unpredictable, it is also unified. For all of these historically specific energies belong to a qualitatively unique situation that, like any individual, is characterized by a "pervasive and internally integrating quality" that holds it together in spite of its internal complexity (Dewey [1930] 1984, 246). This is a "tertiary" or global quality—as distinct from a sensed quality like redness or a felt quality like threateningness. A tertiary quality is the unique quality that characterizes any individual and makes it uniquely recognizable in all its actions, "which makes that situation to be just and only the situation it is." This unique, pervasive quality enables us to feel our way around in dealing with the situation and gives us our sense of what is appropriate in the given situation. "It is this unique quality that not only evokes the particular inquiry engaged in but that exercises control over its special procedures" ([1938] 1986, 109). We constantly sense this pervasive "tertiary" quality as "a 'fringe' by which to guide our inferential movements." It provides "premonitions of approach to acceptable meanings, and warnings of getting off the track" ([1925] 1981, 227). Feeling of quality enables organisms to act with "organic prudence" ([1925] 1981, 229).

The situation begins and ends with primary existential/cultural experience. While secondary or refined experience—science, reflection, intelligence—emerges to deal with specific problems, such experience always returns to the primary situation. Dewey says that "the vine of pendant theory is attached at both ends to the pillars of observed subject-matter" (Dewey [1925] 1981, 11). When Dewey says that the situation guides inquiry, it is clear that the situation is primary experience. This means simply that the situation involves primarily not some theoretical construct or distinction but a real-life problem that we face—something like formulating a workable abortion policy or figuring out how to get single mothers back into the work force. Dewey contrasts these "gross, macroscopic, crude subject-matters in primary experience" with "refined, derived objects of reflection" ([1925] 1981, 15). Existential problems are real problems, not abstract or technical ones. They are problems that affect the quality of our lives and often the continuance of life itself. An existential problem means that something quite real is at stake. These are not "artificial" problems, like questions about "the reality and validity of the things of gross experience" ([1925] 1981, 38), which are generated by outdated philosophy. Existential problems are not minor technical problems of interest only to an overspecialized elite. They are problems with real consequences. They are the everyday problems that generate deep anxiety and dispute.

Hence the existential is the context for and the test of all the nonexistential functions of the situation—thought, ideas, imagination, desires, and so on. All of these are intermediate; they originate in the needs and problems of primary existential experience, "in all its heterogeneity and fullness." And such nonexistential functions must be "brought back to the things of ordinary experience, in all their coarseness and crudity, for verification" (Dewey [1925] 1981, 39). This is why Dewey emphasizes the role of "operations"—existential actions that produce experienceable consequences. "The biological antecedent conditions of an unsettled situation are involved in that state of imbalance in organic-environmental interactions. . . . Restoration of integration can be effected. . . . only by operations which actually modify existing conditions, nor by merely 'mental' processes" ([1938] 1986, 106). Ideas must be turned into operations, which must be performed and their consequences ascertained. For, as Dewey points out, "object thought of and object achieved exist in different dimensions" ([1922] 1988, 173). Hence the need for existential operations and "judgments," whereby we bring generalities to bear on a unique situation. For previous experience, although it may be a help, is in the end no substitute for concrete existential operations and judgments. Each unique situation will have its own existential potentialities that must be taken into account in any recommendations for action.

The situation has a dramatic shape and dynamic. To begin with, a situation rises into our consciousness as a situation only when we become aware of that emotion which is "the conscious sign of a break, actual or impending" (Dewey [1934] 1987, 15). In this situation, habit no longer serves, for various tendencies press for action in different directions; "rival goods present themselves. We are faced by competing desires and ends which are incompatible with one another. They are all attractive, seductive. How then shall we choose among them?" ([1922] 1988, 166). Hence the problematic situation is genuinely indeterminate or uncertain; there are many possibilities that conflict with each other, thus preventing habitual overt action. If we should decide that something can and should be done about it, it becomes a "problem" with a possible solution. Such a problem is also colored by emotion and desire; hence it takes on the form of a drama, involving expectations, crisis, and fulfillment.

Deliberation at first heightens the problem into a crisis. We imaginatively follow out the consequences of each separate impulse and ideal to see where they lead. We try out many possible combinations and configurations. Deliberation is an important "open space" that provides room for all the conflicting elements to develop themselves. Out of this developing crisis, however, something genuinely new begins to emerge. Hence deliberation is also a way of opening us to new consequences or to consequences we had not previously acknowledged. It is a way of "remaking old ends" and creating a "love of new ends" (Dewey [1922] 1988, 138). However, deliberation seeks not just new or remade "ends" or "objects" but "the comprehensive object, one which coordinates, organizes and functions each factor of the situation which gave rise to conflict, suspense and deliberation" ([1922] 1988, 135). The goal of deliberation is a new object or "end" (envisioned consequence) that will organize all of our competing impulses into a new configuration—or, to put it the other way around, competing impulses that find a new configuration in order to achieve a new envisioned consequence. Hence deliberation is not simply a matter of choosing among existing options but of remaking the options and discovering new ends and new configurations.

The denouement is the emergence of working harmony and its subjective correlate, choice. For choice is "the emergence of a unified preference out of competing preferences. Biases that had held one another in check now, temporarily at least, reinforce one another, and constitute a unified attitude." "Choice is made as soon as some habit, or some combination of elements of habits and impulse, finds a way fully open. . . . [w]hen the various factors in action fit harmoniously together, when imagination finds no annoying hindrance, when there is a picture of open seas, filled sails and favoring winds, the voyage is definitely entered upon" ([1922] 1988, 134). "Emergence," as usual, signifies that something which was potentially present has been made manifest and objective. As we have seen previously, the problematic is the situation's way of manifesting emergent harmony, and hence that harmony is always potentially discoverable. This is why Dewey says that "form may then be defined as the operation of forces that carry the experience of an event, object, scene, and situation to its own integral fulfillment." Deliberation is necessary if we are to allow such harmony to emerge. It involves making room and giving time for the harmony to unfold and to rise into our consciousness as sensed "qualitative unity" ([1934] 1987, 136, 137).

This emergent working harmony is dynamic rather than static. Old energies function in new ways; new habits form. The increasing complexity of harmoniously functioning habits results in an "explosiveness." Hence harmony carries within itself the seeds of the problematic. "Increased power of forming habits means increased susceptibility, sensitiveness, responsiveness." When there are many habits, a new one cuts across an old one, with unexpected consequences. "Hence instability, novelty, emergence of unexpected and unpredictable combinations" (Dewey [1925] 1981, 229, 230). In this way stability itself breeds novelty and change. In addition, new coordinations are dynamic, not static, for energies in a new configuration interact differently. The object develops the configuration, and the newly configured energies develop the object. And the new habitual coordination inevitably sets up a chain reaction of changes all down the line. It conflicts with other habits. It unsettles some other area. For example, since I began to change my behavior in relationships from the typical pattern of women in my family, a new harmony has begun to emerge. But as I begin to solidify the new way into a habit, it conflicts with other parts of my life that now also need changing. These consequences are unpredictable, but the fact that change will be needed somewhere is predictable. At some point there will be a new problematic situation. And on it goes.

Dewey insists that the genetic structure of the situation is not, *pace* Stephen Pepper, a "theory of harmony culminating in the great cosmic harmony of the absolute" (1939, 386). That is, the move from problematic to harmonious is not a cosmic guarantee that every difficulty will be resolved into harmony. For Dewey maintains that the "problematic" is not all of contingency but only one limited part of it. Dewey fully acknowledges that there are "cases of conflict that lead to dispersion and disruption" and uses as his example the cases of emotional breakdown described by psychiatrists. However, the "problematic" as he describes it is something quite different; it is a case in which "conflict and tension are converted into means of intensifying a consummatory appreciation of material of an individual qualitative experience" (Dewey [1939] 1988, 36). I take this cryptic phrase to mean that the problematic is by definition a limited and potentially manageable case of conflict. We do not have time to formulate something as a problem with a possible solution if, for example, we are already dead or in the midst of psychic breakdown. Nor do we designate something as a problem if we genuinely believe that there is nothing that can be done about it. We identify something as a problem only when we can think of there being a possible solution. And a problem of this manageable scope implies that there are underlying, enabling structures of mind that are not then problematic. Thus, "in reality, even when a person is in some respects at odds with his environment and so has to act for the time being as the sole agent of a good, he in many respects is still supported by objective conditions and is in possession of undisturbed goods and virtues" ([1922] 1988, 40–41). Underlying equilibrium is still there, and all of these remaining undisturbed habits provide ways of dealing with the problem. Hence Dewey explicitly avoids taking achieved harmony in a specific situation and "illegitimately extending" it to the cosmos as a whole ([1939] 1988, 38).

Existential Roots of Logic

Dewey's general methodological assumption is that if you want to cultivate beautiful flowers you must look away from flowers and turn your attention to humbler things like seeds, roots, and soil (Dewey [1934] 1987, 10). Because he wishes to articulate a more viable picture of the function of logic, he needs to return (imaginatively speaking) to that moment in primary experience at which logic, or the precursors of logic, emerged. For when anything has grown as lopsidedly as logic has, it is worth our while to imagine earlier states at which the existential function might be more evident. So, beginning with the most highly developed logical entities, he traces them back to their existential roots, doing a "natural history" of logic. Here I will look not at the specific situation but at the existential functions in which logic is rooted.

The existential basis of logic is the ecological structure of meaning. In Dewey's terms, meaning is an emergent quality of organic association, a tripartite relation involving at least two persons and a common object. The meaning relation is constituted by a genuine "participation in intent" between the two persons with regard to the object. Behavior becomes "cooperative, in that response to another's act involves contemporaneous response to a thing as entering into the other's behavior, and this upon both sides" (Dewey [1925] 1981, 141). Dewey uses the illustration of a person who points; I look at the object at which she is pointing and enter into her intent with regard to the object—"Bring that flower to me." I then modify my actions, entering into her meaning, and bring her the flower. In so doing I have responded to the gesture not just as a movement but as a "sign" that signifies intent. When I bring her the flower and she waits to receive it we enter into a cooperative activity around that object. We act together, with reference to each other's intent, establishing a division of labor around a genuinely common activity. In so doing we have established, in principle, a new level of cultural or language interactions and a new level of communal activities that are final as well as instrumental.

In this way meaning is first a "property of behavior," a matter of "intent" that is not primarily personal in a private and exclusive sense. It primarily accrues to the act of pointing, which is mutually understood no longer as an organic gesture but as a sign that "means" bringing or carrying. For meaning is an inherently generalizable way of acting with respect to objects. Second, the thing involved gains meaning; it acquires significance in its status in "making possible and fulfilling shared cooperation" (Dewey [1925] 1981, 142). In this example the flower gains the meaning of "portability," which is inherently generalizable to a whole host of other objects.

One of the activities made possible by the structure of meaning is commonsense inquiry. Common sense is our "direct involvement" in the world; and the commonsense world is the world with which we are thus involved (Dewey [1938] 1986, 66). Human purposes with respect to this world are characterized by use and enjoyment ([1938] 1986, 69) rather than by the desire to know things "in themselves," which is a later development. We focus on "the qualitative objects, processes, and instruments of the common sense world of use and concrete enjoyments and sufferings" ([1938] 1986, 76). Common sense has two dimensions—an ability and a set of commonplaces, a body of commonly accepted truths. On the one hand, it is "good sense" or "good judgment," "discernment," "power to discriminate the factors that are relevant and important in significance in given situations," and the ability "to bring the discriminations made to bear upon what is to be done and what is to be abstained from, in the 'ordinary affairs of life'" ([1938] 1986, 67). This is in continuity with that exquisite animal sensitivity that Dewey calls "soul"; human sensitivity, however, must be supplemented by intelligent regulation.

On the other hand, common sense is the "set of meanings which are so deeply embedded in its [a group's] customs, occupations, traditions and ways of interpreting its physical environment and group-life, that they form the basic categories of the language-system by which details are interpreted."

These are our commonly accepted assumptions or axioms, and they are "regulative and 'normative' of specific beliefs and judgments" (Dewey [1938] 1986, 68). These also are in continuity with organic life, for animals too have basic ways of responding to their environment. A crucial difference, however, lies in the fact that in animals these ways are built in and relatively inflexible. Humans, however, are capable of forming those common, cultural meanings that involve a genuine "participation in intent." These are "emergent" ideals that produce genuinely emergent ways of being in the world. These two dimensions of common sense function in "conjugate" relation, as the ability to make judgments and the commonly accepted criteria for making such judgments.

Common sense, in this conjugate articulation, functions to promote human use and enjoyment of the environing world. Common sense as an ability to make wise distinctions and judgments takes form in the various arts of medicine, law, engineering, metallurgy, cooking, sewing, and teaching, as well as in the "fine" arts of dance, literature, painting, theater, and the decotative arts. Corresponding to each of these arts is a body of practical knowledge indicating the qualities of materials and the kinds of processes that are involved in the art. This knowledge consists of "the traditions, occupations, techniques, interests, and established institutions of the group." Such meanings are carried in our "common language system" and are regulative; they "determine what individuals of the group may and may not do in relation to physical objects and in relation to one another. They regulate what can be used and enjoyed and how use and enjoyment shall occut" ([1938] 1986, 118). Common sense, embodied in these arts and in our abilities to make use of them, gives shape to our manifold cultural ways of using and enjoying the world around us.

Thus common sense has an inescapable "horizontal" dimension of interaction between humans and the environing natural/cultural world. However, it also has a cumulative, diachronic dimension that Dewey calls "inference." Whereas animals function according to built-in patterns and responses that are exquisitely synchronized within strict limits, humans have the ability to learn from their experience and utilize that cumulative knowledge in making further decisions. Inference is our conviction that a current problematic situation is suffficiently like some previous experience that we can use some of our cumulative knowledge in approaching the new situation. If inference were not possible at all, we would simply have to start from scratch in every individual situation. But in fact we quite naturally make inferences all the time. We quickly associate qualities with whole events, and jump to conclusions. Dewey says that "the act of inferring takes place naturally, that is, without intention. It is at first something we do, not something which we mean to do. We do it as we breathe or walk or gesture" ([1915] 1985, 69). Of course, spontaneous inference is too "realistic"; it jumps immediately from the footprint to the inferred man, as if he were actually there. We do this largely under the influence of individual and cultural habits ([1915] 1985, 75). But too often jumping to conclusions means that we do as Crusoe does on seeing the footprint: "He can only go on repeating, with continuously increasing fright, 'There's a man about, there's a man about'" ([1915] 1985, 76).

However, gradually we learn that our hasty inferences can get us into trouble. The example of the village matron shows that, in matters of illness and medication, wrong inferences can have lethal results. At this point "the act of response naturally stimulated is turned into channels of inspection and experimental (physical) analysis. We move our body to get a better hold on it, and we pick it to pieces to see what it is" (Dewey [1916] 1980, 349). But this requires detaching the inferred idea from the thing itself. We need to understand that an idea suggests a meaning, not an object; a meaning is a possibility to be investigated rather than an object to be responded to directly. To return to the Crusoe example, he can investigate the footprint and check the validity of his inference without immediately becoming terrified. Hence Dewey's "natural history" of inference or thought involves the conscious, regulated doing of something that has already been done spontaneously.

The ultimate result of commonsense inquiry is a "judgment" whose primary sense is the judgment in a law court. Dewey prefers this image because it is preeminently practical rather than theoretical and because it emphasizes so clearly the crucial role of individualized judgment in concluding the issue. Such judgment has the structure of a proposition with a subject—indicating the legal status of the action in question—and a predicate—indicating the actions that are recommended in response to it—determined on the basis of a comprehensive system of legal meanings. The system is universal in the sense that it applies to no specific person or action but to everything that occurs in our culture. And although this system is universal, the ultimate judgment is singular and individual, trying to take into account the specific needs of the situation and the way in which justice may best be done.

The tripartite structure of meaning ensures that all cultural activities, no matter how highly developed, relate in an intimate way to the environing world. This pervasive ecological structuring means that the existential conditions which form the physical environment enter at every point into the constitution of sociocultural phenomena. No individual person and no group does anything except in interaction with physical conditions. There are no consequences taking place, there are no social events that can be referred to the human factor exclusively. Let desires, skills, purposes, beliefs be what they will, what happens is the product of the interacting intervention of physical conditions like soil, sea, mountains, climate, tools, and machines, in all their vast variety, with the human factor (Dewey [1938] 1986, 485–486). And if nothing human or cultural exists apart from a common environing world, there are, in principle, common elements in all human experience that may be developed and utilized. Commonsense judgment and inference are emergent ways of utilizing this commonality to facilitate human adaptation to the natural and cultural world. Dewey's point is that this may not be done hastily or uncritically—which causes great damage—but carefully, with attention to consequences. It is for this very reason that we have developed logic.

Logic as Refined Instrumentality

The development of highly refined logical forms is part of our attempt to regulate our inferences, to check our system of assumed meanings, to test our judgments so that we are more likely to act wisely in dealing with our world. Logic develops the generality implicit in the structure of meaning, and develops it critically, so that a system of refined and tested meanings is available to us in our inferences and judgments.

If we return to the image of judgment in a court of law, we remember that such a process involves a complex system of legal meanings or principles that fundamentally provide general "ways of acting" that issue in sets of traits defining various legal "kinds." I have in mind such things as the presumption of innocence, the rules of evidence, the principles of common law, all of which issue in categories of murder with or without intent, and corresponding seriousness of punishments. When an event or action comes before the court, we initially use this system of legal meanings to elicit evidence and determine the facts of the case. Can we prove murder or not, and if so, can we prove intent? The outcome here is a provisional judgment that the event in question may be classified as, for example, murder in the second degree. On this basis, we again use our system of legal meanings to determine the appropriate sentence. A lawyer for the defense may adduce mitigating factors which might affect the sentence. The outcome is a judgment in the form of a proposition constituted by subject—the determined offense—and predicate—the recommended sentence. Let me clarify the distinction here between the universal propositions articulating principles of legal procedure and criteria that have no specific reference and the general propositions that state existential identifications made on the basis of adduced evidence.

Keeping this image in mind, let me bring in Dewey's distinction between the two kinds of general propositions—again, universal and generic—that form the proximate subject matter of logic. Universal propositions are definitions; they indicate the properties that must necessarily be present if we are to call something an x, one of a certain kind. They articulate ways of acting that delineate the sets of traits describing "kinds." We determine, for example, that "being mortal" is an "integral and necessary" part of our definition of "being human." On the basis of this logical definition, then, the relation between the two is valid "by definition of a conception." Dewey says that "like ideals, they are not intended to be themselves realized but are meant to direct our course to realization of potentialities in existent conditions—potentialities which would escape notice were it not for the guidance which an ideal, or a definition, provides" ([1938] 1986, 303). General propositions deal with, for example, the existential connection between the "fact of life" and the "fact of death"; here the connection between the two is "a matter of evidence, determined by observations" ([1938] 1986, 255). As in the case of legal judgments, universal propositions state these universal definitions, whereas generic propositions state our identification of something as a member of a kind, based on evidence. As in the legal judgment, the two sorts of logical propositions work in "conjugate" relation in any inquiry. A universal proposition provides a principle for eliciting and determining evidence, resulting in a generic proposition identifying a singular as one of a certain kind. This genetic proposition then encapsulates the "net profit" of the inquiry up to this point and crystallizes what is important for subsequent inquiry ([1916] 1980, 356). Again, another universal proposition directs the determination of further evidence, resulting in another generic proposition.

Each kind of proposition has its own distinct dynamic. Universal propositions are developed in "discourse" according to the lines of "implication." We ask that any development of universal propositions unfold along the lines of "rigorous and productive implication" (Dewey [1938] 1986, 276). If implication is the set of characters that are necessarily "included" in a definition, the two sides of the definition are logically equal. This means that if we have a definition of "rape" as involving, necessarily and exclusively, "sexual penetration" "by force" and "without consent," these three characters are logically equivalent to "rape" but are more specific. We can see that in a rape trial it will be more useful for us to work with the more detailed characters than with the more general term. "Rigor" signifies the logical equivalence; there must be no loss of logical necessity when we move from the more general to the more specific. And "productive" signifies the value of the more detailed logical definition in guiding the determination of evidence in such a situation.

General propositions, however, work along the lines of "inference." This has an existential reference and hence an element of probability and risk that implication lacks. General propositions must enable us either to begin with a "kind" and infer the qualities that are likely to be present if we perform certain operations or to begin with a set of qualities and infer a "kind" identity so that we can treat it in certain relevant ways. For it is evident that we need to be able to locate a given event as accurately as possible within a hierarchy of inclusive kinds, in order to determine its specific affinities and its likelihood of responding in certain ways and not in others.

It becomes evident that if these logical propositions are to work effectively we must have a reliable set of universal propositions that interrelate systematically (Dewey [1938] 1986, 271). That is, their function within inquiry sets definite conditions that must be satisfied if they are to function helpfully ([1938] 1986, 276). Each definition is constituted by necessary interrelated characters which are interdependent. Each character is essential; hence any one character necessarily implies the others. Dewey says that

> If this universal proposition is valid as a definition, it is (1) independent of the existence of creatures marked by corresponding qualitative traits; while (2) it involves the idea that these characters are necessarily interrelated, so that any one of the three characters is meaningless in the *definition* apart from its modifying and being modified by the other terms. In other words, *if* warm-blooded, *then* viviparous, etc. (Dewey [1938] 1986, 340–341)

This interrelation of interdependent characters is "multiplicative," which corresponds to "additive" conjunction in existential matters. Furthermore, "alternation" means that there is implied in the definition a limited and exhaustive number of possible ways of exemplifying this concept (Dewey [1938] 1986, 337). These necessary relations are what we *mean* when we use the term. These sets of propositions have an "if-then" structure. "If, under these conditions, you do this, then this will happen." "If [a, b, and c] are present, then this is a member of *x* kind." They define objects and events in terms of specific, fine interactions. Hence to say that something is of kind *x* is to identify it in terms of a typical series of interactions. To say that it is of kind *y* is to identify it in terms of another typical series of interactions. This "resolution" into detailed and sequential interactions is what allows us to make grounded decisions about what specific action to recommend in order to resolve a situation. We can point to a specific action that must intervene at this specific place in the sequence of interactions, and it will change and redirect the typical interaction so that it produces one result rather than another.

Moreover the terms constituting universal propositions are ordered in various ways: transitivity, symmetry, correlation, and connexity. Transitivity means that propositions are ordered such that they move us quickly down the line.

> Take such terms as "older than" (greater, brighter, etc.), or any property expressed linguistically by a comparative word. If A is more (or less) in any designated trait than B, and B sustains this same relation to C, and C to D, and so on, then A sustains it to the last term in the series, whatever that may be. The terms satisfy the condition of transitivity. Intermediaries may be skipped whenever terms have been constituted to satisfy this form of order. (Dewey [1938] 1986, 329)

Transitivity enables us to make substitutions and hence to move. If we say that whales are mammals and mammals are vertebrates, then we are warranted in saying that whales are vertebrates. We can move down the line. Symmetry means that "things that are equal to the same thing are equal to one another." "Friend-friend" is a symmetrical relation, whereas "kill-killed" is not. Hence symmetry, like transitivity, enables us to substitute one term for another with no loss of rigor. Correlation is equality of relation with respect to scope. "Husband-wife" is correlative, whereas "husband-wives" is not. Connexity is symmetrical transitivity; it is equivalence that grounds "back-and-forth movement in inference and discourse" (Dewey [1938] 1986, 333, 334).

These various kinds of ordering enable us to substitute terms for each other. This promotes inference and enables reasoning to be both rigorous and productive. These various necessary interrelations, being mutually supportive, also make possible *inference* and *implication*. Implication concerns the necessary interrelations of universal propositions, such that any one property or proposition implies another. This is what allows reasoning through a whole chain of necessary connections and interactions, far down the line. This means that when we use a concept like "triangularity," certain more specific properties—like "trilinearity" and "all angles adding up to 180 degrees"—are necessarily implied in that, by definition as it were. Because of necessary relations, we can move around in the system, from generality to specificity. We can move around freely among interrelated terms. *Inference* concerns existential propositions; it means that once we have identified a singular as one of a kind, we can then infer the presence of other qualities not now visible. This anticipation allows us to anticipate what might be there and direct our observations and operations accordingly.

Universal propositions establish the qualities that we take to be necessary to a certain "kind," and also indicate those qualities that are reliable guides for inferential identification. Rather than simply being observed qualities, which may or may not be reliable signs of that kind, universal propositions must depend on qualities that have been proven to be "so involved with one another that, in spite of variations in the circumstances in which they present themselves, the presence of one is a valid sign that the others will present themselves *if* specified interactions occur" (Dewey [1938] 1986, 291). These definitions are not visual pictures or representations so much as they are functional recipes or directions for recognizing certain kinds of properties. "Do this, and if it responds only in this way, and in no other way, it's an *x*." Dewey says that "like ideals, they are not intended to be themselves realized but are meant to direct our course to realization of potentialities in existent conditions—potentialities which would escape notice were it not for the guidance which an ideal, or a definition, provides" ([1938] 1986, 303). In all of these ways, the system of logical universals is a highly developed tool created to facilitate the making of wise and ecologically sensitive judgments.

Toward the Revitalization of Logic as Inquiry

It becomes evident why logic, thought of as a coherent system of universals, has been idealized. For individual propositions are each the net result of such an excruciatingly thorough process of inclusion and exclusion that they become "logical kernels" (Dewey [1916] 1980, 356), highly refined and, therefore, legitimately of great value. And the system does have a symmetry and a transitivity that are mesmerizing to anyone who appreciates such things. The necessity of implication and inclusion is quite fascinating in systemic terms. If one appreciates well designed tools, as I do, this is a tool well worth admiring. I find that a certain degree of appreciative contemplation is quite appropriate and well deserved. However, an understandable appreciation becomes neurotic when it becomes a substitute for using the tool. I suppose that if one is discouraged about the shortcomings of the real world it is quite easy, given a certain personality, perhaps, to look at the system of logical universals as the perfectly ordered and agreed-upon world for which one longs. So it is not surprising that the history of logic is largely a history of attempts to expand and extend the orderedness of this system, as a way, in itself, of bringing order to the world.

However, Dewey's point is that such a system, of itself, can do nothing to bring order to the world. In fact, mis-taking a functional dimension for the whole of Reality—or mis-taking a function for a representation—is, as

Dewey says, one of the "Great Bads" of philosophy. "Working terms, terms which as working are flexible and historic, relative and methodological, are transformed into absolute, fixed, and predetermined properties of being" (Dewey [1903] 1983, 306). Taken "apart from reference to particular position occupied and particular part played in the growth of experience," logical forms become not just relative abstractions (for that is their legitimate function) but "abstractions without possible reference or bearing" and hence "radically meaningless" ([1903] 1983,304). Thus Dewey says that "I know of no way of fixing the scope and claims of mathematics in philosophy save to try to point out just at what juncture it enters experience and what work it does after it has got entrance" ([1916] 1980, 360). Logical universals are valuable not in themselves, but because of what they enable us to do in interaction with existential material. To take this as the whole of reality is to strip off the individual quality that makes life both enjoyable and frightening to us, and to make us look at ordinary life with a jaundiced eye, or with fear and anxiety. In itself it is not a reliable guide to the ordinary world, and if we try to use it this way we will only succeed in convincing ourselves all over again that we must escape from this world into the world of pure logical universals.

However, Dewey's theory of logic makes these logical universals functional rather than absolute, relative rather than isolated. They are not a superior ideal Reality but tools that we develop in the process of using them. They are not to be worshiped and contemplated but used. They have meaning not in themselves but only in functional relation to observed material, and even as they regulate observation they are modified by the results of experience. Moreover, they develop only within a community, on the basis of commonly shared meanings and purposes. Any sense of "coercion" in Dewey's logic is based on the voluntary agreement by all members of a community to submit themselves to the evidence (based on commonly accepted criteria) for the common purpose of acting wisely and with ecological sensitivity. And such universal propositions are merely instrumental to the acquisition of knowledge; we use these universals to develop our thinking. But once we have ascertained the relevant facts we come to the moment of choice and value. All logical activity comes down to the act of judgment, when we must take the logical thinking we have done and on the basis of it determine exactly what specific thing we are logically warranted in asserting as the wise course of action, according to our own values, in this specific situation. Logic cannot enable us to evade this risky judgment, nor can it provide a risk-free algorithm for choice; it can only help us reflect on things and more likely behave "in deference to the connections of things." Hence Dewey says that ultimately his logic is a "logic of individualized situations" ([1920] 1982, 177).

All of this means that logic, for Dewey, is not all of life; it is only a tool for a certain purpose. And although we may well agree with Rorty that there are other purposes in life besides what he calls "prediction and control" (Rorty 1991c, 58), there are times when it can be extremely important to be able to anticipate existential consequences and act accordingly. Having many purposes other than this need not mean that we must disparage this particular purpose or the tools that it has created.

Women and Logic Revisited

I began with my own ambivalence toward logic and Nye's analysis of logic as the "words of power" used by men to silence others. I have also tried to provide a positive reading of Dewey's *Logic*. I realize that the notions of universal conditions and power remain important parts of Dewey's logic and that both remain problematic for feminists. I would, however, point out that though the feminist critique of universality is quite legitimate it does not destroy the validity of Dewey's notion of universality. For what feminists critique is our Enlightenment sense of universality as unproblematic and automatic because built into a rational Reality. Rationally accessible "essences" meant that humans, by virtue of a universal "human nature," were automatically transparent to each other and that group norms automatically reflected what was best for all groups and individuals. And Reason meant that we could use Logic to force agreement and that such rational force was not oppressive because it was an appeal to our own higher selves. I agree with Nancy Fraser and Linda Nicholson (quoting Lyotard) that there just is not as much universality in the world as there used to be (Fraser and Nicholson 1990, 24). This autocratic form of universality, with its uncritical exercise of power, will never again command unquestioning obedience. Nor should it. But we should remember that Dewey spent much of his long career criticizing this very notion of universality. His critique is all the more valuable because it comes from a male philosopher writing within the academy.

However, Dewey offers us more than a critique of absolutized universality. In this connection, let me return to Rorty's analysis of Dewey as "putting power in the service of love." This phrase signifies Dewey's Copernican revolution in logic, a fundamental change of emphasis. For logic is no longer the absolute arbiter of ordinary experience, no longer a fixed higher realm into which we rise in order to escape the vicissitudes of ordinary experience. No longer do the precision and nonexistential quality of logical universals set the standard for Reality or for all of language and experience, thereby denigrating nonlogical experience. No longer does logic provide us with a way of forcing existential difference into the shape decreed by logic. Rather, what comes back into focus through Dewey's Copernican revolution is his deep love and respect for a specific human community whose ordinary experience has primacy and provides the ultimate context for logic.

On the one hand, "power in the service of love" signifies the origins of logic in a communal vocabulary. Logic is not a pre-existing Reality but a human construct. It is a human vocabulary defined by a specific "participation in intent." (This is very close to Rortyan "love" and "solidarity"—more specifically, an "act of social faith" [Rorty 1991d, 33]). Although it is a way of exercising power, this is not *power over* others but *power with* others. It is an exercise in voluntary self-regulation for communally determined goals. The political action of community-building determines the purpose of logic and shapes logic as a tool to serve those human purposes. A pragmatist logic will strive to acknowledge its own purposes and interests so that they can be open to self-criticism and reformulation. It will also strive to articulate its connection with communal experience so that when that experience changes logic may also change.

On the other hand, "power in the service of love" signifies the ultimate purpose of logic. Deweyan logic does involve a turning away from individual difference in order to create common ground. Dewey acknowledges the pain this causes; his unattractive Baconian images in fact deal with the effort required to do this. For authentic common ground is something which is prophetic rather than descriptive; it does not lie on the surface of things but must be struggled for. However, Dewey insists that this turning away is functional rather than metaphysical; for the turn away to find universality is followed by the return to existential difference. Ultimately, universality and difference mutually modify each other. Universality helps us see enough commonality among experiences that we can bring our cumulative wisdom to bear in a new situation; at the same time, existential difference requires the mediation of judgment to custom tailor solutions to the needs of the particular situation. In addition, each particular situation ultimately modifies our cumulative sense of what situations have in common.

Dewey's view of logic is part of his more general way of being in culture. He has insisted that ideals and universals are sterile in themselves and bear fruit only when they work with and are shaped by the needs, limits, and potentialities of a specific situation. Accordingly, he is not interested in Total Revolution, or in separating from culture altogether, but in joining the cultural conversation and changing it from the inside. In Rorty's terms, he would ask that we look for "toeholds" rather than "skyhooks" (Rorty 1991b, 14). The possibilities are great; as Dewey says:

> Women have as yet made little contribution to philosophy. But when women who are not mere students of other persons' philosophy set out to write it, we cannot conceive that it will be the same in viewpoint or tenor as that composed from the standpoint of the different masculine experience of things. (Dewey [1919] 1982, 45).

Dewey's way is to do logic subversively, maintaining continuity with the tradition while simultaneously criticizing it and developing its own ideal possibilities. He would encourage women to join the logical conversation and change it rather than cutting ourselves off from it. This will mean that some of our high ideals will be modified as we attempt to work with concrete situations. But, for Dewey, the price is worth paying if it makes a real change, no matter how small.

So, the question emerges again: what will women do about logic? Will we take Nye's advice and forswear altogether the words of power? Is our experience so radically different that we must create a separate culture *de novo*? I do hear in Dewey's logic a number of possibilities which seem worth developing. I must admit that I continue to have what Adrienne Rich calls "The drive/To connect. The dream of a common language." What I have in mind is not the forcibly imposed "common language" of traditional logic but an authentically common language which honors difference. I refuse to believe that I, as a middle-class, educated, ethnic, christian feminist cannot find common cause—and common meanings—with women of different backgrounds and traditions—and even with men. I no longer think that this is automatic or guaranteed; rather, it is what Dewey calls an "emergent" rather than an "original" function, or what Rorty calls a metaphysically unjustifiable "hope" (Rorty 1982, 208). I continue to believe that all persons live under the same universal conditions of existence and that, as the environmental movement is making dear, we can and must find commonality on basic human issues. I continue to feel a need within my own community for integrality and for some larger theory by which to do ongoing self-criticism and cross-fertilization among our different vocabularies and practices. All of these imply a need for logic in some form. So it seems to me that if women are going to become actively involved in a logic, as I think we could be, Dewey's Copernican revolution might be an excellent place to begin.

As a christian, I continue to be inspired by the prophetic image in the old Jewish scriptures about beating the swords into plowshares and the spears into pruning hooks. What this image says to me is that power in itself is not evil; for there is power which destroys and there is power which nurtures or cultivates. Pruning and plowing are themselves forms of power, but they put power in the service of new growth and human community rather than in the service of oppression. So I continue to believe that it is possible, with concerted effort, to take traditional logic and transform it into an instrument which serves the fruitfulness of individual situations. And I think women can do this, but only if we grasp our own power and enter wholeheartedly into the struggle for cultural transformation.

References

Chaloupka, William. 1987. John Dewey's social aesthetics as a precedent for environmental thought. *Environmental Ethics* 9(3): 243–260.

Dewey, John. [1903] 1983. Studies in logical theory. Reprinted in *John Dewey: The middle works, Vol. 2: 1899–1924*, ed. Jo Ann Boydston. Carbondale and Edwardsville: Southern Illinois University Press.

———. [1915] 1985. The logic of judgments of practice. Reprinted in *John Dewey: The middle works, Vol. 8: 1899–1924*, ed. Jo Ann Boydston. Carbondale and Edwardsville: Southern Illinois University Press.

———. [1916] 1980. Introduction to *Essays in experimental logic*. Reprinted in *John Dewey: The middle works, Vol. 10: 1899–1924*, ed. Jo Ann Boydston. Carbondale and Edwardsville: Southern Illinois University Press.

———. [1919] 1982. Philosophy and democracy. Reprinted in *John Dewey: The middle works, Vol. 11: 1899–1924*, ed. Jo Ann Boydston. Carbondale and Edwardsville: Southern Illinois University Press.

———. [1920] 1982. Reconstruction in philosophy. Reprinted in *John Dewey: The middle works, Vol. 12: 1899–1924*, ed. Jo Ann Boydston. Carbondale and Edwardsville: Southern Illinois University Press.

———. [1922] 1988. Human nature and conduct. Reprinted in *John Dewey: The middle works, Vol. 14: 1899–1924*, ed. Jo Ann Boydston. Carbondale and Edwardsville: Southern Illinois University Press.

———. [1925] 1981. Experience and nature. Reprinted in *John Dewey: The later works, Vol. 1: 1925–1953*, ed. Jo Ann Boydston. Carbondale and Edwardsville: Southern Illinois University Press.

———. [1929] 1988. The Quest for Certainty. Reprinted in *John Dewey: The later works, Vol. 4: 1925–1953*, ed. Jo Ann Boydston. Carbondale and Edwardsville: Southern Illinois University Press.

———. [1930] 1984. Qualitative thought. Reprinted in *John Dewey: The later works, Vol. 5: 1925–1953*, ed. Jo Ann Boydston. Carbondale and Edwardsville: Southern Illinois University Press.

———. [1934] 1987. Art as experience. Reprinted in *John Dewey: The 1ater works, Vol. 10: 1925–1953*, ed. Jo Ann Boydston. Carbondale and Edwardsville: Southern Illinois University Press.

———. [1938] 1986. Logic: The theory of inquiry. Reprinted in *John Dewey: The later works, Vol. 12: 1925–1953*, ed. Jo Ann Boydston. Carbondale and Edwardsville: Southern Illinois University Press.

———. [1939] 1988. Experience, knowledge and value: A rejoinder. Reprinted in *John Dewey: The later works, Vol. 14: 1925–1953*, ed. Jo Ann Boydston. Carbondale and Edwardsville: Southern Illinois University Press.

———. [1948] 1982. Introduction: Reconstruction as seen twenty-five years later. Reprinted in *John Dewey: The middle works, Vol. 12: 1899–1924*, ed. Jo Ann Boydston. Carbondale and Edwardsville: Southern Illinois University Press.

Fraser, Nancy, and Nicholson, Linda. 1990. Social criticism without philosophy: An encounter between feminism and postmodernism. In *Feminism/Postmodernism*, ed. Linda Nicholson. New York: Routledge.

Nye, Andrea. 1990. *Words of power: A feminist reading of the history of logic*. New York: Routledge.

Pepper, Stephen C. 1939. Questions on Dewey's esthetics. In *The Philosophy of John Dewey*, ed. Paul Arthur Schilpp. Evanston, Ill.: Northwestern University Press.

Rorty, Richard. 1982. Method, social science, and social hope. In *Consequences of pragmatism*. Minneapolis: University of Minnesota Press.

———. 1991a. Heidegger, contingency and pragmatism. In *Essays on Heidegger and others*. Cambridge: Cambridge University Press.

———. 1991b. Introduction: Antirepresentationalism, ethnocentrism, and liberalism. In *Objectivity, relativism, and truth*. Cambridge: Cambridge University Press.

———. 1991c. Is natural science a natural kind? In *Objectivity, relativism, and truth*. Cambridge: Cambridge University Press.

———. 1991d. Solidarity or objectivity? In *Objectivity, relativism, and truth*. Cambridge: Cambridge University Press.

CHAPTER FIVE

~

Words of Power and the Logic of Sense

DOROTHEA E. OLKOWSKI

In the conclusion of *Words of Power*, Andrea Nye proudly points to the numerous fallacies she has committed in her dispute with the logicians. In particular, she cites the fallacy that the genesis of an idea is relevant to its truth and falsity and the fallacy that criticism of the logician as a person can count against the truth of that view.[1] She commits these fallacies deliberately because she believes that logic is motivated by the social context, thus it is historically contingent. Her argument for this is that, to have meaning, words must be spoken by a particular person, at a particular place and time, in a particular situation. What this implies is, that without a specific context, language is an abstraction of empty sounds that express nothing and convey no information. With this last statement, I have no fundamental disagreement, especially when we take into consideration how much of language consists of "order words," words that are heard and repeated from person to person or recited, like a prayer, a greeting, or a mathematical formula, though they depend greatly on a shared or familiar context to have the expected impact. Nor do I necessarily differ with her declaration that there is no feminist logic that could supplant the logic she censures. The evidence for this lies in the fact that Nye readily makes use of traditional logic even as she condemns it, or at least, she agrees to many of logic's principle presuppositions such as truth, consistency, and formalization, even as she consciously commits herself to making fallacious arguments, a move that, one might argue, only serves to reinforce the standard she wishes to undermine.

For example, Nye argues against Parmenides who, she claims, fails to be consistent because he makes no connection between the language of logical truth and that of human affairs. Plato is condemned for creating and teaching a method that allows the expert to control truth by controlling the discussion. Nye argues that this is an error that is, in the least, counter to the highest aims of formalization in accordance with which anyone should be able to apply rules to arrive at truths. A similar charge is leveled at Aristotle whose development of the syllogism makes it possible to change one's argument or point of view for the sake of personal or political expediency and who also unflinchingly proclaims "man" to be the chief example of substance. Finally, Stoic logic is condemned for its rejection of the Aristotelian law of excluded middle because it makes paradox impossible to avoid, and paradox is not, presumably, a faithful account (a *logos*) of what is. Additionally, Nye is disturbed that the Stoics did not especially promote a more diverse and less brutal regime either among the Greeks or later among the Romans. In sum, "[a]gainst the force of the authoritative relations that logic structures, a judgment of falsity is inadequate."[2]

Taken as a whole, Nye claims, these systems of logic prove to be inadequate because they either promote authoritarian mastery and control or are irrelevant with respect to the realities of life. Yet, given that logic is recognized by institutions, states, religions, and individuals as the formal expression of rationality and intelligiblity, whether innate or learned, women do not have the option of separating themselves from traditional syllogistic and formal logic in an attempt to create an independent woman's logic or language. Were this even possible, it would mean the abdication of all concern for and involvement in social structures and institutions including such critical orders as language and law, a move that surely would isolate women from society and leave them even more powerless and helpless in relation to a system that would exclude them. Nye's conclusion is that women must learn logical techniques if they are to survive the regimes of power that logic establishes, but, in addition, they must find a way to create institutions that "support a coming together to an adequate understanding of what has happened, is happening, and ought to happen."[3] History, experience, and ethics are thus the realms wherein women would be most active. Given the overwhelming centrality of logic to social institutions, it appears that Nye advocates the development of history, experience, and ethics as realms of practical yet necessarily intellectual or epistemological activity *outside* the sphere of logic. If this is the case, then these spheres of activity would have to be able to produce adequate understandings of life, language, law, and so forth. Nye believes that adequate understanding would arise as the result of women's ability not to speak but to listen and read beneath the level of logic at a level where confusion, need, and weakness prevail. Only here in the field of what she calls our "common humanity" can women and men first, listen and learn then actually begin to speak and communicate one to another outside of the scripted forms of logic.[4]

What would this amount to? What is listening and reading, then speaking and communicating outside or beneath logic? Is it possible to listen, read, and speak intelligibly or even adequately outside or beneath logic? Although it is the case that Nye claims that women must learn institutional logic as a matter of survival only, she theorizes that a second logic and language "beneath" the level of the first is within the realm of the possible and, in fact, may be necessary. On her account, such a logic and language must operate in life wherever we find confusion, need, and weakness, presumably (although she does not say this) without at all subverting the reality and/or the experience of these situations or things that bewilder and confront us with lack and frailty. However, what remains to be answered is precisely the question of what such a logic could be. How can we know what it means to speak below the level of institutional logic? Is such a level, if it exists at all, truly a logic outside logic? Given these questions, it is my intent to examine the very possibility of a realm outside or beneath the sphere of logic.

For a feminist philosopher who has studied phenomenology and poststructuralist philosophy, such a claim is not unprecedented. It immediately brings to mind the work of Maurice Merleau-Ponty, for whom the radical awareness of subjectivity is a radical awareness of language tied to the body. The body, for Merleau-Ponty, is an ambiguous field that seems to correspond to the domain of what Nye calls our common humanity, a situation replete with uncertainty and danger. It is Merleau-Ponty's position that because a certain kind of language, one that is static and predictable and conforms to the dictates of formal logic, there must be another kind of language as well, an expressive and original language emerging from the depths of the body. Yet, as we will see, such a philosophy of the body, a philosophy in which language arises from the depths of the body, will produce a language that suffers from extreme unintelligibility unless it is somehow anchored to or by a formal system of logic. In his attempt to make language expressive, to institute a speaking or writing being whose physical voice resonates in language, Merleau-Ponty encounters the conflict at the heart of bodies and language and language and logic.

Merleau-Ponty begins by examining the "eidetic of language" of Edmund Husserl.[5] It is a logic concerned with the formal properties of signification and their rules of transformation. This pure grammar would ideally make possible, *in any language*, the expression of various propositions signifying existence, negativity, probability, and possibility. Merleau-Ponty's criticism is that pure grammar as a logic of language is possible only on the assumption of sedimented language, long-established language whose meaning and structure are agreed on, universally recognized, and objectified. Pure grammar presupposes that communication is the primary function of discourse and that the purpose of language is, principally, to take up the naming of objects. When symbols are used to represent particular relations, purely conventional meanings are established, and language is protected from shifts in meaning that might open the way to error. Thus it is the function of such a logic of language to replace all confused allusions with precise significations.[6]

Like Nye, Merleau-Ponty objects to the logic of formal properties of language because it neither allows nor accounts for the confusions of everyday life. Following the pure grammar of logic makes language nothing more than a pure sign representing a pure signification, the codification of thought.[7] Unwilling or unable to commit himself to a logical structure that seems determined and lifeless, Merleau-Ponty hopes to make language into a bodily phenomenon. He conceives of a language arising out of the "confusion, need, and weakness" of bodily depths, a language that creates itself independently of the pure grammar of logic and thus is purely original and expressive. While accepting the existence and even the necessity of sedimented language, Merleau-Ponty nevertheless maintains that expressive or creative language is a body; that is, it shares in the passions and actions of the body such that language and bodies intermingle and the external relation of designation is eliminated.[8] However, Merleau-Ponty fails in this endeavor in a manner that, I believe, spells disaster for Nye's project as well. Merleau-Ponty fails because, in seeking to set language free from formal constraints, he restricts it even more by embedding it in the body. What is a language-body? Language that intermingles with the body, that cannot be differentiated from the body remains on the order of pure expression; it can be no more than groans and cries, bodily emanations, regardless of the complexity of the expression. To conceptualize, to argue, to be understood, even on the most common level of humanity, it is necessary, I maintain, to return again and again from the body's physical depths to the surface of intelligibility. And in following this trajectory, Merleau-Ponty is forced to speak a language of pure grammar so he might be able to speak at all.

This is particularly evident when Gilles Deleuze's analyses of the logic of sense are brought to bear on the problem. For Deleuze, we must be careful to distinguish between the confusions of everyday life, which include the qualities of bodies, their physical nature, their actions and passions, and something that is not their opposite yet must be differentiated from bodies—that is, incorporeal events, the logical attributes of propositions, expressed in propositions, though attributed to bodies. The movement through Deleuze's thought that leads to this distinction and the role it plays in Nye's critique of the power arrangements in logic are complicated. I will, however, attempt to provide at least the framework of such an approach.

Nye is not alone in her attempt to make sense of the dominance inherent in logic, yet it is possible to discover this without resorting to fallacious arguments. In the work of French philosopher Deleuze, we likewise find a critique of the logicians directed against their claims respecting the authority and regulatory nature of traditional logical formations. Deleuze argues that Plato laid the basis for attributing a certain kind of authority to logic when he distinguished between limited and measured things with fixed qualities and pure becoming. The former presuppose fixed presents and subjects, while the latter, he claims, is without measure.[9] So much is the latter without measure or limit with respect to qualities, presents, and subjects that not only does it never rest, but it also moves in two directions at once. That is, pure becoming is an infinite identity of both past and future, moving in both directions or senses at the same time, thereby causing future and past, too much and not enough, more and less, and so forth, to "coincide in the simultaneity of a rebellious matter."[10]

What is interesting is that this dualism, as Deleuze calls it, is not what we generally recognize as dualism. We expect dualism to take its place in the distinction between the Idea and matter or Ideas and bodies; between the rational intellectual world and that of sensible materiality. However, in this case, it does not. As conceptualized by Plato, there is a dualism *within bodies* themselves. The dualism exists between that which receives the action of the Idea and that which does not and so is very poorly realized. Thus, for Plato, dualism operates between legitimate copies and false simulacra.[11] Matter within simulacra, insofar as it does not receive the action of an Idea, is pure unlimited becoming. Limited things, on the other hand, are the matter within legitimate copies subject to the action of Ideas. If pure becoming is the simulacra that does not receive the action of an Idea, then its relation to language must be quite specific, for language does not affect the simulacra and speech simply flows over its referent.[12] Of course, it is always possible to contemplate developing two completely different kinds of language: one language designating that which is fixed by the Idea, another expressing becoming. This, I think, is something like Nye's approach and perhaps Merleau-Ponty's as well, insofar as each postulates a language beneath the level of traditional logic or eidetic grammar. The justification for fixing matter by the Idea is that it contributes to a grab for power based on irrefutable conceptual claims for intelligibility, coherence, and hierarchic distribution, whereas when language expresses becoming, none of these claims can be made with any authority. Now, is it enough to leave it here? Can we simply say, "Fine, some bodies are fixed into limited things by language and some are not," or "Some language fixes and some simply flows unimpeded"? The problem with this solution is that it leaves in place a dualism within bodies while creating a second dualism within language. What is left unexamined and unexplained in this is the whole question of how language intersects with bodies or why it does not when it does not, as well as the question of whether a body is simply another linguistic construct referring to something symbolic but never accessible as real.

I want to make clear that none of these alternatives appeal to me. In contrast to the methods advocated by Nye, Merleau-Ponty, and some contemporary feminist postmodern thinkers, another possible approach leads us away from the Platonic problematic toward a different kind of problem and a different kind of solution. Deleuze suggests that we, at least as a start, reconsider the logic of the Stoics. As we have already seen, it is an approach that Nye appears to have rejected for its embrace of paradox and for its failure to produce a more egalitarian society. I would like to suggest that this dismissal of Stoic thinking in its entirety may be precipitous. For while it is true that the Stoics remained apolitical and did not extend their ethics to putting an end to slavery or to the recognition of women as equal to men, nevertheless, they did create a system of logic that is at least not incompatible with those goals. In the very least, Stoic logic appears to me to be far more useful than the descent into confusion and need in breaking up the hegemonic and hierarchical order required by Platonic and Aristotelian forms of thought. And this, I would add, may be all we can expect from logic.

Unlike Plato, the Stoics make several distinctions that Plato does not consider and for reasons which Plato could not entertain. On the one hand, there are bodies characterized by physical qualities, actions, passions, and corresponding "states of affairs." The Stoic conception of bodies is not transposable into Platonic simulacra (matter that fails to be organized by the Idea), for the latter are awaiting the action of an Idea; rather, as the Stoics point out, bodies do have characteristics of their own.[13] All of these bodily characteristics, according to this conceptualization, are determined strictly by how bodies mix with one another, as when metal cuts into skin or water mixes with oil. In addition, however, all bodies are causes (and only causes) of certain effects that are *not* bodily. In a radical reversal of the Platonic scheme, the Stoics claim that although bodies do form mixtures with other bodies, they are also the causes of "incorporeal entities"—that is, of "logical or dialectical attributes"—which are certainly not corporeal things, nor are they facts: they are language events.[14]

Here, following this orientation of thought, we can begin sketching out the extremely complex relation between bodies and language, a relation whose complexity is certain to be underestimated or reduced to some easy formula. Bodies that mix with one another and are the causes of changes in one another certainly exist; as bodies with physical qualities, they are, after all, both active and passive, both engendering and receiving interactions with other bodies. Events, however, as the effects of bodies, do not exist; they do not have the physical qualities that bodies have; they are effects and so are said only to subsist or inhere in relation to bodies.[15] As such, it would be inappropriate to say that language events are substantives (they are not things; they do not exist) or even adjectives, which characterize and predicate substantives. Events are better characterized as verbs, infinitives like *to grow* or *to shrink* that inhere or subsist in bodies as the result of the actions and passions, the intermingling of bodies. Historian of philosophy Émile Bréhier, explains this as follows: when a scalpel cuts through flesh, one body cuts through another body producing an attribute. This attribute is quite particular for it is a meaning attributed to a body. In this instance the attribute is "that of being cut."[16] The attribute is in no way actual (it is not a body in space); Deleuze characterizes it as virtual, something produced at the limit or at the surface of corporeal nature, something real but not a corporeality actualized in space and able to mix with other bodies.

The Stoic distinction between mixtures of bodies in depth and surface events that are the effects of bodies allows for the formulation of clear distinctions between the properties and characteristics of bodies and the properties and characteristics of certain morphological aspects of language (verbs). Physical bodies have depth: metal cuts the skin; mucous fills the placenta; water mixes with wine. But when we utter the words *to cut, to fill, to mix*, they do not mix either with bodies or with one another; rather, they are events of language, the surface effects of the mixing and coexisting of bodies. This is another way of saying that they are attributes of those bodies, but they are attributes expressed in propositions. But in what sense are language events attributes of bodies?

According to Bréhier, the Stoic theory of knowledge makes sensation the starting point and therefore the key to language and knowledge. Knowledge starts with the image (*phantasia*), the impression made on the "soul" by a real object that, for the Stoics, is like the impression of a seal on wax or a modification produced in the air by a color or sound.[17] What is most important in this formulation is that although it is not actualized in space, the impression, nonetheless, is also taken to be something real, something really produced by the object and not simply an effect of Ideas. Furthermore, the "soul" (what I would call the sensory-motor apparatus and memory) may accept or reject that impression of the object.[18] Assent in this matter produces apprehension or perception and the process of giving assent or not is what the Stoics call judgment.[19] Thus, in perception the object is not simply inferred from the image but perception is apprehension of the object. The image must be faithful and the "apprehensive representation" (or image) constitutes one of the criterion of truth.[20]

There is active judgment on the part of the "soul," but it is a kind of judgment that anyone, not just the philosopher, can enact to determine whether the image is faithful and, if faithful, true. Zeno defines perception apprehension as "an image impressed upon the soul, originating in a real object, conforming to this object and such that it would not exist if it did not come from a real object."[21] Each such image contains the unique, personal quality that always distinguishes that particular object from any other object. Thus, "quality" is the first degree of certainty, a certainty that, unlike Platonic Forms or Ideas known only to the philosopher, is available to all. Such "spontaneous reasoning" starts from the perception of things, is not possible without the perception of things, and does not separate itself from the perception of things.[22] Furthermore, wisdom, far from being grounded in nonperceptual activity, is the "accretion and reinforcement" of this initial perceptual certainty. It follows from this that intellectual activity requires grasping the sensible object and that intellectual acts consist in abstracting, adding, composing, and transposing such sensible objects.[23] Thus, there is a necessary relation between the perception apprehension of real things and the production of concepts, but it is a relation that begins with the intermixing of bodies and proceeds to concepts.

Furthermore, associated with sensible things is what can be said about them, what can be expressed or attributed through speech—that is, meanings.[24] What can be expressed is what the soul represents to itself with respect to the thing and not simply what the thing produces in the soul (which is only the image). This is important for logic, which deals with the true or false statements relating to things. What the Stoics seem to want to indicate by this means is that insofar as reasoning arises out of reflection upon sensibles, it cannot arise apart from them, nor can sensibility be reduced merely to the realm of confusion and need. For the Stoics, sensibility is quite explicitly a matter of real impressions and the attributes arising from them that are a function of what soul represents to itself.[25] Additionally, since what is expressed is what the soul represents to itself with respect to the object, this confirms that language, in order to make sense, to be meaningful, must be structured. The question is, how? Bréhier concurs that a complete expression or a simple judgment requires a subject (substantive or pronoun) and an attribute (a verb). But, unlike the Aristotelian syllogism "Socrates walks," the Stoic judgment does not express a relation between concepts. This is because the Stoic subject is always *singular* (it is a reflection that occurs as an effect of a perception), and the attribute is always a verb insofar as verbs are something that happens to a particular someone or something.[26] In this manner, Stoic logic does not depend on the mechanism of the syllogism to connect concepts that are both substances and genera. Instead, it is based on statements of fact about singular subjects. This is what Deleuze means when he says that the event insists or subsists as an effect of bodies that exist.[27] The Stoics retain the syllogism, but the conclusion does not derive from an inclusive relation between two concepts expressed in a categorical judgment. It is instead a relation between facts stated individually through a simple proposition.[28]

However, these judgments and syllogisms are based on language and, in a sense, they are clearly arbitrary. This is because the major premise, which expresses a relation between facts such as that between an antecedent and a consequent, can never be demonstrated. For the Stoics, it is a prediction and nothing more.[29] So Bréhier argues, given the statement "If he has a scar, it is because he has been wounded," the Stoics claim that the sign does not link a present and a past reality. The proposition only connects two statements of fact, both of which are present in the mind so as to be logically identical.[30] The logical relation is expressed in a relation between facts, facts that are observed through the senses and then stated in language. It is a relation between facts that is valid only by virtue of the logical reasoning that unites them. And the "logical reasoning" consists of no more than the simultaneous insistence of two separate facts.

Now the question that arises and that to which Nye seems to be directing her criticism is the question about dualism. Is there a dualism at work here or not? I would argue with Deleuze that a certain kind of dualism is no longer in effect. For it is true that we expect to have to confront the dualism inherent in the categorical philosophy of Aristotle where "all categories are said of Being" but substance is primary.[31] This is precisely the kind of dualism Nye criticizes insofar as she (correctly, I believe) associates it with the grab for power and domination. The problem with this view of Being is that all other categories (notably genus, species, and difference) exist only as modes and accidents of substance that is primary Being, and so they have no "particularity," no existence of their own apart from that distributed to them by substantive Being. Stoic philosophy, on the other hand, recognizes another kind of being; it recognizes that "something" (*aliquid*) subsumes both being and nonbeing, the existence of bodies and the insistence of (language) events or meanings. Being is distributed among bodies, but among bodies as actual particulars, bodies with their particular qualities and quantities, actions and passions, and their states of affairs that are not merely qualifications of substance. On the other hand, there is nonbeing, which is real, though not a sensible body. It encompasses the "sterile, inefficacious, . . . *the ideational or the incorporeal*," the effects in language or in logic of the perceptions and judgements of bodies.[32]

Although there is a dichotomy between bodies and events in the Stoic conception, dualism, as we know it, has lost its meaning in this context. All bodies, not just false copies (*simulacra*), but bodies with depths that also form mixtures always and entirely elude the action of the Idea. This is because intellectual activity consists in grasping the sensible object through its sensible effects on the sensibility of the human being. This means that knowledge is no longer threatened with the untruth of Platonic false copies. Knowledge consists of perception and of judging the perception image as well as the logic expressed in the language associated with perception. Deleuze cautions that language events cannot be *substantives* (they are not things; they do not exist), because for the Stoics, subjects are always and only particular facts. Nor are language events *adjectives* since then they would have to be predicated of substantives. Events, as I stated earlier, are verbs, infinitives such as *to speak* or *to eat* that inhere or subsist in bodies; that is, they are the results of the actions and passions of bodies. Insofar as they are Ideas that are the effect of bodies and not the reverse, they cannot be subject to idealization and so remain "unlimited becoming."

The "unlimited becoming" or radical unintelligibility that Plato attributes to what fails to receive the action of the Idea is precisely what characterizes the language event; it is not a physical property but a linguistic effect, the logical attribute of propositions.[33] I have noted that events are characterized by means of the infinitive form of the verb: *to grow, to cut, to fill*. It is in the infinitive that the "unlimited becoming" of events is expressed. Infinitives clearly are not living presents; bodies act and are acted on in the present, while their incorporeal effects are simultaneously becoming. Each infinitive, *to cut, to fill, to mix*, divides itself infinitely and without limit into past and future, always eluding the present.[34] The infinitive form of the verb can be said to divide itself into past and future because *to cut* or *to fill* has both already happened and is about to happen. The one thing it never is or can be is that which is happening, so it is itself neither active nor passive. Bodies, in accordance with this way of thinking, are beings in depth; they are real, existing in space and, temporally, in the present. In the "depths" of bodies, they coexist with one another in all their parts. They form mixtures, they intermingle "like a drop of wine in the water" or like a poison that spreads throughout the body.[35] On another plane, we find incorporeal acts—what Deleuze and Guattari call the formalization of expression—because what we mean by *to grow, to diminish, to become red, to become green* is something entirely different from the real, spatial, temporally present intermingling in the depths of bodies.[36] These expressions are not states of affairs but incorporeal events at the surface of bodies; they are meanings such as becoming green, becoming poisoned, which becomings are the effects of those bodies' perceptions.

I began by citing Nye's objections to Western logic, focusing on her attribution of domination and control to the makers and users of logical systems. I have tried to show that while Nye is correct in her concern over dualism, the recourse to looking beneath the level of logic for the world of our common humanity governed by confusion, need, and weakness is not an adequate solution. For, unless language is differentiated from bodies, given an order other than that of bodies, the corporeality of bodies and their factuality in the present will overtake language and submerge it in the body's own functions. As Deleuze suggests in *The Logic of Sense*, it will become impossible to differentiate bodily functions such as eating from sense-oriented activities like speaking if there is no logic to organize the words. However, while recognizing and making use of the distinction between bodies and language, the Stoics begin to develop a system of perception, reflection, and concepts that does not immediately justify and organize systems of domination. While it is too much to expect the Stoics alone to have developed all the philosophical conceptions by means of which mind and body can be united, women and minorities can be empowered, and logic ceases to be a tool of entrapment, nonetheless, their example and Deleuze's use of their ideas indicates the kind of work that can be done. We cannot simply revert to the sphere of confusion in the hope of finding logic, ethics, and politics. A society produces the logic, epistemology, ethics, and politics it needs to justify its ongoing, social, political, and ethical practices. As I argued earlier, the justification for fixed Ideas is that they contribute to justifying fixed systems that base their power on irrefutable conceptual claims for intelligibility, coherence, and hierarchic distribution, whereas when language expresses becoming, none of these claims can be made with any authority. Let us not, however, make the mistake of concluding, in Platonic fashion, that logical systems are adequate to produce human and humane values. They are not. Since, if the Stoics are correct, all human ideas begin with perception and reflection, then logic, too, is an effect of sensory-motor phenomena and memory. Let us rather turn our investigation to logics that provide structure without domination, organization without orders, and clarity without absolutism.

Notes

1. Andrea Nye, *Words of Power* (New York: Routledge, 1990), 174.
2. Nye, *Words*, 175.
3. Nye, *Words*, 182.
4. Nye, *Words*, 182–183.
5. Maurice Merleau-Ponty, *The Prose of the World*, trans. John O'Neill (Evanston, Ill.: Northwestern University Press, 1973), 16.
6. Merleau-Ponty, *The Prose*, 4–5.
7. Merleau-Ponty, *The Prose*, 7. See also Dorothea E. Olkowski, "Merleau-Ponty: The Demand for Mystery in Language," *Philosophy Today* 31, no. 4/4 (Winter 1987): 352–358.
8. Merleau-Ponty, *The Prose*, 15.
9. Gilles Deleuze, *The Logic of Sense*, trans. Mark Lester with Charles Stivale, ed. Constantin V. Boundas (New York: Columbia University Press, 1990), 1.
10. Deleuze, *The Logic*, 2, 3.
11. Deleuze, *The Logic*, 2.
12. Deleuze, *The Logic*, 2; Deleuze cites Plato's *Cratylus*, in *Plato*, *The Collected Dialogues*, trans. Benjamin Jowett, ed. Edith Hamilton and Huntington Cairns (Princeton, N.J.: Princeton University Press, 1961), 421–474, 437*ff*., for the argument that simulacra fall below the level of the idea.
13. Deleuze, *The Logic*, 4.
14. Deleuze, *The Logic*, 4–5.
15. Deleuze, *The Logic*, 5.
16. Deleuze, *The Logic*, 5; Deleuze cites Émile Bréhier, *La Théorie de incorporels dans l'ancien stoicism* (Paris: Vrin, 1928); published in English as *The Hellenistic and Roman Age*, trans. Wade Baskin (Chicago: University of Chicago Press, 1965), 11–13.
17. Bréhier, *The Hellenistic*, 38.
18. For a complete articulation of the role of the sensory-motor systems and memory, see Olkowski's *Gilles Deleuze and the Ruin of Representation* (Berkeley: University of California Press, 1999), especially chapter 4.
19. Bréhier, *The Hellenistic*, 38.
20. Bréhier, *The Hellenistic*, 39.
21. Bréhier, *The Hellenistic*, 39.
22. Bréhier, *The Hellenistic*, 40.

23. Bréhier, *The Hellenistic*, 39, 41.

24. Bréhier, *The Hellenistic*, 41.

25. A similar case for this argument could be made using, for example, David Hume's notion that the mind must be "qualified" or it could be made using a less strongly realist version of the cognitive science argument that sensory-motor systems and emotion are necessary aspects of reason.

26. Bréhier, *The Hellenistic*, 41.

27. The Stoic conception of how perception produces ideas remains somewhat vague in relation to contemporary scientific accounts. However, I begin to work through this question in chapters 3 and 4 of *Gilles Deleuze and the Ruin of Representation*.

28. Bréhier, *The Hellenistic*, 42.

29. Bréhier, *The Hellenistic*, 43.

30. Bréhier, *The Hellenistic*, 44.

31. Deleuze, *The Logic*, 7.

32. Deleuze, *The Logic*, 7.

33. Deleuze sometimes characterizes these language events as "dialectical" attributes by which he does not mean to imply that the past and future are synthesized in the infinitive. Instead, past and future inhere in time and divide each present *infinitely*; thus, they are mutually exclusive. The Stoics used the notion "dialectic" to refer to one of the two parts of logic, the other being rhetoric. Dialectic, in turn, consists of two parts: the *lekta*, literally, things said; and how the human voice is articulated to say things. See Michael Frede, "Principles of Stoic Grammar," in *Essays in Ancient Philosophy* (Minneapolis: University of Minnesota Press, 1987), 303.

34. Deleuze, *The Logic*, 5.

35. Gilles Deleuze and Félix Guattari, *A Thousand Plateaus, Capitalism and Schizophrenia*, trans. Brian Massumi (Minneapolis: University of Minnesota Press, 1987), 86.

36. Deleuze, *The Logic*, 6.

PART TWO

LOGIC AND EMPIRICAL KNOWLEDGE

CHAPTER SIX

~

On Mapping a Transdisciplinary Approach to Reasoning

RACHEL JOFFE FALMAGNE AND MARIE-GENEVIÈVE ISELIN

Feminist critiques have exposed the social situatedness and the gendered location of rationalism, and they have unmasked the exclusionary deployment of rationalist norms. In particular, recent analyses have focused on logic as a central component of this power/knowledge system. These critiques, many of which are contained in the present volume, interrogate the foundational status of logic, problematize some key logical constructs, and expose the hegemonic function logic has served. In this chapter, we take these critiques as a point of departure to argue for the necessity of articulating a transdisciplinary approach to the study of inference, and we explore some theoretical and methodological issues entailed in such a project.

This discussion is motivated by two convictions. First, although we take critique to be essential, we believe that one of its most useful applications is to yield a novel reconstruction of a domain, be it a provisional reconstruction. From a philosophical point of view, this implies developing new theoretical constructs informed by the critique and reconceptualizing inference to replace the grounding that rationalism provided. Some reconstructive works of that nature are exemplified in this volume.

The second contention is that such ends necessitate a transdisciplinary approach, in which philosophically based modes of analysis and empirically based research inform one another dialectically and are integrated methodologically. The purpose of this chapter is to provoke transdisciplinary thinking on the form that this integration might take. For the empirical component of this project, this involves the development of new methods and it entails complex issues of focus and genealogy. In a manner parallel to the philosophical reconstruction just mentioned, the traditional psychological research on reasoning, which, as we argue later, is grounded in rationalist philosophy, must be reconfigured or transformed along lines suggested by the critique.

The relations between theory construction and empirical research, always complex, are particularly intricate with respect to feminist theories of logic and feminist epistemology: theories of this kind have quasi-normative as well as descriptive aims, which complicates the issues. One of the central aims of this chapter is to explore the dialectic between empirical research and feminist theory construction and to begin reflection on the status of empirical data for this type of theory. In the discussion to follow, an illustrative study of reasoning processes is used as a vehicle for exposing the metatheoretical, theoretical, and methodological issues entailed in such a transdisciplinary reconstructive project. The research is grounded in an interdisciplinary model of the gendering of the social order and of the constitution of subjectivity. Reasoning processes are considered within that framework, using a design and interpretive method informed by feminist critiques of logic and feminist perspectives on epistemology. Some exemplary findings from the study are presented to stimulate, among scholars with various disciplinary histories, an exploration of the relevance of these (and other) kinds of findings for theories of logic.

Another aim of this chapter is to address the issues of knowledge construction involved in designing the method of this (or other) research within the context of the broad agenda just sketched, issues that concern in particular the design of the interview, the identification of research participants, and the construction of the descriptive language for moments[1] of reasoning. That the particular methodological choices will configure the knowledge produced is, of course, an intrinsic feature of the research process. However, the matter is particularly consequential when it comes to attempting to produce new, feminist theories of logic. The tensions that present themselves at each juncture in this research will serve as a medium for exposing issues.

The first section of the chapter selectively reviews some philosophical analyses that constitute the point of departure of this project. The next section poses more explicitly the central problematic. A quick review of traditional cognitive research follows, which sets the context for issues of empirical methodology. An interdisciplinary theoretical framework for the research is then discussed, and the illustrative empirical study is introduced briefly. Issues of methodology and method along with some illustrative findings are considered critically in the following sections. The final section returns to the question regarding the use of empirical research in theory construction with concrete reference to this research.

Logic and Rationalism under Critical Scrutiny: A Selective Review

Several converging lines of feminist critique subvert the foundational status of logic as an epistemic norm. On the most general level, the situatedness of knowledge that standpoint theorists, feminist epistemologists, and 'postcolonial' critics[2] have exposed extends to logic itself. Both individual knowers and communities of knowers have particular social locations. The knowing subject is not generic; she or he is concrete and has an historically specific, intersectional social location. This means not only that the knowing subject is viewing the world from a particular standpoint in the material and discursive relations that structure the social world, but also that her or his self as knowing agent is constituted by these discourses, practices, and material conditions. Thus, knowledge is situated in both these ways (e.g., Alcoff and Potter 1993; Fox 1993; Hartsock 1983; Collins 1990; Harding 1990a, 1990b, 1993, 1998; Anzaldua 1990; Mohanty 1991). Most relevant for the discourse of logic, the situatedness of knowledge bears not only on substantive knowledge but also on standards of justification: there is no "view from nowhere" that would yield absolute standards of justification. Norms for evaluating knowledge claims are situated in particular social locations and used at the service of the power relations that configure the social. Just as this is the case in any discursive domain, in particular for science as discourse (Longino 1990; Code 1993; Harding 1990a, 1990b, 1993, 1998), it is the case for logic as well.

At a more specific level, the foundational status of logic has also been subverted by feminist critiques of rationality, in particular regarding the relations between rationality and masculinity. These relations are at once historical, symbolic, social, and psychological, and they thus form an intricate system of mutually constitutive processes. As Genevieve Lloyd (1984, 1993) submits, reason is part of the content of *symbolic* maleness specifically, where symbolic gender is distinguished from psychological gender: Rationality and symbolic maleness can be appropriated by concrete women or concrete men (we return to this point in a later section, where we also discuss the interplay between the two). Jane Flax (1993) shows how Kant's original formulation of the Enlightenment ideal of reason was grounded in assumptions about gender and was linked to his desire (as a socially constructed man, we might add) to have the male child separate from the private and the family, thereby outgrowing his initial dependency on the mother. So, although, ostensibly, reason was to be universal for Kant, it was in effect explicitly formulated for (white Western privileged) males only. Thus, historically, the rationalist, normative formulation of reason by Kant hinges on a particular social construction of gender.

In her sophisticated analysis weaving cultural history and psychology, Susan Bordo (1987) illuminates how the problematic that led Descartes to formulate the ideals of detachment, clarity, and objectivity of pure thought was a product of his historical cultural context and individual anxieties. She describes Descartes's trajectory as a "'flight from the feminine', a 're-imaging of knowledge as masculine'"(5) in response to the cultural broadening of the seventeenth century and the epistemic anxieties that followed. These critiques of rationalism as a masculinist construction indirectly bear on logic as well, as an instrument of rationalism. In particular, though Bordo's critique of objectivity mainly applies to the scientific method, it also ramifies to logic, in that the formalism of logic reflects similar assumptions about the possibilities of detachment and closure.

The foundational status of logic is subverted most directly by recent analyses that specifically mark logic as the object of critique. In her influential historical critique of different moments in the history of Western logic from preclassical times to modern mathematical logic,[3] Andrea Nye (1990) argues that logic must be considered not as an independent formal system to be evaluated through technical criteria but as a human creation driven by a purpose, and that it must be historicized. She documents both the motivations that drove the development of each logic and the social function it has had as an instrument of power either by making factual truth secondary to logical validity in the case of Aristotle or by essentially obliterating the human user of language in the case of Frege. Nye suggests that logic may be inherently hegemonic for these same reasons.

From a different theoretical perspective, Luce Irigaray (1985; see also Hass, chap. 3 of this volume) posits that because it makes the representation of the feminine impossible, logic is not neutral, contrary to its definition and ambition. She contends that logic is in fact built to resist the expression of sexual difference, which is fundamental. Indeed, logic's structures embody a cultural desire for sameness, symmetry, definiteness, and closure. In her analysis of three concepts central to logic, Irigaray critiques the constraining views of negation as contradiction, of identity as solid, singular, and definite, and of generality, which should be reconceptualized as more than, and different from, mere summation. Both Irigaray and Nye, in arguing that classical and modern logic are inherently flawed because of their fundamental aspiration to abstraction and formalism or because their structure fundamentally silences certain groups of people, conclude implicitly or explicitly that logic inherently embodies systems of domination and that (any) logic is antithetical to feminist theories of knowledge.

Others articulate a different kind of resolution and instead attribute the oppressiveness of logic to particular logical constructs or properties. Thus, Val Plumwood (1993; chap. 1, this volume) analyzes Western dualisms, in which dichotomies are constructed not merely as distinctions but as hierarchical relations, and one member is backgrounded, stereotyped, and defined only relative to the dominant member (e.g., reason/emotion, mind/body). Plumwood also points out how the two are hyperseparated and their differences radicalized. She observes that classical negation is similarly based on hyperseparation. The negated term is a homogeneous universe that only consists of everything that is not contained in the positive term: it thus cannot be identified independently from the latter. Plumwood insists that the oppressiveness of logic lies not in the abstraction of logical thought but in the specific content of the dominant logical theory. She suggests that alternatives such as relevant logics and relevant negation are better suited to nonexclusionary modes of reasoning and nonoppressive practices.

Marjorie Hass (1999) likewise explores a radically different logic involving notions of negation that avoid the metaphysical and discursive problems of classical negation and that are inspired by feminist discourse. Distinguishing between difference as contradiction and difference as distinctness, she suggests a nondualistic reformulation of negation that would honor the fluidity of thought stressed by Irigaray (Whitford 1988) and others. Dorothea Olkowski (1997; chap. 5, this volume), drawing from a perspective informed by Gilles Deleuze's theory and by phenomenology, does concur with Nye that the oppressiveness of formal logic lies in its abstraction but submits that it is possible to imagine a logic based on statements of fact about singular subjects and grounded in bodily phenomena such as perception and memory, along the lines explored by the Stoics. From a different, Quinean perspective, Lynn Hankinson Nelson (1997; Nelson and Nelson, chap. 7, this volume) argues that logic, as one element in an interdependent system of knowledge, can, in principle, be revised based on feminist epistemology and methodology. These proposals are formulated on philosophical grounds. In the next section, we argue that, as such, they constitute one strand in a transdisciplinary conversation.

On the Dialectic of the Analytical and the Empirical

The work just discussed is crucially important. However, if we, feminist theorists, are to avoid reproducing on new grounds the problems of masculinist theory and developing new canons for thought and 'rationality' (albeit, this time, on alternative grounds), feminist theory cannot rely on analysis alone (Falmagne 1997, 2001). In other areas of feminist theorizing, it is widely accepted that theory must start from women's lives (e.g., Smith 1987; Harding 1990b) for two linked reasons, epistemic and political. Epistemically, since knowledge is grounded in the structural location that the knower occupies in the social order, women, who have been marginalized in the production of knowledge, are more likely to uncover social contradictions that are invisible to the dominant group (hooks 1990), and their thinking may exhibit tensions that subvert the dominant system. Politically, the principle is to make the lives of concrete women the focal data that inform theory. For similar reasons, the contention here is that, if we are to avoid performing analytic domination (Falmagne 1997, 2001), empirical work must be part, in some way, of the reconstructive project for logic and that theory must be informed *jointly* by feminist analysis and by the thinking of concrete women, each occupying a particular location in ethnic/racial, socioeconomic, and cultural formations. Theory cannot merely rely on what we think are sound ways to think.

It is interesting (and perhaps a reflection of disciplinary histories) that, although these principles are generally heeded in other areas of feminist theorizing (and in other areas of feminist philosophy, as reflected, e.g., in Narayan and Harding 2000), feminist writings on logic or epistemology have been, paradoxically, rationalist in style. They have developed through conceptual and political analysis, not in dialogue with empirical work. Although feminist writings on logic do, of course, draw on interdisciplinary feminist analyses of the social order, some of which are grounded in the social sciences, the point here is that, methodologically, the mode of theorizing on which they rely generally does not involve a dialogue with empirical work. Nelson (1997) and Nelson and Nelson (chap. 7, this volume) are one exception to this statement, pointing toward such an interplay.

In stating that theory must be informed jointly by analysis and by the thinking of women as a complex group, "jointly" is centrally important. The relation between analysis and empirical research is dialectical. But the exact form of the interplay between analysis and data indexed by the term *jointly* is, of course, an open issue. In what way exactly can research on reasoning inform feminist theory and critique? What kind of data is relevant to this task, and what is the form of their relevance? Reciprocally, what are the strategic and methodological ramifications of feminist theory for empirical research? What empirical questions flow from these theoretical frameworks? For feminist social scientists with a frame of reference grounded in feminist epistemologies, the task is to develop an empirical research program motivated by feminist theory as one strand in the transdisciplinary project that is at stake here.

It is our hope that the arguments developed here and the exploratory empirical work we describe later may stimulate a transdisciplinary examination of these questions. The term *transdisciplinary* connotes the idea that the interdisciplinary dialogue, in which disciplinary methodologies are preserved, is not sufficient to advance this task. It is necessary to develop an approach that subsumes analysis, empirically based theorizing, and empirical work under the same methodological space. We return to these matters in the concluding discussion.

The motivation for conducting the exploratory study here was to let these issues regarding the articulation of the theoretical and the empirical present themselves in the concrete context of developing a method and to let the tensions unfold productively. Likewise, this chapter is intended to raise questions rather than propose answers. We present the exploratory study as a vehicle for exposing issues and tensions and for beginning to think them through collectively.

Psychological Research on Inference: A Preliminary Contextual Note

There is a history of research on reasoning in psychology. Although its presuppositions and most of its methodology must be rejected or transformed for the task at hand, it needs to be reviewed briefly here because it does constitute part of the genealogy of this project.

As a whole, the existing psychological research on inference originated in rationalist philosophy and is shaped by this historical origin. This has continued to be the case despite the fact that many rationalist assumptions have been relaxed, transformed, and woven with other assumptions and also that wide differences exist among psychological theories. Most theories reveal their rationalist origin directly or indirectly, whether they spell out rationalist thought processes or whether they argue for alternatives that are motivated by rejecting those assumptions (Falmagne and Gonsalves [1995] provide a review). For instance, one recent controversy centers on whether a naturalized logic in the form of some kind of system of formal principles might be involved (Braine 1993) or whether that assumption must be abandoned entirely and people's reasoning is instead driven by situational principles (Cheng and Holyoak 1985), beliefs (Evans 1989), or mental models of the material world (Johnson-Laird 1986). Thus, the rationalist origins of that area of research are still present in trace form. That is, questions have centered either on logic or on its naturalized successors, either positively or negatively. The centrality of logic as point of reference remains present in the rhetoric that rejects it.

Research on inference that is guided by feminist critiques of logic and feminist epistemologies must start from a different point, not presupposing the centrality of logic either positively or negatively. Thus, the exploratory study described next and the more extensive studies we are currently conducting in this research program explore in particular the variety and nature of the knowledges the interviewees bring into their reasoning process, and it does not constrain at the outset how these knowledges will be described. The interview format and the data-interpretative method were specifically designed to avoid centering the theoretical lenses on whether the women display evidence of formal principles. The effort is to liberate the study from the rationalist discourse that has shaped both the field and our own thinking and to broaden the lenses so as to break out of the historically narrowed focus of previous work.

Originally, the study of reasoning in psychology aimed to assess whether logic had psychological reality as a system underlying human thought processes. That focus has been reformulated to some degree recently. In line with the pragmatic turn in philosophy and linguistics, there is now increasing emphasis on the pragmatic context of thought and of language, and some theories maintain that inference is embedded in immediate situations (Barwise 1989), governed by pragmatic factors (e.g., Cheng and Holyoak 1985), or embedded in processes of communication (Sperber and Wilson 1986). However, importantly, those accounts remain fundamentally decontextualized, because the theoretically relevant context they invoke is the immediate situation, not the societal context. In keeping with the tradition of cognitive psychology, psychological theory and research on reasoning attempt to describe a universal reasoner and a lone individual.

A feminist paradigm, in contrast, takes reasoners to be social agents who occupy particular locations in the social order and who are constructed in particular ways by the cultural discourses and social practices in which they participate. The next two sections describe the theoretical framework and the method of the present exploratory study, which strives to capture participants' grounded particularity.

The Societal Matrix of Subjectivity and Thought

The theoretical framework in which the research is grounded is systemic in scope. The social world is seen as a system that involves social structures, economic structures, and ideological formations. Ideological formations are the conceptual frameworks that are taken for granted and that shape social practices, social institutions and social subjects, along the lines discussed in particular by Dorothy Smith (1987, 1990); Michele Barrett (1992); Joan Scott (1988); Myra Marx Ferree, Judith Lorber, and Beth B. Hess (1999); and others. Social, economic, and ideological processes support and reinforce one another in a dialectical way. Individuals are constituted as social subjects through these processes and contribute to social reproduction by instantiating these processes in their behavior, their subjectivity, and their thinking. Thus, individual functioning, in particular individual reasoning, is considered within an integrated, systemic theory (Falmagne 2000b).

Extending Michael Omi and Howard Winant's (1994) notion of racial formation, this theory sees gender, 'race'/ethnicity and class as *social formations* that include social, institutional, symbolic, and ideological elements and that configure cultures and societies in these complex ways. The theory takes gender, 'race', and class to be intersectional social formations, an intersectionality long recognized by feminists 'of color' and working-class feminists (e.g., Mohanty 1991; Collins 1990; Tokarczyk and Fay 1993), and more recently addressed by others (e.g., Marx Ferree et al. 1999). Thus, gender is construed through its intersections with 'race'/ethnicity and class and is seen as culturally and historically situated.

The social formations of gender, 'race', and class have both material and discursive aspects, which are closely intertwined and implemented institutionally. Materially, gender, 'race', and class organize social groups, power relations between these groups, economic functioning and access to resources, and division of labor. Discursively, they configure those symbolic representations and ideologies that regulate social practices and individual subjectivity. Ideologies of gender, like ideologies of 'race' and class, and in intersection with them are translated into legal, educational, and other institutional texts and practices that implement and reproduce these ideologies. Smith in particular (e.g., 1990) makes clear how ideological discourses, in their material manifestations through institutions and texts, exercise semiotic control over social practices and individual subjectivity (see also Marx Ferree et al. 1999; Narayan and Harding 2000; and contributors therein). The notion of social formation captures the fact that these ideological, symbolic, economic, social, and psychological processes support one another in a systemic manner.

We draw from this theoretical framework to study the individuals who actively participate and are embedded in this system. Analytically, as has been noted by others as well (e.g., Lloyd 1993), it is important to distinguish structural gender, symbolic gender, and psychological gender. *Structural gender* refers to those social roles historically constructed through normative ideologies of gender, social practices, and institutional arrangements. *Symbolic gender* denotes the meaning and discourse of masculinity and femininity in a society at a particular historical time. *Psychological* gender, in intersection with 'race' and class, is constructed by social agents living in that structural and symbolic world, through a dialectic between processes of social constitution and the individual's agency in appropriating, resisting, transforming, or modulating available cultural discourses. The notion of a dialectic is crucial here in marking that individual and societal processes are coconstitutive. Within her or his particular racial/ethnic, class, and cultural niche, the reasoner's subjectivity and mode of thought are constituted through this dialectic (Falmagne 2000b). These notions constitute the interpretive frame through which participants' modes of reasoning and forms of knowledge are understood here.

An Illustrative Exploratory Study

As stated previously, the major purpose of this exploratory study was to let the concrete process of developing a method within this transdisciplinary agenda reveal areas of tensions for further reflection. Additionally, it also aimed to develop methodological tools for this new line of research, in particular an interview method, a domain of ordinary life situations for interviewees to discuss, and a method of data analysis.

The study included fifteen women college students from widely different ethnic/racial and cultural backgrounds, who were asked to reason about situations in which they had to adjudicate contradictory, mutually exclusive possibilities—for example, contradictory diagnoses about a medical problem, contradictory accounts in hypothetical legal situations, and other analogous situations. Each woman was interviewed about her upbringing and family background, her family's ethnic/racial and socioeconomic location, and her cultural trajectory. Two in-depth interviews followed that focused on the woman's reasoning and her reasoning norms. One or two hypothetical situations were presented to the woman as models of the kinds of situations in which we were interested, and she was encouraged to think of situations from her own life in which she had to adjudicate contradictory possibilities, a route many women took. A flexible interview method was developed to probe the women's reasoning, with a focus on the kinds of knowledges they brought into their reasoning process and the kinds of epistemological norms they seemed to hold.

Initially, the full purpose of the study was explained, the woman's questions were answered fully, and she was assured that she was a full participant whose input the researcher valued. The interview was conducted as a conversation and was largely guided by the woman's responses (we return to this aspect of the method in a later section when discussing the tension between openness and focus). This approach appeared largely to succeed in reducing the power differential built into interview settings.

The data analysis focused on moments of reasoning and aimed to develop a new descriptive language (a set of provisional descriptive categories) for the knowledges and resources brought into the reasoning process, for the women's personal epistemological norms about what constitutes sound reasoning, and for the discourses that seemed to be reflected in their reasoning at various moments, with particular attention to whether there appeared to be tensions between dominant and resistant discourses in their reasoning. The method attempted to be as inductive as possible but was guided interpretively where appropriate by constructs and frameworks derived from feminist theoretical writings. (We return to this point later when discussing the construction of the descriptive language.)

In examining the specific resources deployed at various moments of reasoning, one element from the cognitive psychology methodology was retained: We use a fine-grained mode of analysis to examine thought processes, attempt to characterize the ingredients of the reasoning process as it unfolds in real time, and describe their interplay. However, this methodology is deployed here within a feminist frame of reference, as just described. The frameworks and constructs yielded by feminist critiques of logic and feminist epistemologies serve as a 'listening frame' during the interview and as resources for the inductive development of the descriptive vocabulary.

The overall data analysis is designed so as to generate both (1) a characterization of each woman as a full human being grounded in her societal context and (2) cross-sectional constructs transcending individual particularities. The provisional descriptive categories of moments of reasoning served the latter aim. To meet the former aim, individual profiles of each woman's life context and reasoning through the various problems were developed. Four abbreviated profiles are included in the appendix as illustrations.

In examining various aspects of method in more critical detail, the next four sections focus on the tensions resulting from the broad agenda that animates this research. This study proposes to reconfigure the study of reasoning on new ground informed by feminist critiques and to develop a new theoretical vocabulary for this reasoning domain. These aims create tensions for the strategic issues concerning the selection of the research participants, the design of the interviews, the construction of a descriptive vocabulary, and the dialectic of the particular and the general in describing the responses and narrating the findings (see Falmagne [2001], for a more extended discussion of these issues).

Women as the Starting Point of Feminist Theory

The study focuses on women for methodological reasons, so as to have women's thinking be the starting point of the process of developing a new, feminist theoretical language and new analytic and descriptive tools about reasoning. Because theory must be developed from a foundation of multiplicity from the onset, women were recruited so as to maximize the variations in their ethnic/racial and socioeconomic location, as well as in their cultural trajectories.[4]

The choice to interview women is a particular resolution of a complex theoretical issue. It stems from a social constructivist view on subjectivity and thought, not from an assumption that men as an empirical group are rational and that women, as an empirical group, are not, an assumption that we see as misguided. The rationale underlying this choice pertains to the dialectical relation between structural, symbolic, and psychological gender. Many of the analyses reviewed earlier expose the *symbolic* association between rationality and masculinity. However, since human development is shaped by society and culture, those symbols have repercussions for real, concrete human beings. We are constituted as knowing agents by symbolic representations, social practices, cultural discourses, and our structural positioning. Consequently, the ideal of detachment and the separation of reason from emotion that the rationalist worldview promotes have been instrumental in constructing gendered aspects of the social order, in particular the subjectivities of Western privileged white men. To be sure, this is not a passive process. Subjectivity and thought are constituted by the dialectic between these structural and discursive elements, on the one hand, and individual agency, on the other, which appropriates, transforms, or rejects these elements. However, while agency is an integral part of this dialectic, agency is constrained, and its local deployment does not overshadow the systemic forces.

In other words, the connection between gender and rationality involves a complex circular dialectic among the symbolic order, social structure, social practices, and individual functioning. Historically, it does remain that logic as a cultural and institutional system shares men's social location, at least in the 'West', and standpoint-theoretic and other discussions of situated knowledge have clearly shown that this is consequential. The choice of starting this research by studying women is theoretically motivated by these considerations and by the conjecture that listening to women with lenses derived from feminist critiques (to mix perceptual metaphors) would therefore be more likely to yield novel constructs so as to subvert the rationalist approach to the study of reasoning. Thus, the study does *not* aim to uncover modes of reasoning 'specific to women'. Rather, it heeds bell hooks's and others' depiction of the margin as a "space of radical openness" (hooks 1990) and uses women as informants because of their marginal social location as a group in relation to the 'ownership' of rationalist norms.

As is clear from the preceding section, gender is understood here in terms of the complex interactions through which it is constructed in specific ethnic/racial, cultural, and socioeconomic settings. For this reason, the particularities of reasoners' social location and experience are essential elements of the interview and interpretive method. However, importantly, in the same way as it does not aim to identify modes of reasoning specific to 'women', the study does not aim to identify differences between prespecified intersectional groups of women. The reasoner's societal niche and cultural history are used *interpretively* to understand her thinking, not causally and not as a basis for generalization to her group(s). We return to this issue, and to its data-analytic and narrative aspects, in a later section, when discussing the dialectic of the particular and the general.

Interview Design: Tension between Openness and Focus

Complex choices attend the delineation of the reasoning domain as it is developed in a theoretical space opened up by feminist critique. Methodological choices configure the theories that are constructed. In a general sense, this issue faces all qualitative research, but its particular form is shaped by the specifics of the research. Here, the issue pertains specifically to this feminist reconfiguration of research on 'deductive' inference, and in that capacity it involves the problematics of transforming that research and redefining deductive inference while preserving referential continuity between the old and the transformed domain. As Elizabeth Wilson discusses (1998; see also Falmagne 2000a), reconfiguring a domain entails, in part, transforming it while 'inhabiting' it. Wilson writes, with reference to a deconstructive critique of cognitive psychology: "Deconstruction has its effect by inhabiting the structures it contests. . . . A deconstructive reading of cognitive psychology places itself internally to that domain, and it is reliant on that domain for its coherence and efficacy" (29). Likewise, the issue here is how to transform the domain of 'deductive' reasoning without vacating it and in doing so abandoning it to its traditional construction.

Thus, while the aims of this research imply removing the constraints of traditional methods and dislodging the narrow rationalist definition of what constitutes deduction, these aims also imply keeping the focus on a certain 'deductive' domain of reasoning even while reconfiguring it. Roughly, the research focuses on reasoning processes in contexts in which people assess the entailments of particular assertions, adjudicate contradictory accounts, or evaluate the soundness of arguments. Thus, in posing the hypothetical problems that served as model situations, problems centering on moral dilemmas were avoided (although the women were of course free to switch to such problems[5]), because these have been studied by others within a different theoretical framework and with a different genealogy (Gilligan, e.g., 1982). Decision-making situations strictly governed by cost–benefit considerations rather than by exploring the entailments of assertions were avoided as well.

But drawing those distinctions presupposes a pretheoretical demarcation between domains of reasoning, demarcation that can be challenged. On the other hand, to leave the field wide open essentially entails abandoning the study of 'deduction' to the rationalist tradition. Thus, there is a critical tension between openness and focus. While an unconstrained net preserves the natural intertwining of thought, delineating the domain of reasoning rests on pretheoretical distinctions, which are then imported into the construction of findings and of theory. At the same time, however, delineating the domain of reasoning preserves referential continuity between the untransformed and the transformed domain. Practically, what emerged from this tension was to offer each woman one or more hypothetical ordinary life situations involving contradictory accounts and encouraging her supply situations from her own life instead if these came to mind (e.g., contradictory theories she might have encountered in her classes or other situations), and many women did so. Yet, even though the hypothetical situations were stressed to be mere models and women brought up a wide range of situations, they of course constrained the universe of reasoning.

A similar tension is inherent in the design of the interview. The interview was flexible and largely shaped by the woman, yet it was guided contextually by broad concerns pertaining to the way in which she constructed the problem, the knowledges and resources she brought into her reasoning at different moments, and the interplay of these resources. In addition, attention and time were given to the contrasts between reasoning situations and to the way in which the woman's reasoning could be understood in the context of her societal location and formative discourses. These concerns were broad, and the 'inductive' orientation of the listening method implied devoting full attention to the woman's responses while remaining attentive to dialectic between these responses and the frameworks and constructs introduced by feminist critiques. Yet, while the interview was flexible and the approach 'inductive', a guiding thread circumscribed what could have been produced.

The inevitable fact that the questions that served as the guiding thread of the interview constrain the nature of the 'data' takes on a particular force in this research, because the conscious agenda, both in feminist theories and epistemologies and in the present research, is to develop a theory of knowledge on new ground. In that context, the way in which preconceptions and available discourses impact the generation of 'findings' is of focal concern. Likewise, the issue of domain definition, while integral to any research, is dramatized in this attempt to construct an approach to inference on new ground, because the demarcation of the reasoning domain is itself a theoretically meaningful and unstable problem. Yet, again, these observations do not entail shifting to an open-ended approach, for reasons just discussed, and thus the tension remains. It will color the appraisal of the import of these (or other) 'data' for theories of logic.

Construction of the Descriptive Language

One aim of this research is to develop a descriptive language for reasoning liberated from the logicist hegemony that has molded this area of research. The epistemological issues involved in constructing this language are closely related, from the data-analytic angle, to the issues of interview design just discussed.

This descriptive language is guided by feminist theories, but in a dialectical way. New analytic categories are constructed by listening to the participants' language and mode of thinking with an open ear, although an ear wearing the filters of feminist theory broadly conceived.[6] Thus, the process involves being *oriented* inductively (with the recognition that pure induction is not possible) but with the analytical guidance of feminist theories of knowledge. The dialectic between this 'inductive' mode of processing and feminist constructs in the text analyst's mind is expected to produce descriptions that are both faithful to the 'data' in a suitable sense and relevant to feminist theorizing. As one example of a category developed through this method, some participants seemed to draw on a mode of knowledge we coined as "standpoint knowledge." The constructs of standpoint theory enabled us to hear particular presuppositions underlying the responses and to identify distinctions between these kinds of responses and others that might appear similar on the surface (see the later section on modes of knowledge). At the same time, because the aim is precisely to develop a transdisciplinary methodology for studying inference, existing feminist discussions of logic or epistemology cannot dictate or restrict what is attended to. Metaphorically, they should suggest a register for listening but not particular notes.

The (ubiquitous) theory-laden character of data, a feature of both qualitative and quantitative research, is particularly complex in qualitative research, because qualitative methodology is interpretive. Therefore, the data-analytic tools are explicitly theoretical. As illustrated earlier, this becomes crucial when one aim is to dislodge the normative hegemony of logic, and the other is to inform the development of feminist theories of logic and reasoning through a transdisciplinary methodology.

The Dialectic of the Particular and the General

There is an inherent tension between preserving the richness, concreteness, and particularity of responses and participants, and capturing cross-sectional patterns. This tension has epistemic as well as narrative dimensions. Epistemically, for reasons discussed previously, it is important to understand each woman in her full particularity, as a whole person functioning in a complex social matrix and grounded in the context of her life and her social location. At the same time, if the understanding gained from empirical research is to be somewhat cumulative, the outcome of the study cannot be a collection of individual contextual narratives. Thus, two principles follow. First, it is important to be attuned to convergences or contrasts that may emerge across particularized participants. Second, it is important to develop an analytic language for identifying moments of reasoning, the use of which transcends particular participants. For these reasons, the data analysis is twofold. It includes the descriptive categories cutting across participants discussed in the previous section, and it includes narrative profiles that describe each woman's modes of reasoning as well as her social location, cultural and family history, and pertinent life context.

A key feature of the methodology is that societal context is used interpretively, not causally and not as a basis for generalization. The aim is to particularize the woman to understand aspects of her reasoning more fully, not to make causal attributions regarding aspects of her context or yield generalized inferences about modes of thinking characterizing her (predefined) intersectional subgroup. Both these moves are misguided: They hamper the examination of grounded variations within groups, perpetuate historically dominant categories, and fail to consider thinkers as whole persons functioning in a complex social matrix (Falmagne 2000b). Although, of necessity, there are implicit generalities underlying any social interpretation, it is important to see that these are *used interpretively to understand a particular reasoner.*

Yet, along with the primacy of the particular, one wants to have gained from a participant an understanding that can enhance one's understanding of other participants as well, to some degree. If a broader understanding of reasoning in social agents is to be achieved, meaningful condensations are necessary. There must be a degree of (selective) transferability to these interpretations. Individual reasoning patterns must be described, both in their diversity and situatedness, and in terms of potential commonalities that might emerge through a contextual understanding of each woman. Hence the two principles are in productive tension, a tension that has both epistemic and narrative dimensions. Epistemically, the two principles jointly entail attempting to understand grounded variations within groups. General statements that may emerge from this approach, either about women in particular locations or about broader patterns, are not abstract generalizations but "concrete generalities" (a notion adapted from Ilyenkov [1982/1960]; see also Falmagne 1995a). On this view, meaningful general statements are claims that focus on the interrelatedness of diverse reasoning practices understood in their fully specific social and historical context, rather than claims that abstract common denominators between thought patterns or between women from a social group. Narratively, this approach implies that every moment of narrating, when patterns are discussed, necessitates deliberate rhetorical strategies to block mistaken causal readings and mistaken categorical generalizations to the group or subgroup.

A Glimpse at Modes of Knowledge and Other Constructs

Several distinct modes of knowledge are reflected in the women's reasoning at different times and in their epistemological commentaries. The following are merely representative, not exhaustive, of this ongoing analysis. We offer them as stimuli for considering the ramifications of this kind of data for theories about logic.

1. *Empiricist process:* The woman's reasoning is a search for facts, with the explicit or implicit notion that "facts speak for themselves." Often, but not always, perceptual metaphors, usually visual ("I do know

that they have the evidence and that helps me out a lot because if I can see it and I can touch it, then I know it's real."), are used. It appears that, in the participant's view, facts are unmediated by processes of selection or by inferential processes. The source of knowledge resides in facts, not thought.

2. *Rationalist process:* In this process, rational understanding is given primacy. The woman pursues paths that will generate a coherent (to her) explanation that she can rationally endorse. In sharp contrast to the previous approach where the main burden is on empirical 'proof', knowledge here is attained mentally and evaluated according to rationalist norms. One woman provides a clear example in the medical situation: "First I would like to understand the facts, and then I could understand the reasoning for why I would have to take that medicine. . . . I mean, there has to be a relationship between what is wrong with my body and their explanation for what is wrong with my body and what they will . . . give me to make my body better. . . . I have to see the relation." Thus, her truth criterion lies in her own understanding. In later segments, this woman will show complex interweavings of different modes and indicate that what counts as rational varies situationally, so this excerpt must not be interpreted as capturing her overall epistemology, but rather as reflecting a rationalist moment.
3. *Balanced rationalism:* Logic and rationality are instruments of knowledge but only when articulated with other processes and used functionally according to broader goals. Two elements are crucial here: logic is highlighted (an emphasis not always present), and it is only one component of a system of knowledge (a construal that departs from pure rationalism). It is their conjunction that characterizes this mode of knowledge. For instance, "Anna" (see the appendix) praises rationality but defines it functionally, in terms of goals and values in particular contexts; abstract rationality oblivious to its function is inappropriate. "Sonia" provides a different example; her rationalism is grounded in practical knowing and social knowledge to form an integrated epistemic approach to problems.
4. *Knowledge by immersion:* Knowledge is acquired by direct contact with the problem situation. This notion occurred infrequently but is sufficiently distinct to warrant singling out. For instance, one woman, in describing a relative's problem, insisted that they had to bring the relative to live with them, so that they would be with her at all times and, crucially, through being with her, would be able to understand the problem. This type of knowledge rests on processes of perception

and/or understanding that are only possible with intimate experience. The knowledge gained is concrete because it is contextualized and relies on direct and rich contact with details.

5. *'Liberal' view:* This is a relativistic conception of knowledge that often uses language such as "each person has their point of view." This pattern foregrounds equality and appears to be guided by a concern for not privileging any point of view. The term *liberal* attempts to capture that driving concern. This view does not appear to be grounded in an articulated epistemology, in sharp contrast with the next two categories.
6. *Standpoint knowledge:* This is an articulated conception in which knowledge is grounded in the standpoint of the knower. Unlike the 'liberal' view, there is an explicit assumption that the knower is part of the knowing process and that knowers are constituted by their material conditions which give them a partial view on the world. One woman, asked to discuss her thoughts on the opposing views about welfare, states that she would have to go and live with people on welfare to know what their problems are and how they are thinking; a knowledge of their problems as they see them is not possible otherwise. Thus, for her, a person's thinking is grounded in their circumstances. This view differs from a 'liberal' view by articulating explicitly the relation between material conditions and modes of thought. It differs from the 'knowledge by immersion' in that (in this example) one does not gain knowledge of other people's thinking through direct, intimate contact per se; rather, living there gives one access to the standpoint of these knowers.
7. *Subjective knowledge:* In this articulated perspective, knowledge is inherently subjective and personal. This view of knowledge foregrounds the person herself as the individual source of knowledge. This construct is similar to what Belenky et. al. (1986) have described for their "subjective knowers." Here, however, the construct characterizes not the woman as a knower but the mode of knowledge instantiated in a moment of reasoning through the woman's response to a particular problem.
8. *Concrete/historicized knowledge:* Abstract knowing is called into question for misrepresenting the complexity of phenomena and therefore yielding misguided conclusions. Interestingly, this epistemic view and the reasoning processes instantiating it were often found in highly articulate, sophisticated responses. For instance, one woman expressed a sharp critique of macroeconomics, insisting and illustrating that

economic theories needed to be historicized and contextual. Likewise, Sonia criticizes unwarranted inferences from one country's political events to another, inferences that ignore each country's history and political particularities.

9. *Pragmatist epistemology:* The reasoning process, rather than relying on factual knowledge as does the empiricist process, or on mental understanding as does the rationalist approach, is driven by a quest for "what works" (a phrase often used by some participants). For instance, in the medical situation, the women would try out one treatment then another, rather than evaluating the doctor's reasoning. Likewise, "Leah," in discussing competing theories of education, is explicitly pragmatic in using as a criterion "what works for me" or what is practical.
10. *Trust:* Though not exactly a mode of knowledge, trust as a resource for reasoning appeared unexpectedly as an important theme in several interviews. Perhaps it can be put, in some cases, in relation to Collins's (1990) and others' consideration of "personal accountability" in evaluating arguments. Our data show interesting distinctions regarding the basis of trust and its nature. For some, trust is a substitute for knowledge: One relinquishes one's role in the knowing process by relying on a well-intended person. For example, Leah trusts her family doctor for having her interests at heart and because he knows her and her family. In that case, trust is one ingredient of an approach that has been construed as a relational and interpersonal, not primarily epistemic problem. For other participants, trust is merely a mode of deferred knowledge: The woman knows that she does not have enough substantive knowledge in the subject and defers the work to an expert, but one whom she has mentally appointed based on her own evaluation of his/her expertise, and one whose reasoning she does monitor. For instance, Sonia's trust is based empirically on the doctor's accuracy record, not on interpersonal connection or on the doctor's goodwill. Also, her trust does not override rational explanation; she would probe the logical and empirical basis for the doctor's inferences and she requires a satisfactory explanation, which is a rationalist criterion. So here, trust is an ingredient of an epistemic approach.
11. *Uses of the self:* In the interviews we conducted, different ways of using the self in reasoning through a contradictory situation have caught our attention. These uses differ across participants but can also be present at different moments for a participant. (i) Sometimes *the*

self is used as a model for inferring the thoughts or behavior of one of the protagonists ("Usually when someone tells me one thing and someone else tells me another thing, I take half and half because I know I do that when I'm hurt and I tell someone about it. I tell my side, and my side's usually not the objective side."). (ii) At other times, *the self is used as a criterion*, almost an empirical observation, for evaluating the accuracy of theories. For instance, one woman commenting on what would lead her to endorse a particular personality theory says, "Um, things that I would agree with or things that would remind me of me or [if] I had a similar thought in the past and I found it here and the theory explains it more." Here, one's self and its psychological makeup is used as a test case to evaluate a theory, in contrast with the previous case, in which the self is used as a concrete model from which to infer other people's feelings or behavior. (iii) Finally, another use of the self identified so far is for the woman to take *her own view as an anchor*, a more cognitive use: "I would [. . .] sort of decide whether or not this theory fits or doesn't fit my own thoughts." Here, the self is neither a concrete model nor a test case but rather an epistemic agent whose views serve as a standard: convergence only works in this case if the theory (or the other person's testimony) fits the woman's own view; otherwise it is discounted. The woman's own conception is not disconfirmable.

12. *Assemblages of information:* Interesting distinctions emerge in the ways in which different lines of information are brought together in the reasoning process. (i) Sometimes, when evaluating an account, the woman relies on the *convergence* of different lines of evidence. For instance, one woman, addressing a legal situation, states, "[Y]ou have medical testimony. . . . Look at everything. . . . Like if she wasn't at work [and] her wounds mirrored exactly what her testimony was like [and] neighbor's witness accounts of the perpetrator constantly harassing her." (ii) Distinct from this approach is an *overlap* method, in which there is an attempt to see what elements are in common between those presupposed by a statement and those actually found ("I'd have to check and make sure that my symptoms and the symptoms of their diagnosis [match]. I check for extra symptoms or symptoms that they say I have that I don't have."). Thus here, the woman scrutinizes the degree of overlap, in the set-theoretic sense, between her set of individual symptoms and the set corresponding to the diagnosis, in contrast to the example of convergence mentioned previously, where different testimonies all point to one conclusion. (iii) A different,

interesting approach is the use of a '*puzzle* framework' in which the different kinds of information complement one another, as they do in a puzzle, and must form a coherent story in which all the parts "fit" together in a way that makes sense ("You know, if you . . . think on it long enough and if you have, if you have all or most of the pieces to this puzzle."). (iv) Contrasting with the puzzle framework is a *network view* in which it is the relations between elements that is focal, not the elements themselves, and everything must be connected through understandable links. In contrast to the puzzle frame, the required relation among elements in a network view is not necessarily one of complementarity but can be a relation of entailment, for instance.

Epistemic Norms

Some of the modes of knowledge and assemblages of information just discussed are indicative of different epistemologies, but there are other, more complex indicators as well. In reviewing these, it is important to remember that both reasoning processes and epistemic norms are modulated by the nature of the situation being reasoned about, and we are thus not characterizing participants but rather 'moments' of reasoning.

For instance, "making sense" surfaced as a rich, polysemous marker; determining whether something "makes sense" appears to be a criterion used by many women for evaluating different arguments, opinions, diagnoses or theories. It appears to reflect different personal epistemologies and to have vastly different meanings across participants and situations, including (1) making sense intuitively, generating a feeling of coherence with the woman's existing beliefs; (2) well supported by the evidence adduced by the protagonist; (3) resulting from a reasoning process the woman considers reasonable on the part of the protagonist; (4) grounded in a mode of knowledge she finds appropriate (e.g., sufficiently contextual as opposed to relying on abstract knowledge, in the case of one woman); (5) making sense substantively, in terms of what she knows about the phenomenon; (6) making sense logically, structurally; (7) relying on a satisfactory explanatory structure, well spelled out.

Also, the women's explicit responses to epistemological probes, as well as their spontaneous reasoning, reveal different kinds of interweaving among logic and other kinds of knowledges. The following are representative and, of course, would need extensive illustrations to be fully explicated. (The sketches in the appendix may be useful, meanwhile.) (1) Logic is the guiding principle, other knowledges (contextual, personal, or other, depending on the participant) are supportive only. (2) Logic is merely a default, other knowledges are primary (social, personal or other, depending on the participant). (3) Logic is necessary but insufficient, it needs to be integrated with standpoint knowledge (see "Simone" or Sonia). (4) Logic is a common ground for communication, but not the basis on which knowledge is attained; it is inadequate as epistemic norm. (5) Logical thought is supported by mild emotion but incompatible with strong emotion (see Anna).

Of particular interest is the interplay between intuition and thinking and the different forms this interplay may take. In some cases, intuition is a heuristic guide, which needs to be supplemented by rational or factual evidence, as illustrated by one woman who states that, in attempting to sort out different diagnoses, her intuition would generate a "70 percent or 30 percent" assessment only and that she would need the final confirmation to come from a scientific medical source. In other cases, it is intuition that leads to definitive knowledge; factual evidence has limited probative value and needs to be confirmed by intuition. One woman states, "If I was a juror, I would look at the facts . . . and I would make my best judgment on the facts, but *with* that [her emphasis] I would use my intuition, like 'Are they just acting weird on the stand, do they seem uncomfortable? Do they make me uncomfortable? . . . And I would just use the intuitive feelings that I've had.'" The woman later adds, "I think facts and my intuition weigh the same." In these two cases, intuition and other modes of thinking based on fact or reason complement each other synergistically. A very different pattern is reflected in other passages, which convey a tension between intuition and rationality as different discourses of knowledge.

Interesting tensions appear to be present in some of the women's responses, tensions that illustrate the dialectic between cultural discourses of knowledge and individual agency in constituting modes of thinking and subjectivity. In some women's interviews, one hears the cultural discourse of rationality, which they appear to have appropriated, while also hearing implicit or explicit dissatisfactions with it, or resistant attempts to reinterpret the meaning of rationality. Anna provides a clear example but several other women illustrate such tensions in different ways. For instance, one woman's responses appear to reflect a tension between relying on "rational" processes as a path to knowledge and a standpoint epistemology. Another woman, in her approach to a legal dilemma, oscillates between a procedure relying on logic and a process relying on personal knowledge. In these examples, the pattern is less one of interweaving different kinds of knowledge into an integrated approach, than one of unstable tension and shift between cultural discourses and resistant discourses in the women's thinking.

Status of the 'Data' for Feminist Theories about Logic

As discussed earlier, this empirical work is one component of a transdisciplinary reconstructive project. It is premised on the view that if feminist theorizing about logic and reason it is to avoid the same rationalist mode of theorizing as that afflicting traditional theories of logic, the theorizing must be informed *in some way* by the actual thinking of concrete people, concrete women each occupying a particular location in ethnic/racial, socioeconomic, and cultural formations. Conversely, empirical work must be designed along lines suggested by feminist critiques.

The relations between empirical research and theory construction are always complex. Theory and data are mutually constitutive: Theoretical lenses shape and constrain what we 'see' in ways that have been well elaborated on. However, a new layer of complexity emerges when it comes to feminist theories about logic, because logic, like epistemology, has normative as well as descriptive aims. In its traditional forms, of course, logic has functioned as a regime of truth in the Foucaultian sense in Western societies in its capacity as an epistemic and linguistic norm. But even though feminist reformulations of logic and feminist epistemologies reject the hegemonic use of systems and norms, of necessity they retain a quasi-normative quality, and this is inherent in their aim: to define principles of sound inference, in some sense of "sound," albeit on new terms, and to define grounds of justification for knowledge claims.

Thus, at issue is the relation between data such as those sketched here and a theory that has both descriptive and normative aims. Those two aims are interwoven and indeed the boundaries between the descriptive and the normative are not without ambiguity, yet the two aims are distinct in substance. The first aim, which animates substantive theory construction of the kind typical in the social sciences, is to develop a theory that represents, on some criterion of adequacy, the empirical phenomena as they have been constructed and described. This is perhaps the more straightforward enterprise of the two. However, even so, it is affected by the epistemic and narrative issues discussed in the previous sections, regarding tensions between openness and focus in the design of the interview, and regarding the dialectic of the particular and the general in describing the women's responses. The construction of the descriptive language raises one additional issue as to whether the problems of logic exposed by feminist critics are confined to the normative function of logic or whether they contaminate its use for descriptive purposes and whether, therefore, to include abstract principles as part of the descriptive language entails performing a rationalist move and undermining the critical and reconstructive aims of the research.

Regarding the quasi-normative aims of feminist theories of logic, two interlocking questions emerge. The first concerns the impact of the methodological decisions involved in an empirical study such as this one on the theory that is developed. For instance, the demarcation of the reasoning domain is a theory-laden and unstable problem, the resolution of which affects the implication of 'findings' for theories of logic. Likewise, the particular resolution of the tension between openness and focus in the design of the interview configures the scope and the nature of the data produced. Narrowly restricting the domain and strongly structuring the interview is likely to generate data that are less conducive to radical reformulations of logic than are data obtained with a methodology that reveals the complexity of thought. Although we believe that the present research illustrates one provisionally adequate resolution of these tensions, the data are, as always, contingently related to the specifics of the method.

The second, and central, question concerns the status of the constructs developed here for feminist theories of logic. How should such quasi-normative theoretical reformulations use empirical results like those generated by this research? For example, how does the mode of knowledge identified here as "balanced rationalism" prompt the development of a new paradigm or a reformulation of the relation between the two classical categories of "empiricism" and "rationalism," which are usually construed as opposed to each other? In addition, can the many and significant uses of the self we described help rethink a theory of knowledge where the identity of the knower is an active tool in her deductive strategies? If logic is revisable based on data from the external world, as Nelson (1990) and Nelson and Nelson (this volume) have maintained, then one question is whether and how it is revisable based on data of the kind reported here or similar data. Clearly, feminist theories of logic or of inference are not mere inductions from what women do; moreover, women's modes of thinking are diverse. As we have argued, it is necessary to develop an approach that subsumes analysis, empirically based theorizing, and empirical work under the same methodological space, and to begin transdisciplinary thinking about the status of particular 'data' in the quasi-normative process of theory construction.

One methodological choice in this research was guided by a principle that, we would like to suggest, ought also to inform the development of theory. To do justice to the richness, concreteness, and particularity of responses and participants, the constructs and descriptions in the data-analytic language of this research are concrete in that they embrace reasoning moments in their full specificity, as evidenced in women whose being and thinking is particularized sociohistorically. The descriptive constructs are not abstract categories but provisional pointers to distinct patterns, and the patterns are understood contextually with reference to the particular woman's social location, cultural and family history, and pertinent life context and with reference to the pertinent interview context. Thus, each woman is understood in her full particularity, as a whole person functioning in a complex social matrix and grounded in the context of her life and her social location. The convergences or contrasts that may emerge do so across particularized participants. The analytic language for identifying moments of reasoning transcends particular participants and the constructs involve an element of generality, but generalities in this approach are concrete and remain contextualized. The suggestion is that feminist theories of logic likewise be grounded in the individual thought patterns of particularized women, both fully specified and fully contextualized and that generalizations be concrete in the sense just discussed. To theorize fully contentful and richly contextualized forms of deductive thought honors feminist principles and circumvents the rationalist style that has been called into question.

By illustrating one way of conducting empirical research on reasoning that is anchored in a feminist perspective, and by exposing some of the dilemmas that an integration between empirical work and theoretical formulation poses, it is our hope that this chapter initiates a conversation across disciplinary boundaries on these and related questions.

Notes

The research reported here and the writing of this chapter were supported by Grant 200000081 from the Spencer Foundation to Rachel Joffe Falmagne.

1. People in general, and women in the study presented later on, often show different modes of reasoning depending on the situation or problem they reason about and sometimes different approaches to the same situation at different times. We thus speak about moments of reasoning rather than about an overall epistemology.

2. The quotation marks are intended to reflect the misleading nature of the term 'postcolonial': the postcolonial era has not arrived yet.

3. Nye does not consider contemporary alternative logics.

4. With respect to this commitment to develop theory from a foundation of multiplicity of locations, the fact that the women interviewed were college students was a limitation, but it was motivated by pragmatic constraints in this exploratory study. The women recruited were from very diverse cultural backgrounds and ethnic origins.

5. Although the problems were presented to the women as 'truth-seeking', epistemic episodes in which contradictory assertions needed to be adjudicated, women

actively *constructed* the functional context for their reasoning, as, for example, epistemological, ethical, or interpersonal.

6. The descriptive language involves categories, as languages do. However, importantly, these categories are not classification tools. The categories serve a heuristic function as 'provisional pointers'. They form a language enabling one to speak and to identify contrasts. These provisional categories are revised or enriched or transformed on an ongoing basis as concrete instances present themselves in the transcripts, especially if these instances are borderline or in tension.

Appendix: Illustrative Narrative Sketches (Abbreviated)

Sonia was born in Argentina in an intellectual Jewish family, raised in Mexico among educated Latin American immigrants, and educated in British schools. She states being encouraged by her parents to study, read, and discuss issues. Her Jewish identification is qualified: she disassociates from the Mexican Jewish community but gets along well with Argentinean Jews, whom she describes as very integrated. She speculates that her outsider's position in the different contexts in which she has lived has strongly influenced her thinking in leading her to envisage other's viewpoints.

Her approach to the suggested problems as well as the examples she supplies are broadly grounded historically and politically. "One reasons every time one opens a newspaper." One theme in her responses is that the most reliable knowledge is that gained directly from her own observations and judgment—that is, empirical knowledge but mediated through her. In the absence of such "direct" knowledge, she must rely on what she reads, but that is clearly a default. Likewise, inferences from similar contexts are acceptable defaults but must be qualified with concrete, specific knowledge about the problem situation. Thus, contextual and historical knowledge is central. At the same time, her thinking relies on rational argument. Her responses to the various situations contain many instances of explicit deductive reasoning, but always contextual and grounded in her world knowledge. Her epistemological norms, in response to explicit probes, are consistent with her spontaneous reasoning on this: logic and empirical knowledge are inseparable in evaluating the validity of an argument. In contrast to other women for whom rationalism and practical knowing seem to be in discursive or epistemic tension, there is no evidence of tension for this woman. Instead, what comes across is an integrated approach drawing on social knowledge and deduction.

For Sonia, evaluating an argument requires knowing the author and his or her views. For instance, in evaluating a newspaper's argument, the author's general views function as one premise of her reasoning, along with the author's explicit argument, and are an important basis for the inferences she draws; she clearly believes in the coherence and continuity of persons. Though she discusses articulately the importance of the logic of the argument, the argument is good only if the premise of the author fits the way she would have viewed the situation and is in her view factually true. Her explicit normative views are in line with her reasoning on this point: an irrational way of thinking is "one that uses wrong premises to reach a conclusion."

Sonia states being interested in considering opposing views only when her own knowledge is limited and her convictions weak, and mostly to see whether there may be new information or a new perspective that she has not considered. Interestingly, although throughout her interviews she shows clear epistemic awareness, there is a discrepancy here between her initial assertion that her outsider's status has initiated her to the existence of different points of view, and her reliance on her own reasoning and judgment throughout the problems. In assessing these opposing views, one key element is the location (social, generational, political) of the informants who are at the source of these views. Thus again, knowledge is grounded, contextual, and historical.

Simone, a young Black woman from Jamaica, has been in the United States for four years. For most of this time, she lived and attended school in a racially and ethnically mixed, predominantly working-class part of greater Boston, which she liked very much and where she had many friends from Jamaica, the United States, Barbados, and other countries. Recently she moved to a predominantly white, upper-middle-class suburb of Boston that she does not like and where she states she has no friends. Her mother is a nanny, and her mother's husband does not work. In her first year at college, she plans to explore her interests, but she enjoyed accounting and math in high school and wants to pursue these subjects.

She initially appears suspicious of the (white European) interviewer and of the study, but an extended conversation on the study and the investigator's life history and interests appears to succeed in minimizing the power inequalities inherent in this situation and in establishing trust and mutual interest in the focus of the interviews.

One consistent theme in Simone's reasoning about the various situations is distrust of the motives of the protagonists; this consideration, which she often mentions first, governs her reasoning strategies—for instance, in the medical situation, where she evokes the possibility of deception: if three opinions differed, she would suspect that either her condition is serious and the doctors are concealing it, or she is not ill and they are inventing a diagnosis. She also evokes the possibility of an error in the doctor's reasoning or of the lab's confusing her test samples and those of another patient and recommends replicating the tests.

Simone presents several situations from her life. One is an algebra course, in which the teacher insists on a decompositional method that she finds unnecessarily complex and that differs from the method she learned in high school. She herself prefers to rely on straightforward equations, argues that other students were taught these as well, questions the confidence of her teacher, and suspects that her real motive is to promote the book she is writing, supporting this claim with deductive arguments. By her own account, no argument from the teacher could change her view: Simone relies on her own epistemological criteria of a valid approach to algebra, simplicity and understanding of the principles.

One other example is her current course on Africa and the world. Her discussion of the colonization of Africa weaves her social knowledge of imperialist motives, her psychological knowledge of the mechanisms of deception, and her own deductive inference from both knowledge bases into a political and psychological analysis of European strategies of infiltration. A critical distrust of political motives guides her analysis, which also relies on a psychological model, but her argument is deductive throughout. In another situation she brings up, she would rely on her observations of the protagonists' behavior and on what she can infer from certain actions, rather than on their words, because of people's untrustworthiness: people's actions and statements are foremost driven by interest.

Thus, one central form of knowledge brought into Simone's reasoning is social knowledge. However, interestingly, the epistemic markers "I think" she tends to use in stating her conclusions indicate that she is aware of the deduced status of her conclusion. So while she relies on her own judgment and social knowledge, she maintains an epistemic critical distance about the conclusions she derives on that basis. Her discussions are generally structured according to clear deductive processes, and she trusts her own rational evaluations of evidence. She appears to have secure confidence in her own judgment, though she states so on one occasion only. Her approach to reasoning, overall, embodies an implicit reliance on the epistemic advantage of marginality described by many feminists of color, whose writings she is presumably unfamiliar with.

Leah is a white woman from a mixed Jewish/Christian second family in upstate New York, where her father and stepmother ran a small family business. She describes her neighborhood as middle-class, though she does not seem to have given prior thought to that question. Her neighborhood was predominantly white, as was her rural elementary school, but her high school had a diverse student population, which she enjoyed.

Her responses to the dilemmas reflect a 'liberal' view on knowledge: each person has his or her own approach to a problem and handles it in his or her own way, all equally valid relative to that person. Her relativism appears to be based in a concern for not privileging one approach over another. Thus, this is not a 'standpoint' relativism, for which knowing is grounded in the person's location and conditions, but an individualistic relativism: her criterion for defining a valid solution is subjective (what the person feels comfortable with) and pragmatic (what "works" for the person). This pragmatic construal is also the main determinant of her own approach to several of the hypothetical dilemmas. "What works" is a recurrent linguistic marker throughout her discussion.

Likewise, Leah defines 'liberally' what would constitute a rational approach to a dilemma: what is best differs for different people and each person can decide. When questioned in depth about her view on rationality, she maintains that everyone is rational but in their own way and that each person is entitled to his or her opinion. However, she then spontaneously defines as irrational someone unwilling to listen to the other side. There seems to be a struggle between a liberal discourse and a need to articulate a normative judgment about irrationality.

In the medical situation, in adjudicating both diagnoses, her main theme is her trust in her family doctor, based on her faith in his good intentions and in the rapport they have. Thus, her trust is based on the quality of the relationship and her subjective comfort (rather than on his past performance or the quality of his reasoning). She makes no reference to needing to evaluate the doctor's inference or the basis for his diagnosis.

In the legal situation, Leah's reasoning focuses on concrete material evidence (multiwitnessed alibis or fingerprints); character evidence is secondary as compared to material "proof," because "people can change." She describes herself as liking concrete things. Her first statement, however, is that she would listen to both sides of the evidence. Although this approach would be natural in a legal situation, her offering that statement is an interesting discursive positioning, in light of her general commitment to a liberal approach. She does offer a complex view of facts: there are real facts, but they could be different for different persons. While initially she presents those differences as, implicitly, irreconcilable, she then recommends to discuss diverging perceptions until consensus is reached. There is a fact of the matter, and listening to others is a good way to improve one's reasoning. So she slides between what appears to be an objectivist notion of factual evidence and a subjectivist notion. This may reflect a tension between two conflicting discourses, an empiricist discourse and a liberal discourse grounded in individual subjectivity.

Anna is from Norway from a middle-class family, has lived in the United States for one year, speaks English fluently if with occasional expressive strain, tried studying mathematics but disliked it, and turned to psychology. She describes Norway as having little ethnic diversity and being a closed country, not open to strangers but loyal to its own. Her interviews reveal a strong interest in the question of what is rational and what is objective, two notions she spontaneously brings up in her commentaries. She displays complex, elaborate views on these questions, both spontaneously and in response to probes. Her view can be capsulized as balanced rationalism: in adjudicating competing diagnoses she relies on the doctor's knowledge and ability to explain, and she uses her own understanding as a criterion for a credible diagnosis; however, overall, she criticizes "cold" reason, the rationality she advocates is a rationality of purpose, not of process: rational thinking has integrity in relation to the goals of the thinking. Although she affirms logic as a tool of argumentation, hers is not a disembodied logic but a logic grounded in values.

Interesting shifts in Anna's responses suggest a struggle between conflicting discourses: the cultural discourse of rationality, and a resistant discourse in which rationality is relativized in relation to values, goals, and context. Her responses also slide between two meanings of "rational": the standard sense and a broader sense that she is attempting to redefine. She contrasts rationality with emotion according to a complex (or conflicted) theory: rational thinking is useful in conflict situations, whereas emotions impair her ability to solve problems, but she later insists that emotion is necessary—strong emotion interferes with rational thinking, but mild emotions are healthy and support thought. From another angle, while she stated earlier that her father was helpful to her about a life dilemma because "he is very rational and [does not let his emotions interfere]," and she repeatedly praised rationality with some qualifications, she later states, in response to a straightforward request for clarification, "I think he's not a great family father because he's always so clear, like he doesn't see, like he probably doesn't focus on feelings so much because—um, feelings can get in the way of thinking rationally. That's how he sees it. Um, and like, he always said—like things should—it's a little bit difficult; can you repeat the question one more time?"

Her response, and the surprising statement "it's a little bit difficult; can you repeat" (when the original question was merely a request for her to explicate her earlier statement), suggests a struggle between two voices: her father's voice, which she attempts to articulate, and hers. Later, she characterizes herself as rational also, but in a different sense—that is, in that her choices would be guided by her values, not only by "objective" considerations.

When probed for clarification, Anna asserts, interestingly, that it is males who have defined the rational as being superior and involving no feelings, and she distances herself from that norm, when this was exactly her own definition of rationality earlier. Thus, she spontaneously critiques what she sees as the historically masculinist construction of rationality. When juxtaposed with her initial claim that rationality (in the traditional sense) is useful, her resistant comments here are particularly interesting, another manifestation of what appears to be an epistemological struggle. This is a clear illustration of the dialectic among the cultural discourse of knowledge, her enculturation into that discourse, and resistant knowledge construction.

References

Alcoff, Linda, and Elizabeth Potter. *Feminist Epistemologies*. New York: Routledge, 1993.

Anzaldua, Gloria. "Introduction." In *Making Face, Making Soul: Creative and Critical Perspectives by Feminists of Color*, ed. Gloria Anzaldua. St. Paul, Minn.: Aunt Lute, 1990.

Barrett, Michele. "Words and Things: Materialism and Method in Contemporary Feminist Analysis." In *Destabilizing Theory: Contemporary Feminist Debates*, ed. Michele Barrett and Anne Phillips. Stanford, Calif.: Stanford University Press, 1992.

Barwise, Jon. *The Situation in Logic*. Stanford, Calif.: Center for the Study of Language and Information, 1989.

Belenky, Mary Field, Blythe M. Clinchy, Nancy R. Goldberger, and Jill M. Tarule. *Women's Ways of Knowing: The Development of Self, Voice and Mind*. New York: Basic Books, 1986.

Bordo, Susan. *The Flight to Objectivity: Essays on Cartesianism and Culture*. Albany: State University of New York Press, 1987.

———. "The View from Nowhere and the Dream of Everywhere: Heterogeneity, Adequation and Feminist Theory." *American Philosophical Association Newsletter on Feminism and Philosophy* 88, no. 2 (1989): 19–24.

Braine, Martin D. S. "Mental Logic and How to Discover It." In *The Logical Foundations of Cognition*, ed. John McNamara and Gonzalo E. Reyes. Oxford: Oxford University Press, 1993.

Cheng, Patricia W., and Keith J. Holyoak. "Pragmatic Reasoning Schemas." *Cognitive Psychology* 17 (1985): 391–416.

Code, Lorraine. *Epistemic Responsibility*. Hanover, N.H.: University Press of New England, 1987.

———. "Taking Subjectivity into Account." In *Feminist Epistemologies*, ed. Linda Alcoff and Elizabeth Potter. New York: Routledge, 1993.

Collins, Patricia Hill. *Black Feminist Thought: Knowledge, Consciousness and the Politics of Empowerment*. New York: Routledge, 1990.

Crawford, Mary. "Agreeing to Differ: Feminist Epistemologies and Women's Ways of Knowing." In *Gender and Thought: Psychological Perspectives*, ed. Mary Crawford and Margaret Gentry. New York: Springer, 1989.

Denzin, Norman K., and Yvonna Lincoln. *Handbook of Qualitative Research*. London: Sage, 1994.

Evans, Jonathan St. B. T. *Bias in Human Reasoning: Causes and Consequences*. Hove, U.K.: Erlbaum, 1989.

Falmagne, Rachel Joffe. "The Abstract and the Concrete." In *Sociocultural Psychology: On the Theory and Practice of Knowing and Doing*, ed. Laura Martin, Katherine Nelson, and Ethel Tobach. Cambridge: Cambridge University Press, 1995a.

———. "Logic and Domination." Paper presented at the Annual Meeting of the International Pragmatics Association, Amsterdam, 1995b.

———. "Toward a Feminist Theory of Inference: Exploration of a Crossdisciplinary Methodology." Paper presented at the enGendering Rationalities Conference, Eugene, Oregon, April 1997.

———. "Deconstructing Cognitive Psychology: A Critical Opening. Review of E. A. Wilson." *Neural Geographies: Feminism and the Microstructure of Cognition.*" *Theory and Psychology* 10, no. 2 (2000a): 277–282.

———. "On the Gendered Foundations of Culture, Thought and Development." In *Towards a Feminist Developmental Psychology*, ed. Ellin K. Scholnick and Patricia H. Miller. New York: Routledge, 2000b.

———. "The Dialectic of Critique, Theory and Method in Developing Feminist Research on Inference." In *Issues in Theoretical Psychology*, ed. John Morss, Niamh Stephenson, and Hans van Rappard. New York: Springer, 2001.

Falmagne, Rachel Joffe, and Joanna Gonsalves. "Deductive Inference." *Annual Review of Psychology* 46 (1995): 525–559.

Flax, Jane. *Disputed Subjects: Essays on Psychoanalysis, Subjects, Politics and Philosophy*. New York: Routledge, 1993.

Fox, Pamela A. "Recasting the 'Politics of Truth': Thoughts on Class, Gender and the Role of Intellectuals." In *Working Class Women in the Academy: Laborers in the Knowledge Factory*, ed. Michelle M. Tokarczyk and Elizabeth A. Fay. Amherst: University of Massachusetts Press, 1993.

Gilligan, Carol. *In a Different Voice*. Cambridge, Mass.: Harvard University Press, 1982.

Haack, Susan. *Philosophy of Logics*. New York: Cambridge University Press, 1978.

Harding, Sandra. "Feminism, Science and Anti-Enlightenment Critiques." In *Feminism/Postmodernism*, ed. Linda Nicholson. New York: Routledge, 1990a.

———. "Starting Thought from Women's Lives: Eight Resources for Maximizing Objectivity." *Journal of Social Philosophy* 20, nos. 2/3 (1990b): 140–149.

———. "Who Knows? Identities and Feminist Epistemology." In *(En)gendering Knowledge: Feminists in Academe*, ed. Joan E. Hartman and Ellen Messer-Davidow. Knoxville: University of Tennessee Press, 1991a.

———. *Whose Science? Whose Knowledge? Thinking from Women's Lives*. Ithaca, N.Y. Cornell University Press, 1991b.

———. "Rethinking Standpoint Epistemology: What Is 'Strong Objectivity'?" In *Feminist Epistemologies*, ed. Linda Alcoff and Elizabeth Potter. New York: Routledge, 1993.

———. *Is Science Multicultural? Postcolonialisms, Feminisms and Epistemologies*. Bloomington: Indiana University Press, 1998.

Hartsock, Nancy. "The Feminist Standpoint: Developing the Grounds for a Specifically Feminist Historical Materialism." In *Discovering Reality: Feminist Perspectives on Epistemology, Metaphysics Methodology and Philosophy of Science*, ed. Sandra Harding and Merrill Hintikka. Dordrecht: Reidel, 1983.

Hass, Marjorie. "Can There Be a Feminist Logic?" In *Is Feminist Philosophy Philosophy?* ed. Emanuela Bianchi. Evanston, Ill.: Northwestern University Press, 1999.

hooks, bell. "Choosing the Margin as a Space of Radical Openness." In *Yearning: Race, Gender and Cultural Politics*. Boston: South End, 1990.

Ilyenkov, E. V. *The Dialectics of the Abstract and the Concrete in Marx's Capital*. Moscow: Progress, 1982. (Original Russian edition 1960.)

Irigaray, Luce. "Le Langage de l'homme." In *Parler n'est jamais neutre*. Paris: Minuit, 1985.

Jessor, Richard, Anne Colby, and Richard A. Shweder. *Ethnography and Human Development: Context and Meaning in Social Inquiry*. Chicago: University of Chicago Press, 1996.

Johnson-Laird, Philip N. "Reasoning without Logic." In *Reasoning and Discourse Processes*, ed. Terry Myers, Keith Brown, and Brendan McGronigle. New York: Academic Press, 1986.

Lennon, Kathleen, and Margaret Whitford. "Introduction." In *Knowing the Difference: Feminist Perspectives in Epistemology*, ed. Kathleen Lennon and Margaret Whitford. New York: Routledge, 1994.

Lloyd, Genevieve."Maleness, Metaphor, and the 'Crisis' of Reason." In *A Mind of One's Own: Feminist Essays on Reason and Objectivity*, ed. Louise M. Antony and Charlotte Witt. Boulder, Colo.: Westview, 1993.

———. *The Man of Reason: 'Male' and 'Female' in Western Philosophy*. London: Methuen, 1984.

Longino, Helen. *Science as Social Knowledge: Values and Objectivity in Scientific Inquiry*. Princeton, N.J.: Princeton University Press, 1990.

Marx Ferree, Myra, Judith Lorber, and Beth B. Hess, eds. *Revisioning Gender*. Thousand Oaks, Calif.: Sage, 1999.

Mohanty, Chandra. "Introduction: Cartographies of Struggle." In *Third World Women and the Politics of Feminism*, ed. Chandra Mohanty, Ann Russo, and Lourdes Torres. Bloomington: Indiana University Press, 1991.

Narayan, Uma, and Sandra Harding, eds. *Decentering the Center: Philosophy for a Multicultural, Postcolonial and Feminist World*. Bloomington: Indiana University Press, 2000.

Nelson, Lynn Hankinson. "Feminist Perspectives on Logic." Paper presented at the enGendering Rationalities Conference, Eugene, Oregon, April 1997.

———. *Who Knows? From Quine to Feminist Empiricism*. Philadelphia: Temple University Press, 1990.

Nye, Andrea. *Words of Power*. New York: Routledge, 1990.

Olkowski, Dorothea. "Words of Power and the Logic of Sense." Paper presented at the enGendering Rationalities Conference, Eugene, Oregon, April 1997.

Omi, Michael, and Howard Winant. *Racial Formation in the United States: From the 1960s to the 1990s*. New York: Routledge, 1994.

Over, David, and Ken I. Manktelow. "Rationality, Utility and Deontic Reasoning." In *Rationality: Psychological and Philosophical Perspectives*, ed. Ken I. Manktelow and David E. Over. London: Routledge, 1993.

Plumwood, Val. "The Politics of Reason: Towards a Feminist Logic." *Australasian Journal of Philosophy* 71, no. 4 (1993): 436–462.

Quine, W. V. O. *Philosophy of Logic*. Englewood Cliffs, N.J.: Prentice Hall, 1970.

Scott, Joan Wallach. *Gender and the Politics of History*. New York: Columbia University Press, 1988.

Smith, Dorothy. *The Everyday World as Problematic: A Feminist Sociology*. Boston: Northeastern University Press, 1987.

———. *Texts, Facts and Femininity: Exploring the Relations of Ruling*. London: Routledge, 1990.

Sperber, Dan, and Deidre Wilson. *Relevance: Communication and Cognition*. Cambridge, Mass.: Harvard University Press, 1986.

Tokarczyk, Michelle M., and Elizabeth A. Fay. *Working Class Women in the Academy: Laborers in the Knowledge Factory*. Amherst: University of Massachusetts Press, 1993.

Whitford, Margaret. "Luce Irigaray's Critique of Rationality." In *Feminist Perspectives in Philosophy*, ed. M. Griffith and Margaret Whitford. London: Macmillan, 1988.

Wilson, Elizabeth. *Neural Geographies: Feminism and the Microstructure of Cognition*. New York: Routledge, 1998.

CHAPTER SEVEN

Logic from a Quinean Perspective: An Empirical Enterprise

LYNN HANKINSON NELSON AND JACK NELSON

Our project in this discussion is modest. We explicate W. V. Quine's arguments for the view that logic and mathematics are empirical enterprises—more specifically, that each is part of the overall enterprise of science—and what we take to be significant implications of these arguments.[1] One implication is that logic and mathematics confront experience as part of our overall theory of nature and are interdependent with other theories that together constitute it. Another is that, although logic and mathematics are deeply interwoven throughout other theories, neither is above revision. Thus, however unlikely it may seem from present vantage points, should developments in more obviously empirical sciences call for revisions or abandonment of some aspects of contemporary logic or mathematics, there will be *choices made* between, on the one hand, adopting the new theories and making the adjustments in logic or mathematics they call for and, on the other, giving priority to accepted aspects of logic and mathematics, and modifying or abandoning the new hypothesis or theory incompatible with these.

The relationship between our discussion and the topic of this volume is, then, this: Insofar as feminist and other contemporary theorizing in the sciences may lead to significant revisions in scientific theories, or to the development of new theories incompatible with some currently maintained, Quine's arguments suggest that these developments *could* carry implications for logic. Of course, we cannot predict such developments now, but neither, given Quine's arguments, can we rule them out. In explicating Quine's positions and their implications, our discussion illustrates how, from the perspective of a thoroughgoing empiricism, it is reasonable to explore relationships between logic and theorizing in other arenas, including that undertaken by feminist scientists. We will not argue, and indeed we do not believe, that current or foreseeable developments in feminist theorizing, or any other empirical theorizing, have been shown to constitute a challenge to currently accepted theories or principles of logic. We seek to explicate Quine's arguments as to why and how developments in other empirical sciences could constitute a basis for revising theories or principles of logic.

To claim that such choices *would* arise in situations such as that earlier described is not to claim that the available options will or should be weighted equally. As Quine (1966b) notes, there may be good reasons for making adjustments in newer theories rather than, say, in logic; he, among others, views conservatism to be an important epistemic virtue. As logic and mathematics are interwoven throughout the more obviously empirical parts of our theories of nature and both shape and reflect the various commitments of these theories, revisions in logic or mathematics are far less likely than revisions in other theories. Finally, Quine (1963, 42–43) also recognizes more "distance" between statements of logic and mathematics and the "experiential periphery"; this, too, makes revisions in these theories less likely.

Nonetheless, if we accept the arguments Quine offers, it does follow that as our other empirical theories develop, we may choose to revise portions of currently accepted logic and mathematics. Such revisions are not limited to the development of new branches to deal with particular and "special" domains (e.g., quantum physics). Aspects of generally applicable and classic theories in logic could be revised or abandoned in response to developments in other sciences. This is not to say that we may come to view some statements of current theories in logic or mathematics to be false. It is to say that a future theory might not include them.

In explicating Quine's views concerning logic, we emphasize his arguments against the analytic/synthetic distinction and his arguments for holism. Our emphasis on the first line of argument will not surprise readers familiar with philosophy, although it is likely that some will not concur with aspects of our analysis. We also take Quine's arguments for holism, developed subsequent to the publication of "Two Dogmas of Empiricism," to explicate the view, only mentioned in that essay, that the analytic/synthetic distinction and verificationism (the application of the verification theory of meaning to individual sentences) are "at root identical" dogmas (41).

Quine's arguments against both dogmas, and those we advance concerning their implications, presume empiricism, a history of empiricist inquiry, and naturalized philosophy of science. We do not here argue for empiricism or naturalism. We also do not respond to critiques of Quine's arguments which seek to revive the analytic/synthetic distinction and, thus, the view of logic as a nonempirical enterprise. None in our opinion succeeds.[2] We also do not presume readers' familiarity with the developments within the empiricist tradition to which Quine's arguments are a response or that those familiar with these developments will concur with our interpretation of them. Accordingly, we begin by locating Quine's arguments in relation to developments in the empiricist tradition.

Quine's Project

David Hume held that there are two kinds of truths: those resting on the "relations of [among] ideas" and those resting on "matters of fact." An alleged example of the former is "A pentagon has more sides than a square"; one of the latter is "The Nineteenth Amendment gave women the right to vote." The former is, or so the story goes, made true by the relations among the "meanings" of 'pentagon', 'square', 'more', 'side', and so on. Given that these terms mean what they do, the sentence could not but be true. Its truth is therefore certain but also uninformative—it tells us nothing we did not know already by knowing the meaning of the constituent terms. But "The Nineteenth Amendment gave women the right to vote" is otherwise. To know of this amendment is to know a bit of history, an event that happened when and as it did, but might not have happened or might have happened differently.

By dividing truths into these two kinds, known later as "analytic" truths and "synthetic" truths, Hume set a new standard for intellectual respectability and an agenda for future empiricists. For Hume's successors, reasoning concerning analytic statements was to yield the truths of logic and mathematics. Synthetic truths were to be the domain and product of science. Everything else is nonsense.

Thus, the agenda Hume set for future empiricists is this: Show how all claims we want to hold as meaningful—as either true or false—derive either from relations of ideas or matters of fact.

In the two centuries following Hume's death, philosophers and mathematicians labored to complete Hume's agenda. On the "relations of ideas" side, they sought to show that all of logic and mathematics consists of analytic truths. It was hoped that, for mathematics and logic, truth could be identified with provability. That is, a statement of mathematics or logic would be true if and only if it were a theorem in an appropriate formal system. This project, pursued by David Hilbert in the first decades of the twentieth century, came to a halt in 1931 when Kurt Gödel proved that truth and provability cannot be identified, even for arithmetic truths.[3] Although Hilbert's project was abandoned, efforts continued to show that logical truths and mathematical truths are different in kind from empirical truths; for example, they are true by definition or by convention.

The empiricist part of Hume's agenda—that of showing that all synthetic truths are empirical claims whose support rests ultimately on sense experience—was pursued assiduously by members of the Vienna Circle and, after that group dispersed, by Carl Hempel, Ernst Nagel, Karl Popper, and, most important in Quine's intellectual development, Rudolf Carnap. Those working in the tradition from the 1930s through the 1960s thought, like Hume, that every truth could be accounted for either on grounds of logic (relations of ideas) or of sensory experience (matters of fact). In broad strokes, they sought to develop a coherent account of empirical knowledge that identified the meaning of a sentence with the method or process or content of the procedure used to verify (or reject) the sentence and that revealed how all empirical knowledge rests, in the end, on sensory experiences.

The driving force behind this endeavor was twofold. First, it was assumed that all we initially know is what is immediately presented to us through our senses, and hence that claims that go beyond this immediate presentation need to be justified by or replaced with claims about sense experience. Second, it was assumed that sentences reporting sensory experience, or the sensory experiences themselves, are cognitively privileged—they are unmediated, and because they are, they offer no room for error. Given these two assumptions, it follows that if we can either reduce all the empirical claims we care about to sensory experiences or claims about them, or alternatively replace those claims with claims about sensory experiences, we will have eliminated the possibility of error, will have placed science on a firm foundation, and will have decisively refuted the skeptic.[4]

Carnap's approach was perhaps the most formal. He attempted, in his *Der logische Aufbau der Welt*, to develop a "language" of sensory experience that in theory could supplant ordinary language. As Quine (1963) describes it, the project of the *Aufbau* was that of "specifying a sense-datum language and showing how to translate the rest of significant discourse, statement by statement, into it" (39). Although Quine studied under Carnap in Prague in 1933 and continued to be influenced by him at least through the 1950s, he became uneasy with the Humean agenda as early as 1936, when "Truth by Convention" first appeared. In that article Quine does not argue that mathematics is not reducible to logic ("There is no need here to adopt a final stand in the matter" [80]). But he does argue that logic itself cannot be construed as true by definition:

> But if we are to construe logic also as true by convention, we must rest logic ultimately upon some manner of convention other than definition: for it was noted earlier that definitions are available only for transforming truths, not for founding them. (Quine 1966b, 81)

Quine next explores whether various other conventions might be the basis for the truths of logic and mathematics. He concludes that it is unlikely, showing that logic itself is needed to explicate both logic and mathematics.

"Truth by Convention" is important because it shows that if logic and mathematics consist, in the end, of analytic truths, those truths cannot be definitional truths. Later, in "Two Dogmas of Empiricism," Quine argues that other varieties of and explanations of analyticity fail, leaving no room for giving an account of mathematical truths and logical truths distinct from that given for the truths of science generally. In "Truth by Convention," Quine hints at the view he will later maintain concerning why we tend to see the truths of mathematics and logic as having a special status (e.g., being analytic or true by convention). They have no such special status, but they do permeate all of science, and therefore changes to them would have implications for every part of science. They are, then, the "statements which we choose to surrender last, if at all, in the course of revamping our sciences in the face of new discoveries" (95). We invent doctrines of analyticity and truth by convention to explain why we are reluctant to give up or modify the claims of mathematics and logic. In other words, it is our unwillingness to abandon claims of mathematics and logic that explains why we think they must be true in some special way, rather than their *being* true in some special way that explains why we are unwilling to abandon them. There is, as we next explore, more than a little of Quine's later holism here.

Thus, as early as 1936, Quine set the stage for his subsequent rejection of the analytic/synthetic distinction in "Two Dogmas of Empiricism." We review the arguments of that article in the next section and conclude here by noting the agenda already laid out, in broad strokes, in "Truth by Convention." Quine is committed to maintaining both the truth and the importance of the claims of logic and mathematics, and he is unable to avail himself of the Humean defense of these disciplines (that they rest on relations of ideas).

"Two Dogmas of Empiricism"

Quine published "Two Dogmas of Empiricism" in 1953.[5] In it, he rejects outright the analytic/synthetic distinction and verificationism—that is, the verification theory of meaning as applied to individual sentences.[6] The first of these empiricist doctrines has, as noted earlier, its roots in Hume's distinction between relations of ideas and matters of fact. The second empiricist doctrine rejected in "Two Dogmas," verificationism, emerged as the basis of a strategy of completing one half of Hume's agenda, that of showing how all empirical knowledge flows from experience.

In "Two Dogmas," Quine adopts the device of showing that common, and superficially promising, defenses of the analytic/synthetic distinction invariably turn out to presuppose, rather than elucidate, the notion of analyticity. An investigation of the nest of interrelated notions, analyticity, synonymy, interchangeability *salva veritate*, and necessary truth yields, Quine notes, an argument that "is not flatly circular, but something like it. It has the form, figuratively speaking, of a closed curve in space" (30). We now review the salient pieces of this closed curve in space.

Kant's view, Quine claims, can be taken to be that "a statement is analytic when it is true by virtue of meanings and independently of fact" (21). Quine finds meanings to be "obscure intermediary entities" that are "well abandoned" in favor of an investigation of "the synonymy of linguistic forms." Instead of talking of meanings, we can talk, given the notion of synonymy, of two linguistic forms, two sentences, or two words, meaning the same if and only if they are synonymous. So we are making progress, if we can give an account of synonymy. The progress is this: Analytic statements fall into two subclasses: logical truths and statements that can be turned into logical truths "by putting synonyms for synonyms" (23).

Quine's example of a logical truth is "No unmarried man is married," and his general characterization of a logical truth is "a statement which is true and remains true under all reinterpretations of its components other than the logical particles" (22), these exemplified by "'no,' 'un-,' 'not,' 'if,' 'then,' 'and,' etc." An example of a statement that is not a logical truth but yields one through the substitution of synonym for synonym is "No bachelor is married," where 'bachelor' and 'unmarried man' are taken to be synonyms.

This first part of the closed curve seeks to explicate analyticity in terms of synonymy, which, Quine contends, "is no less in need of clarification than analyticity itself" (23). In the second section, Quine explores and rejects the view that synonymy rests on definition. On this view, 'bachelor' is supposedly defined as, and is therefore synonymous with, 'unmarried man' (24). The problem, Quine argues, is that ordinary definitions, dictionary definitions, are not stipulations but reports on usage. "The lexicographer is an empirical scientist, whose business is the recording of antecedent facts" (24). The lexicographer reports on linguistic usage, including on the usage of two terms as synonyms for one another; he or she does not create usage or synonyms.[7]

Quine next turns to the notion of interchangeability of terms *salva veritate* as a possible explication of synonymy. The proposal is that expressions are synonymous if they are everywhere interchangeable without changing the truth or falsity of the containing statement. The problem here is that such allegedly clear synonyms as 'bachelor' and 'unmarried male' are not so interchangeable. For example, 'Unmarried male' cannot be substituted for 'Bachelor' in

> 'Bachelor' has less than ten letters

without turning the above truth into the falsehood

> 'Unmarried male' has less than ten letters

(Quine's example, 28).

To make the substitutivity test work, we have to limit substitutions to whole words. The word spelled *b-a-c-h-e-l-o-r* does not occur as a whole word in the prior example, though its name (formed by placing single quotation marks around that word) does. Appearances notwithstanding, the word we are discussing that is allegedly synonymous with the expression 'unmarried male' no more appears in

> 'Bachelor' has less than ten letters

than does 'cat' in 'catapult'.

So far so good (assuming the notion of 'wordhood' is unproblematic). But to make the substitutivity test work—to prevent its declaring such coreferential but nonsynonymous expressions as 'the first president of the United States [under the Constitution] and 'the second husband of Martha Washington' synonymous—we will have to consider substitutivity not only within such ordinary contexts as

> The first president of the United States was married to Martha Washington

but also such contexts as

> Necessarily the first president of the United States was married to Martha Washington.

That is, while the expressions 'the first president of the United States' and 'the second husband of Martha Washington' are intersubstitutable in the first context, *salva veritate*, they are not in the second.

> Necessarily the first president of the United States was married to Martha Washington

is presumably false while

> Necessarily the second husband of Martha Washington was married to Martha Washington

is presumably true.

But, Quine now reminds us, to attach 'necessarily' to a statement is just to claim that the statement is analytic. That is,

> Necessarily bachelors are unmarried

is best understood as

> 'Bachelors are unmarried' is analytic.

So our curve in space has closed itself. We can explicate analyticity in terms of synonymy, synonymy in terms of intersubstitutivity *salve veritate*, including in contexts governed by 'necessarily', and such necessity in terms of analyticity.[8]

Quine next turns his attention to his second target, "The Verification Theory and Reductionism." Historically, discussions of "Two Dogmas of Empiricism" have centered on Quine's attack on the analytic/synthetic distinction and have largely ignored the second dogma, verificationism (perhaps because many defenders of the analytic/synthetic distinction have no sympathy for verificationism). Indeed, at first it seems odd that Quine would see these two positions as paired or related dogmas. Upon reflection one might conclude that having rejected the analytic/synthetic distinction, Quine had no choice but also to reject verificationism, precisely because he does not want to abandon the meaningfulness of logic and mathematics. That is, if the only criterion of meaningfulness is verification by sensory experience, then mathematics and logic appear to be meaningless; for surely there are no sensory experiences that can be taken to confirm (or disconfirm) the alleged truths of mathematics and logic. This unlikely view of logic and mathematics—as consisting of important nonsense—is one A. J. Ayer (1946) was willing to take in his explication and defense of verificationism in *Language, Truth, and Logic*. Being unwilling to follow Ayer, one might conclude that Quine has no choice but to reject verificationism as a theory of meaning.

But this is not the motivation for Quine's rejection of verificationism. Quine does not take the truths of mathematics and logic to be unverified by the standards of verificationism. He notes in "Two Dogmas" that "as long as it is taken to be significant in general to speak of the confirmation and infirmation of a statement, it seems significant to speak also of a limiting kind of statement which is vacuously confirmed, *ipso facto*, come what may; and such a statement is analytic" (41). In other words, Quine grants that "the truth of statements does obviously depend both upon language and upon extralinguistic fact" (41). If we allow sentences to be candidates for truth and falsity *individually* (i.e., one by one), it follows that we can explicate analytic sentences as the limiting case, those in which "the linguistic component is all that matters," where the role of extralinguistic fact is nil. Given verificationism, the truths of logic and mathematics and perhaps all commonly termed analytic statements are vacuously verified, verified "come what may" by way of experience.

Hence, were verificationism to stand, it would, by itself, constitute a basis for an explication (and thus reinstitution) of the analytic/synthetic distinction, analytic statements being those that are verified come what may. So if the analytic/synthetic distinction is to be banished as an insupportable dogma, so must verificationism. In fact, Quine asserts not just that the analytic/synthetic distinction is a consequence of verificationism but also that "The two dogmas are, indeed, at root identical" (41).

It is not immediately obvious that verificationism does follows from the analytic/synthetic distinction—that is, that the two are identical. We return to this issue later. We turn now to Quine's attack on verificationism.

We stress again that Quine does not reject the verification theory of meaning—the thesis that the meaning of sentences just is their empirical content—but verificationism, the applicability of this theory of meaning to most sentences taken individually.[9] Quine holds verificationism to be closely connected with, if not equivalent to, radical reductionism—the view that "Every meaningful statement is . . . translatable into a statement (true or false) about immediate experience" (38). In "Two Dogmas," his argument against verificationism and radical reductionism takes the form of what might be called "dismissal by charitable reinterpretation." Radical reductionism goes back at least to Locke and Hume, who in Quine's words "held that every idea must either originate directly in sense experience or else be compounded of ideas thus originating" (38). Tooke improved on this idea by moving the focus from ideas to terms, allowing the doctrine to be rephrased in "semantical terms by saying that a term, to be significant at all, must be either a name of a sense datum or a compound of such names or an abbreviation of such a compound" (38). But such a doctrine, Quine maintains, is

> unnecessarily and intolerably restrictive in the term-by-term critique which it imposes. More reasonably, and without yet exceeding the limits of what I have called radical reductionism, we may take full statements as our significant

> units-thus demanding that our statements as wholes be translatable into sense-datum language, but not that they be translatable term by term. (38–39)

Devising such a translation scheme for statements into sense-datum language was the goal of Carnap's *Aufbau.* Although Quine finds Carnap's attempt, especially his constructions utilizing "the whole language of pure mathematics" (39) impressive, he believes the whole project is ultimately doomed to failure, because Carnap

> provides no indication, not even the sketchiest, of how a statement of the form 'Quality *q* is at *x;y;z;t*' [a point instant] could ever be translated into Carnap's initial language of sense data and logic. The connective 'is at' remains an added undefined connective; the canons counsel us in its use but not in its elimination. (40)

Carnap abandoned his radical reductionism project subsequent to publishing the *Aufbau.* Others, Quine notes, continued to hold that

> to each statement, or each synthetic statement, there is associated a unique range of possible sensory events such that the occurrence of any of them would add to the likelihood of truth of the statement, and that there is associated also another unique range of possible sensory events whose occurrence would detract from that likelihood. (40–41)

In "Two Dogmas," Quine does not produce and criticize the arguments of those who continued to hold radical reductionism after Carnap abandoned it. Rather, he makes a "countersuggestion"—a charitable reinterpretation of the verificationism and radical reductionism of the *Aufbau*—namely, that "our statements about the external world face the tribunal of sense experience not individually but only as a corporate body" (41). The countersuggestion is holism—one of the two key doctrines that Quine was to spend the rest of his career elucidating and defending (the other being the explication of how experience constrains theories—i.e., of how we can have holism and empiricism).

We turn to holism in the next section, considering arguments Quine subsequently offered for it and some of its significant implications. Here we note that the arguments Quine gives against the analytic/synthetic distinction, the "closed curve in space" we have explored, are not decisive arguments. Quine's strategy is rather to put the onus on those who want to rehabilitate the analytic/synthetic distinction. And this he does. His challenge was and remains this: If the analytic/synthetic distinction is to be maintained, then either the notion of meaning must be resuscitated and clearly enough explicated so as to provide grounds for deciding whether the "meaning" of one term is or is not included within that of another term (Kant's original notion); or the notion of cognitive synonymy must be explicated, without appealing to analyticity; or the notion of substitutivity *salva veritate* must be explicated, without appealing to contexts that presuppose analyticity but are strong enough to distinguish between coextensionality and synonymy. Since the publication of "Two Dogmas," Quine's critics have taken up this challenge, offering views of meaning or synonymy, or of modal operators such as 'necessarily', that purport to break the "closed curve in space." None, in our opinion, succeeds.

Finally, we return to Quine's claim (generally neglected in the literature) that the "two dogmas are . . . at root identical." If they are, then those who find verificationism implausible or unacceptable should take the same view toward the purported distinction between analytic and synthetic statements. Quine's argument to the effect that if verificationism can be defended, then so too can the analytic/synthetic distinction, is reasonably clear and has already been reviewed. Is there an implicit argument in the other direction?

Perhaps. If there is an analytic/synthetic distinction, then it makes sense to distinguish the role of linguistic convention and the role of extralinguistic fact in determining the truth or falsity of a given statement. Analytic statements are those in which "the linguistic component is all that matters." Synthetic statements are those whose truth values are not determined by the linguistic component alone. So if we are able to distinguish analytic statements from synthetic ones, then it must be that we are able to identify the factors that determine the truth values of the latter, their linguistic and nonlinguistic components, on a statement-by-statement basis. So for each synthetic statement we can identify the extralinguistic elements, the elements of experience, that are relevant to its truth or falsity. But then we are free to identify the meaning of the statement with those extralinguistic elements. And this is just what verificationism does. So, in this sense, verificationism does follow from the analytic/synthetic distinction, if one is prepared to identify meaning with the experiences relevant to a synthetic statement's truth or falsity. Traditional empiricists were ready to do this, but not all contemporary philosophers are traditional empiricists.

Holism

We have noted that holism is offered in "Two Dogmas" as a countersuggestion to the analytic/synthetic distinction and verificationism, dogmas Quine views as "at root identical."[10] There is, in this article, no full-blown argument for holism, no lengthy explication of it, and no exploration of how it transforms empiricism. Yet, holism is a substantial and significant doctrine. It argues for the tentativeness of all theories and beliefs, from the most abstract of logic and mathematics, and the most theoretical of the theoretical sciences, to the most down-to-earth, commonsense theories and beliefs. If it is correct, correspondence theories of truth go by the board and, with them, any possibility of construing empiricism as a theory of truth. Holism argues against the plausibility of "metalevel" theories of truth and for truth as immanent, à la Tarski. If there is a future for empiricism, it is as a theory of evidence: a theory about how the evidence provided by the senses serves as the basis for warranted beliefs and of how language does contribute to "meaning" but not in a way that can be isolated on a sentence-by-sentence basis. If holism holds, foundationalism also goes by the board; there are no Archimedean standpoints. We work, to paraphrase Quine, as scientists, laypersons, and philosophers, *from within*—from the vantage point of an evolving body of theory we inherit and seek to improve, on the basis of experiences significantly shaped by this very same body of theory. Working from within this theory, we indeed take the claims we find to be warranted to be true. But truth is immanent and the firmest of warrants is provisional (Quine 1981, 22).[11]

We begin our explication of holism by identifying two theses that are intertwined with it. The classic statement of holism, given in the last section of "Two Dogmas," begins:

> The totality of our so-called knowledge or beliefs, from the most casual matters of geography and history to the profoundest laws of atomic physics or even of pure mathematics and logic, is a man-made fabric which impinges on experience only along the edges. (42)

The first intertwined thesis is that all of science broadly construed is our own construction, and that even the apparently most disparate parts are, in fact, interconnected—hence Quine's metaphor of a fabric (and of a network, a field, and a web). The paragraph of "Two Dogmas" also notes:

> A conflict with experience at the periphery occasions readjustments in the interior of the field. Truth values have to be redistributed over some of our statements. Reëvaluation [*sic*] of some statements entails reëvaluation of others, because of their logical interconnections—the logical laws being in turn simply certain further statements of the system, certain further elements of the field. . . . But the total field is so underdetermined by its boundary conditions, experience, that there is much latitude of choice as to what statements to reëvaluate in the light of any single contrary experience. (42)

This is the second intertwined thesis of holism: that a recalcitrant experience can force an adjustment in the network of theories to which we are committed, to the totality of science. But such an experience cannot force a change of commitment to any particular belief or component sentence of science. This is because "No particular experiences are linked with any particular statements in the interior of the field, except indirectly through considerations of equilibrium affecting the field as a whole." This is the overarching thesis of holism: our theories of nature face experience as a collective body, not sentence by sentence, not even particular theory by particular theory. They do so because there is no one-to-one relationship between most sentences of this body and specific experiences. Thus, the thesis of holism is a consequence of taking the verification theory of meaning seriously—of taking seriously the thesis that a chunk of language has empirical meaning only if there are experiences that will confirm or disconfirm it. There are no such confirming or disconfirming experiences for most individual sentences. There are for sentences taken collectively, for bodies of theory, for our whole going theory of the world (for science broadly construed). So it is only sentences taken collectively—bodies of theory, or our whole going theory of the world—that have empirical meaning. Empirical meaning or content is spread across the sentences that together can be tested against experience. (Quine claims that some individual sentences—observation sentences and their kin as he defines them—do meet the verificationist test for empirical meaningfulness; these claims are not relevant to the present discussion.[12])

Thus, faced with recalcitrant experience or intertheoretic conflicts, we make decisions concerning which sentence or sentences of a theory to regard as vulnerable and which to hold firm. Theoretical virtues, such as conservatism, simplicity, fecundity, and so forth, figure in such decisions; but neither they nor experiments dictate a particular outcome. All of our theories, and all of our judgments concerning them, are tentative. How large or how all-embracing a network of sentences must be to have empirical content is not yet clear.

It is obvious that the empirical content of the more obviously esoteric sentences that figure in scientific theories and practice is a function of the broader body of theory in which those sentences are contained. Consider, for example,

> These chipped stones, found near fossil remains of *Australopithecus*, indicate tool use.
>
> Members of species tend to behave in ways that maximize their fitness.
>
> The vibrations of this spot of light on this celluloid ruler measure the electrical resistance of that coil. (Duhem 1991, 145)

Each sentence presupposes extensive and sophisticated bodies of theory. The first presupposes notions of fossils, a now-extinct species, and tools. It further presupposes a body of theory that makes it plausible to link chipped stones with tool making. The notion of "fitness" presupposed in the second is, of course, technical and varies by school of thought; the notion of "species" is also theoretical and has evolved a pace with developments in biology. In the case of the third sentence, it is a substantial body of theory that relates the spot of light to the electrical resistance of the coil. As Pierre Duhem (1991, 145) notes, if a novice asked the researcher undertaking this experiment what the relationship is between the electrical resistance of a coil and the phenomena perceived, it is likely the researcher would recommend that the novice take a course in electricity.

Substantial bodies of theory are also presupposed in scientific predictions. Consider:

> Tools used in conjunction with hunting or gathering will be found near fossil remains of *Australopithecus*.
>
> Female lions will display behaviors that will tend to increase the number of their genes replicated in the next generation.
>
> If an observer "plunges the metallic stem of a rod, mounted with rubber into small holes, the iron [will oscillate] and, by means of a mirror tied to it, [send] a beam of light over to a celluloid ruler." (Duhem 1991, 145)

Behind each prediction lies a substantial body of theory, as becomes obvious when we note that should one of the predictions not be borne out, we would need to make adjustments somewhere in the theory that yielded the prediction. But the failed prediction does not itself identify where the adjustments should be made. Indeed, the problem might not lie in the specific body of theory with which we associate the prediction. As his references to "the totality of our so-called knowledge and beliefs" indicate, Quine holds that empirical content is shared more broadly than our assumptions about boundaries separating the sciences from one another, or from common sense, would suggest. In *Word and Object*, for example, Quine notes:

> Theory may be deliberate, as in a chapter on chemistry, or it may be second nature, as is the immemorial doctrine of ordinary enduring middle-sized objects. In either case, theory causes a sharing, by sentences, of sensory supports. In an arch, the overhead block is supported immediately by other overhead blocks, and ultimately by all the base blocks collectively and none individually; and so it is with sentences, when theoretically fitted. (1960, 11)

We can also get a sense of the content of the interdependence reflected in Quine's use of an arch metaphor by considering the structure he attributes to the network of theories we maintain. There are sentences "deeply embedded" in the network (in the "interior" in the sense both that they are furthest from the periphery of experience and that they are interwoven through other theories), sentences "closest to the periphery" of experience, and a host of sentences in between. The characterization of holism that appears in "Two Dogmas" and that just cited from *Word and Object* suggest the view that the more embedded a sentence is, the more its relationship to specific stimulus conditions is a function of (is mediated by) other sentences.

Quine's discussion in "Posits and Reality" of what he called "the molecular doctrine" pulls together the foregoing points. The essay was written before the development of technologies that enable observations of molecules. In this sense, but only in this sense, is Quine's discussion dated. What he says about the nature of the evidence that supports theories that posit molecules is also generalized to the evidence for all theories, including those of logic and mathematics.

> According to physics, my desk is, for all its seeming fixity and solidity, a swarm of vibrating molecules... no glimpse is to be had of the separate molecules of the desk; they are, we are told, too small.
>
> Lacking such experience, what evidence can the physicist muster for his doctrine of molecules? His answer is that there is a convergence of indirect evidence, drawn from such varied phenomena as expansion, heat conduction, capillary attraction, and surface tension. The point is that these miscellaneous phenomena can, if we assume the molecular theory, be marshaled under the familiar laws of motion. . . . [A]ny defense of [the molecular doctrine] has to do . . . with its indirect bearing on observable reality. The doctrine has this indirect bearing by being the core of an integrated physical theory which implies truths about expansion, conduction, and so on. (1966a, 233–235)

On the one hand, theories that posit molecules (or other physical particles too small to directly observe) provide systematic explanations of a wide range of phenomena, including common-sense phenomena. This, together with other virtues of the doctrine of molecules (e.g., simplicity, familiarity of principle, and scope), is among the benefits of adopting the theory. On the other hand, what warrants such theories (i.e., what constitutes evidence for them) is their ability to link sensory stimulations to sensory stimulations. This criterion applies to all theories.

> Having noticed that man has no evidence for the existence of bodies beyond the fact that their assumption helps him to organize experience, we should [do] well, instead of disclaiming evidence for the existence of bodies, to conclude: such, then, at bottom, is what evidence is, both for ordinary bodies and for molecules. (238)

Despite Quine's mention of "ordinary bodies," it might seem that although clearly theoretical sentences have empirical meaning only as part of broader bodies of theories (as holism asserts), this is not so for more mundane sentences—such as 'The mail carrier will come again tomorrow' or 'There is an apple on the counter'. But Quine points out that there is also a substantial body of theory lying behind claims such as these. Commonsense sentences about bodies presuppose physical object theory, according to which there are middle-sized objects (such that we say "Here's an apple," rather than "It's apple-ing"), of which apples are examples (but "red" and "on" are not). To learn physical object theory is to learn that apples and lots of other things are discrete objects (unlike snow which is scattered about in blankets or drifts), and we learn this theory as we learn language and master the principles of individuation (as we learn 'a', 'the', 'an', etc.). Such principles, together with the notion (also part of physical object theory) that middle-sized objects are relatively enduring, makes it possible to wonder, to paraphrase Quine, if the apple on the counter is the one noticed yesterday.

We have only begun to explore what such relatively simple sentences as 'There is an apple on the counter' presuppose (consider, e.g., the "is" of predication and the predicate 'is on the counter'). But perhaps what we have said is sufficient to understand what Quine is urging. Even if we learn this particular sentence by mimicry, we do not learn every sentence this way. The child who masters this sentence will eventually be able to come up with 'My doll is on the table' and 'My doll is *not* on the table', never having heard either sentence. At this point, we say that she or he 'has caught on' to at least some of our most basic *theory* of the world concomitantly with catching on to our theory of language.

This same body of theory, which tells us what to expect by way of the behavior of various kinds of objects, can yield the prediction "If no one has eaten it, this apple will still be on the counter in the morning." "Seeing a body *again*," Quine (1987) notes, "means to us that it or we or our glance has returned from a round trip in the course of which the body was out of sight" (204; emphasis added). The notion of 'seeing again' requires a sophisticated notion of "the corporeality of things" (204).

It is an implication of Quine's arguments against the analytic/synthetic distinction, and those just summarized for holism, that most sentences—of the obviously empirical sciences, of common sense, and of logic and mathematics—have empirical content only as part of broader bodies of theory and that it is such broader bodies that yield predictions. How extensive a portion of our currently maintained theories need we consider in making a judgment about any particular hypothesis or claim? Much more, of course, than just the hypothesis or claim in question. But normally, Quine maintains, we do not need to consider the whole of a going theory of nature to adjudicate some specific hypothesis or theory. Rather, he suggests that what he terms a "moderate or relative holism" will generally suffice (1960, 13). "What is important," Quine suggests in "Five Milestones of Empiricism," "is that we cease to demand or expect of a scientific sentence that it have its own separable empirical meaning" (71).

We noted earlier that holism argues for the tentativeness of all of our theories and theorizing, and it is by now clear how it does so. Lacking an algorithm or formula for determining what sentence or sentences some set of observations confirms or falsifies, there is no place for dogmatism. A further implication of Quine arguments for holism is that we have no "unmediated access" to the world around us. We work within a network of theories we inherit, and do our part to contribute to them. And this network itself is connected multifariously to experience, directly confronting it only at the edges.

We also noted that, if holism is correct, correspondence theories of truth go by the board. Again, the reasons why are now obvious. If holism is correct, then we are not in a position to relate most sentences, taken individually, to stimulus conditions that would verify them, and correspondence theories presuppose a dichotomy between theories and the world, or language and the world. The only relationship reasonably explored is that between systems of sentences and the triggerings of our sensory receptors, a relationship that more appropriately underwrites the notion of warranted belief than it does the notion of truth.

Conclusion

We devote our concluding remarks to a brief consideration of issues that are a matter of some debate in the biological sciences and are understood by some to call for (or at least to suggest the need for) rethinking aspects of widely held views about the logical form of mature scientific theories.

Many philosophers of science, including Quine, hold that first-order quantification will constitute the canonical notation of an overall theory of nature. In *Word and Object*, Quine argues that by current lights, our "most serious" and inclusive theory of nature will be able to formalized in first order logic.

> Taking the canonical notation thus austerely . . . we have just these basic constructions: predication, universal quantification, and the truth functions. . . . What . . . confronts us as a scheme for systems of the world is that structure so well understood by present day logicians, the logic of quantification of calculus of predicates. . . .
>
> Not that the idioms thus renounced are supposed to be unneeded in the market place or the laboratory. . . . The doctrine is only that such a canonical idiom can be abstracted and then adhered to in the statement of one's scientific theory. *The doctrine is that traits of reality worthy of the name can be set down in an idiom of this austere form if in any idiom.* (1960, 228; emphasis added)

We have elsewhere argued that Quine does not have any particular universe of discourse or domain in mind for an overall theory of nature.[13] And, in the passage just cited, Quine notes that recognizing first-order quantification as the canonical form of an overall theory of nature just settles "the logic" of the theory, not the sentences it counts as true.

Consider, then, recent debates within biology about whether the emphasis on discrete objects and their discrete effects, an emphasis that seemed appropriate to classical physics, is an appropriate emphasis in the biological sciences. In recent years, some biologists, including some prominent feminists, have argued that, in these respects, physics is not a good model for structuring biological explanations and models. For example, Ruth Bleier, Ruth Hubbard, and Evelyn Fox Keller all criticize models of cellular protein synthesis that assume or posit "discrete genes" and their "discrete effects," on the grounds that such models obscure the actual complexities of the biological processes involved.

Concerning such models, Bleier (1984) maintains:

> Not only can a complex behavior pattern or a characteristic not be linked to a gene or a gene cluster, there is not even any single cause and effect relationship between a particular gene and a particular anatomical feature. . . . Any gene's action or expression is affected, first of all, by its interactions with many other genes . . . [and] occurs only within an environmental milieu and [is] affected by it. (43)

Hubbard (1982) also argues for less linear and more complex models: "Genes (DNA) impart specificity, but so do other molecules (e.g., RNA, proteins, and even carbohydrates and lipids), and so do many processes that occur within organisms and in the interactions in which organisms engage with their environments" (65). Finally, Keller (1985, 132) offers a more general argument that a biology characterized by an emphasis on "order" (not exclusively on "lawlike" relationships), rather than physics, should serve as a model for all serious science.

If these theorists are correct about the nature of biological processes, then it may be that first-order quantification will prove inadequate for the canonical form of scientific theories, or at least for biology. If this is so, it may be that finding an adequate formal system to express the claims of biology (at least as these theorists and others envision it) requires abandoning or modifying some presently held principles of logic. We emphasize that this *may* be the case. Whether Keller, Hubbard, and Bleier are correct about the nature of biology and biological processes is still an open question. So, too, if they are correct, it remains an open question whether finding an adequate vehicle for expressing the claims of biology will require abandoning or modifying presently accepted principles of logic, rather than merely rejecting first-order quantification theory in favor of some alternative system of logic that is itself consistent with presently accepted principles of logic.

Although brief, our consideration of the possible implications of debates in biology and the philosophy of biology for logic serves to reemphasize what we take to be the more significant consequences of those of Quine's arguments we have considered. These include that logic is an empirical enterprise, and thus not immune to revision, but also that, given the interweaving of logic throughout our largest theory of nature, any such revisions will emerge concomitantly with developments in other empirical sciences.

Notes

We are grateful to Marjorie Hass and Rachel Joffe Falmagne for their invitation to contribute to this volume, their patience, and their suggestions and also to Paul Roth and Gary Thrane for their suggestions. With the exception of the introductory material and conclusion, this discussion is largely excerpted (with minor revisions) from Nelson and Nelson (2000). Thanks, as well, to Dan Kolak, editor of the series in which this monograph appeared, for permission to reprint parts of this work.

1. We emphasize science for two reasons. The first is because Quine emphasizes science and we are concerned to explicate his arguments; that said, it is arguable that Quine uses the term narrowly in some contexts and broadly in others so that it denotes, in addition to the sciences "proper," at least commonsense theorizing about physical objects and subdisciplines within philosophy (e.g., naturalized epistemology and philosophy of science, and formal logic). We also emphasize science (in the narrow sense) because we think, for reasons to become clear in the larger discussion that should revisions in logic be called for, it will be due to developments in other empirical sciences.

2. Indeed, in his own later work Quine does provide limited versions of the analytic/synthetic distinction and of synonymy, but these apply only to Quinean observation sentences and their kin (see, e.g., Quine 1990, 17).

3. The substance of Gödel's result is, in Quine's words, that no deductive system, with axioms however arbitrary, is capable of embracing among its theorems all the truths of the elementary arithmetic of positive integers unless it discredits itself by letting slip some of the falsehoods, too. Gödel showed how, for any given deductive system, he could construct a sentence of elementary number theory that would be true if and only if not provable in that system (Quine 1966b, 18–19).

4. Readers may notice a tension here. Science is by its very nature public, an enterprise conducted within a community of investigators sharing (or disputing) assumptions, techniques, and theories. Sensory experience is, again by its very nature, private, perhaps even incommunicable. The attempt to reduce science to, or replace it with, claims about sense experience is, therefore, on the face of it implausible if not a nonstarter. We take it to be part of Quine's major contribution to philosophy of science and epistemology that he not only saw this tension but also took as his challenge the relating of science to sense experience while not abandoning the public for the private, the communicable and testable for the unstructured and incommunicable fleeting present of sensory experience. Whether he succeeded in bridging the tension remains controversial. See, for example, "Empiricism Reconstituted" in Nelson and Nelson (2000).

5. It first appeared in 1951, in *Philosophical Review.*

6. Quine's target in "Two Dogmas" is verificationism as promulgated by the members of the Vienna Circle. He is attacking the view that individual sentences have empirical content, and that this content is "the method of empirically confirming or infirming" them. His own view, explicated in the next section, is that most individual sentences have empirical content or meaning only to the extent that they are parts of larger theories or chunks of theories that can be tested against experience. That is, he maintains that verificationism works as a theory of meaning of larger linguistic units—whole theories or significant chunks thereof—and also for a special class of sentences (observation sentences and their kin) that will not concern us here. But see also Nelson and Nelson (2000).

7. Quine does grant that there is "an extreme sort of definition which does not hark back to prior synonymies at all: namely, the explicitly conventional introduction of novel notations for the purposes of sheer abbreviation" (26). An example is when a logician introduces the expression 'iff' as an abbreviation for 'if and only if'. Although this is "a really transparent case of synonymy created by definition," it is clear that such cases of synonymy cannot save the notion of analyticity. Not every analytic truth that is not a logical truth can be turned into a logical truth by appeal to an explicitly conventional introduction of a synonymous term. See also "Truth by Convention" where Quine argues against the plausibility of the view that mathematics and logic are true by convention.

8. We have omitted portions of Quine's arguments specifically directed at Carnap's defenses of the analytic/synthetic distinction. Of some historical interest, they are not central to Quine's basic argument.

9. See n. 4. Indeed, we maintain that Quine does not abandon the verification theory of meaning and, indeed, that its assumption is key to his arguments for indeterminacy of translation. See Nelson and Nelson (2000).

10. Although we here explore the classic statement of Quine's holism as it occurs in "Two Dogmas," it is worth noting that there are precursors to it in Quine's earlier writings. In "Truth by Convention," Quine argues that conventional definitions do not really establish a separate kind of truth—'truth by convention'. Of "the apparent contrast between logicomathematical truths and others," Quine (1966b) notes:

> Viewed behavioristically and without reference to a metaphysical system, this contrast retains reality as a contrast between more and less firmly accepted statements. . . . There are statements which we choose to surrender last, if at all, in the course of revamping our sciences in the face of new discoveries; and among these there are some we will not surrender at all, so basic are they to our whole conceptual scheme. Among the latter are to be counted the so-called truths of logic and mathematics, regardless of what further we may have to say of their status in the course of a subsequent sophisticated philosophy. (95)

11. See also Nelson (1995) for an extended discussion of more general implications of holism for feminist science scholarship.

12. See Nelson and Nelson (2000, chaps. 2, 4, 5, and 7).

13. See Nelson and Nelson (2000, 54–69).

References

Ayer, A. J. *Language, Truth, and Logic*. New York: Dover, 1946.

Bleier, Ruth. *Science and Gender: A Critique of Biology and Its Theories on Women*. New York: Pergamon, 1984.

Duhem, Pierre. *The Aim and Structure of Physical Theory*, trans. P. P. Wiener. Princeton, N.J.: Princeton University Press, 1991. (Originally published 1954.)

Hubbard, Ruth. "Have Only Men Evolved?" In *Biological Woman: The Convenient Myth*, ed. Ruth Hubbard et al. Cambridge, Mass.: Schenkman, 1982.

Keller, Evelyn Fox. *Reflections on Gender and Science*. New Haven, Conn.: Yale University Press, 1985.

Nelson, Lynn Hankinson. "Feminist Naturalized Philosophy of Science." *Synthese* 104, no. 3 (1995).

Nelson, Lynn Hankinson, and Jack Nelson. *On Quine*. Belmont, Calif.: Wadsworth, 2000.

Quine, W. V. "Posits and Reality." In *The Ways of Paradox and Other Essays*. New York: Random House, 1966a.

———. "Truth by Convention." In *The Ways of Paradox and Other Essays*. New York: Random House, 1966b. (Originally published 1936.)

———. *Pursuit of Truth*. Cambridge, Mass.: Harvard University Press, 1990.

———. *Quiddities: An Intermittently Philosophical Dictionary*. Cambridge, Mass.: Harvard University Press, 1987.

———. "Things and Their Place in Theories." In *Theories and Things*. Cambridge, Mass.: Harvard University Press, 1981.

———. "Two Dogmas of Empiricism." In *From a Logical Point of View*, 2d ed. New York: Harper & Row, 1963.

———. *Word and Object*. Cambridge, Mass.: MIT Press, 1960.

CHAPTER EIGHT

~

Saying What It Is: Predicate Logic and Natural Kinds

ANDREA NYE

Along with generational differences between successive "waves" of feminism and political differences between various ideological versions of feminism, there is another maturing process characteristic of feminist philosophy. In a movement away from sectarian controversy and away from narrow focus on the victimization or the vindication of women, feminist philosophers have found that the questions they raise about women's condition engage not only social theory but deeper issues of meaning and existence. Feminist philosophy in this mode becomes not just philosophy of women or of gender but philosophy itself, as new paradigms of philosophical inquiry develop that better represent understanding free of androcentric bias. The point of such a philosophy is not to give a reading of knowledge or meaning advantageous to women, or even "from a woman's point of view," but to develop epistemologies, metaphysics, and ethics in new "feminist voices" (Kourany 1998). Much recent feminist philosophy has been critical, concentrated on ways in which androcentric or masculinist prejudice supposedly taints or distorts existing theory. Much recent feminist philosophy has been defensive, explaining and defending women's perspectives. Feminist philosophy in a constructive mode goes even further, to analyze deep structures of thought that generate self-consistent but distorted views of the natural world and explore alternative paradigms for naming and engaging with reality.

Perhaps no area of philosophy has remained more resolutely barricaded against any such feminist invasion of "philosophy proper" than logic, but it is in the above spirit of feminist reconstruction that I raise the following questions about predication. My aim is not to expose current philosophical logic as sexist or to suggest a "woman's way" of reasoning. Nor is my aim to solve logical puzzles as generated within current logical paradigms. Instead, I hope to show that biologists' struggle with predications that group individual organisms into species and species into higher taxa is not well represented in terms of the currently dominant predicate logic developed by men like Gottlob Frege and Alfred Tarski and, more currently, Willard Quine and Donald Davidson. To go one speculative step further, I express doubt whether presuppositions of the "mathematical" approach to logic advance understanding of scientific debates about the nature of species.

Some of the earliest feminist voices in logic addressed the question of the identification of individuals. Jaakko Hintikka and Merrill Hintikka's (1983) paper "How Can Language Be Sexist?" suggested that the currently accepted extensional view of meaning—the view that the meaning of a concept is the "extension" of that concept—represents only one way to understand how individual things are named and characterized in language. In this chapter, I continue their line of thought. When the identification of the objects of science is taken for granted, and consequently when the set inclusion of those objects is also taken for granted (i.e., an individual either is or is not a member of a set), the nature and purpose of science may be misrepresented. Science becomes holistic and self-consistent rather than critically assessable engagement with reality.

The principle of noncontradiction, often thought to be the foundation of logic, is relatively superficial in contrast to the principle of predication, to saying what things are. It is in primary moments of engagement between speaker and reality that any truth must be rooted. Predications, the fruit of those engagements prior to logical inference, provide substance on which logical principles operate. Without predication there is nothing to be true or false, nothing to be consistent or inconsistent, contradictory or coherent. But the essential act of observing or stating that something is such-and-such or has such-and-such has occupied little attention in mainstream philosophy of logic. Although logicians can claim success in solving technical problems in set theory or modal logic, predication remains something of a mystery. Predication, however, is of primary interest in a feminist approach to logic in the aforementioned sense of involvement and engagement with reality.

No matter how propositions are combined, no matter how inferences from one proposition to another are warranted, to have a proposition in the first place requires that words be put together in a way that says something about something. No truth or inference can be established without that primal combination of terms, as was first noted by Socrates. Not all words go together to say something, he explains to Theaetetus in the *Sophist*. Saying something is not just stringing words together in succession but requires a fitting together of two kinds of words, names and predicates.

> [W]hen "lion," "stag," "horse," are spoken and all the other names of things that do those actions are uttered, such a string of words does not amount to saying anything. For in neither case do the words uttered indicate the action or the inaction of anything existing or not existing, not until verbs are mixed with names. Then the words fit and say something, which is simply the first combination and really the first and simplest of things that can be said.[1]

Thaeatetus's perplexity as Socrates tries to elucidate this mysterious "fit" has not been dispelled.

How disturbing the mystery of predication can seem to logicians is seen in an article by Peter Geach (1968). Aristotle, Geach charges, strayed from an "initial" current insight into predication to initiate "a disaster" "comparable only to the Fall of Adam" (47). Like Adam, "traditional" logicians that followed Aristotle were guilty of "depravity" that plunged logic into a "long degeneration" relieved only by occasional bouts of "repressed logical conscience" (50). Only when Frege and Russell replanted a fertile seed of logical precision was the crude simplicity of the "Egyptian or Cimmerian darkness" into which logic was plunged somewhat redeemed (59). The sin, according to Geach, is to get predication wrong. Aristotle reduced the difference between subject and predicate, making two kinds of terms interchangeable. In one form of the syllogism, a middle term is used twice, once as subject and again as predicate. Not only does this leveling of difference between subject name and predicate name create the possibility that a term can be predicated of itself threatening semantic paradox. More important, said Geach, it gets ontology all wrong. The world is not made up of one kind of thing but two kinds of things: individuals and sets into which individuals are gathered.

The source of the ontological orthodoxy that made the Aristotelian view of predication heresy for Geach is, of course, current mathematical logic. Frege's achievement as one of the founders of this logic was to give an account of predication free of any taint of Aristotelian travesty. To say something is something is not to assert similarity between two objects or two forms. What allows something to be said about something is asymmetry between logical subject and predicate, an asymmetry that for logical purposes, Frege argues, can be understood in mathematical terms. Just as a mathematical function is different from a quantity or argument substituted in its variable spaces, so a linguistic predicate is different from the various items of which it is true or false. The logical subject of a predicative sentence is an argument plugged into a concept. When a mathematical function is paired with a numerical argument a numerical value results, when a conceptual function is paired with an object argument, a truth value—the sentence is either true or false—results. A concept or predicate correlates object arguments with truth values the same way a mathematical function correlates number arguments with numerical values.[2]

One problem with this current mathematical interpretation of predication is its apparent superficiality. In the Aristotelian scheme of things, real forms or essences are presumably available to mark criteria for deciding whether an individual "instantiates" or "partakes of" a form. The criteria for whether an object falls under a concept—in Fregean terms, for whether a function yields the value true for a specific argument—is not so clear. In mathematics proper, numbers have numerical characteristics by virtue of which they are gathered into sets. The "value range" of a linguistic concept (the class or set of objects for which a concept yields the value true) can seem to be a shifting shadow whose sharp edges are reliably sketched only by logical fiat. In mathematics, sets with the same extension can, for the most part, be taken as equivalent regardless of how those individuals are specified without causing much difficulty.[3] In linguistic contexts, concepts that indicate the same set of individuals do not always have the same meaning. As Frege (1970) explains the problem in "Sense and Reference," the value ranges of concepts can have the same members (yield the value true for the same arguments) but the term that stands for them not be substitutable in every sentence. "Animal with hearts" may have the same members as "animal with kidneys," but a person might believe a man has a heart and not believe a man has a kidney. To address this problem, Frege retains a vestige of Aristotelian essence in the form of the "sense" of a concept. A sense, says Frege, is the way we pick out a set of objects, and the same set of objects may be identified by different senses.

Decades earlier, Alfred Tarksi (1944) is credited with finally eliminating the last vestige of Aristotelian sin by devising an explanation of predicative generality with no embarrassing regress to extralogical senses or meanings. He uses the notion of "satisfaction." The open sentence "*x* is a rose" is satisfied by a given plant if that plant is a rose. More specifically, the open sentence is satisfied by a function that maps the variable unto the entities over which the variable ranges—in this case plants—so that the sentence is true. "*x* is a rose" is satisfied by just those plants of which "rose" is truly predicated. Satisfaction occurs for a closed sentence without variables ("the plants in your garden are roses") when the objects to which the subject of the sentence refers correlate with some of the objects mapped by the function that satisfies the open sentence, when, in other words, they are some of the objects that make up the "value range" of the concept which the predicate designates (the set of objects of which the concept is true). Although Tarski's formula is for formal languages with finite vocabularies and defined conditions for satisfaction, philosophers such as Donald Davidson claim his analysis for the logic of natural language.

If the use of singular terms or phrases such as proper names or "this plant right here" might seem to introduce a reference to physical fact that cannot be accommodated as satisfaction, some philosophers have gone on to show that for logical purposes, singular terms might be eliminated. Quine, drawing on Russell's theory of descriptions, substitutes a combination of variables and predicates for singular terms. To say that a given individual did something or has some property is to say that someone—someone who has certain identifying characteristics and is the only one with such characteristics—did something or has some property.[4] In the end, Quine argues, all that is needed are Frege's open sentences, quantified formulas, into which lists of objects can be substituted, objects designated by the concepts. The result is Quine's famous "ontological relativity." Depending on choice of concepts and theory, the world has in it different objects; theory itself can only be evaluated holistically according to its consistency, simplicity, and by how well it serves human needs themselves understood within theoretical restraints.

When singular terms are eliminated, it seems as if all that is left are, if not essences, then sets: in the simplest of sentences a set specified as having a single member in the subject place and a set marked by the predicate that may or may not include the single member of the subject set. In fact, says Strawson (1967), even for Quine, the asymmetry in grammatical form between subject and predicate remains in the background. Quine hopes that with a canonical notation "the general program [of logic] can proceed without the intelligibility of its whole apparatus of theoretical notions appearing to rest on our grasp of the functioning of these definite singular terms" (80). But, Strawson insists, to make it clear why the paraphrases that stand in for singular terms cannot themselves be put in predicate position, the original distinction between subject and predicate, and between individual and class, is necessary. Sets can be subjects of sentences only by analogy.

Philosophers such as Saul Kripke have gone even farther to preserve predicative reference. Problems of reference to individuals do not go away when you substitute descriptions for proper names, Kripke (1980) says. If you no longer have to determine the reference of a name, you have to determine what is the rigidly designated "extension" of a name (29n). Furthermore, some supposed predicates indicate extensions which are rigidly designated.

Natural kinds, such as species, Kripke argues, are identified in original ostensive baptisms and indicated with a continuity that establishes stable subjects for scientific theory. On this view, "Rosa rugosa" is not an open-ended class category but a subject whose real nature will be determined by science. But without a way to identify the subjects of science independent of theory, Kripke's real essences become articles of simple faith: faith that the theories of science are about real objects. No object can be indicated without a predicate, no individual plant without indicating a "plant," no plant species without indicating a group of "organisms"; but for Kripke, what is a plant, a species, an organism, is determined by what science claims is a plant, a species, or an organism.

No matter what elaborate technical devices are used, essential and irreducible and at the heart of logic remains a primal combination of terms, terms that indicate a spatiotemporal entity and terms that say something about that entity. The person who perhaps best expresses the stubborn irreducibility of predication is Davidson, staunch defender of Tarskian truth theory. Davidson (1984) comments:

> [A]n absolute theory of truth [such as Tarski's] doesn't really illuminate the relation of satisfaction. In Tarski's method satisfaction is a relation between predicates and entities of which the predicates are true. The problem is that Tarskian truth theory does not tell us what satisfaction is, it says only that an entity satisfies 'x flies' if and only if that entity flies. If we ask for a further explanation or analysis of the relation, we will be disappointed. (217)

If one simply adds a new predicate, Davidson goes on, one would not know "*how to go on to the next case*" [Davidson's italics].

> For the definition . . . will explicitly limit the application of satisfaction to a fixed finite list of predicates (and compounds of them). So if a theory (or definition) of satisfaction applies to a given language and then a new predicate, say "x flies" is added, it will follow that 'x flies' is not satisfied by an object that flies—or by anything else. (217)

Tarski's truth theory, Davidson explains, is not meant to explain reference or even truth, but only "reveals how the truth of every sentence of a particular [language] depends on its structure and constituents," where language means a language with a given and finite vocabulary. But Davidson argued, this is not a significant difficulty (218–219). The truth of propositions can be assured without reference and without defining satisfaction. What corresponds to reality are not terms that directly indicate individuals or properties and not atomic sentences that correspond to fact. A perfectly good interpretation of correspondence to reality can be given in terms of "satisfaction." To say a sentence is true or corresponds to the facts is to say that a sentence is satisfied by a function (a sequence of objects, or ordered or unordered pairs of objects). For closed sentences without free variables, Davidson argues, this definition comes closest to our commonsense view of correspondence. John loves Mary is satisfied by John and Mary. Either every possible ordered pairing we can make of individuals satisfies and the sentence is true, or none do and the sentence is false. "Closed" sentences—sentences without variables—have no priority based on observation or ostension but are derived as instances from appropriate open sentences. In other words, language must be understood and evaluated holistically. Theory comes first and particular predications are derived from theory, according to how well a theory works for human purposes (47–49, 222).

But is it a rose? And does it smell as sweet? How does a botanist, for example, determine the species of a newly discovered plant or a zoologist distinguish various related species of animal? Does she simply apply the current botanical or zoological nomenclature as best she can? Does she put the plant or animal into whatever scheme seems most convenient according to her, or her employer's, interests? Although the avowed and fervent commitment of contemporary logicians such as Quine and Davidson is to science as the only truth, their actual interest in the history of botanical or zoological predication is minimal. When the issue of predication comes up, it comes up in the context of solving problems in philosophy not science. Quine (1969), for example, in his discussion of "Natural Kinds," begins not with the extensive debates in past and current biology about the identification of species and genera but with logical puzzles popular at philosophy conferences, such as the odd and paradoxical category "grue" invented by the philosopher Nelson Goodman (114–115).[5]

From his conclusion as he insists on the irreducible distinction between subject and predicate, it seems that Strawson is motivated not by problems in science but by well-worn philosophical controversies between Platonists and nominalists.[6] Similarly, Kripke came to the rigid designation of "gold" or "tigers" not from interest in chemistry or biology but from problems of identity across the possible worlds of modal logic, worlds that are themselves projections of philosophical concepts of necessity and contingency. The examples of natural kind identification and misidentification that Kripke cites are fictional, invented to illustrate philosophical points and unlikely to occur in any actual scientific context. "Suppose the explorers who attributed these properties [four-leggedness] to tigers were deceived by an optical illusion and that the animals they saw were from a three-legged species, would we say that there turned out to be no tigers after all?" "Suppose we discover an animal which, though having all the external appearances of a tiger, . . . has an internal structure completely different from that of a tiger. . . . Let's say they were in fact very peculiar looking reptiles" (1972, 120). In addition to the wildly counterfactual nature of these examples, Kripke's confident answers—the three-legged tiger is a tiger; the reptilian tiger is not a tiger—depend on assumptions about the nature of species in dispute among biologists.

Whether a species is a lineage, a genetic pool, an internal structure, or something else, has been debated throughout the last several centuries, in the midst of controversy that has deep historical roots in the early modern period. In the seventeenth and eighteenth centuries, Europe saw a deluge of specimens of new and unknown organisms collected by naturalists and travelers in newly discovered colonized territories. If by the terms of set-theoretic or truth-theoretic standard logic nothing true could be said about these new objects, as is claimed by Davidson, that logic was not respected by practicing biologists. Nor were they content to simply build new theoretical constructs to serve their, or their patron's, human needs and interests. Instead the identification and naming of new organisms was the occasion for profound questioning of the relation between knowledge and natural diversity, and further of the origins and meaning of life itself.

Putting together new subjects and predicates was an important part of that questioning. Individual things are not irreducibly diverse. If they were, names would be the only language and theorizing would be impossible. A rose is a flowering plant not an accidental chunk of matter, a tiger is a body plan and a dynamic organic system not a chance aggregate of parts. The fact that in nature there are similarities and analogous structures accessible to careful and methodical observation makes science possible. Repeating forms and processes make up the expanding predicative subject matter of natural science. The seminal insight of Aristotelian logic—the intuitive observation that an individual substance "is something"—inspired an intense and productive outpouring of scientific energy in the early modern period as new specimens were collected and examined. Whatever mathematical logical sin might seem to have been committed, far from impeding and restricting botanical science, traditional class logic descended from Aristotle fostered a fertile and energetic mix of theorizing about the plants and animals that arrived in Europe by the shipload to be catalogued and studied in natural history collections and herbaria. Linnaeus, often accused of retrograde commitment to classical logic, devised a remarkable perspicacious and flexible system of plant taxonomy based on flowering parts, a system that he constantly revised and changed in the light of new plant varieties and which he subjected to ongoing questioning as he observed processes of reproduction, development, and hybridization. Antoine Laurent de Jussieu with his clusters of defining characteristics, Georges Cuvier with his tables of functional body plans for natural genera and orders, Geoffrey St. Hiliare with his insight into formal organic structure, and many others researched successfully under the broad banner of finding the essences of living things. Immanuel Kant, maligned by both mathematical logicians for a naive adherence to traditional logic and by evolutionists for his claim that mechanistic explanations were insufficient in biology, reviewed in his *Critique of Judgement* the great variety of theses about the nature and the history of life current at the end of the eighteenth century.[7] Individual organisms, it was now clear, were too diverse to be lined up and gathered into groups in any facile way. Old taxa defined by specified value ranges or lists of members were inevitably unsettled and redefined with the discovery and study of new objects. Subject and predicate categories were in constant dialogue, predicates stretched, distorted, reworked to accommodate new observations and findings, individuals redescribed in terms of new predicates.

From the standpoint of the current mathematical logic, this struggle to establish natural kinds, although it might seem "fundamental to our thinking," is alien to logic. As Quine (1969) puts it, the diversity of species theorizing was due to the poorly developed state of biological thought in the eighteenth and nineteenth centuries: "It is a mark of the maturity of a branch of science that the notion of similarity or kind finally dissolves so far as it is relevant to that branch of knowledge. That is it ultimately submits to analysis in the special terms of that branch of science and logic" (121). Natural kind talk, based on some innate spacing of stimulations, as well as animal expectation or habit formation, may be useful for children learning language (125). It may be useful for the undeveloped naturalist who has not yet progressed to proper quantitative method, but it is "logically repugnant" (116). "We are baffled when we try to relate the general notion of similarity significantly to logical terms" (117). In set theory, things go into sets in any and every combination; things can be the joint members of many sets. If natural kinds seem a special kind of set central to inductive reasoning and prediction, in fact, "the very life of science," that only means that science is "rotten" at the core. No, insists Quine, the "muddy savagery" (134) of the "animal" sense of kind may have its use in more primitive times; but as knowledge matures we "rise from savagery" (135) to devise "lusty" (136) set-theoretic concepts that express functional mechanisms.

In biology, Quine argues, liberation from "savagery" came with the theory of evolution.[8] This allowed biologists finally to identify natural kinds properly and logically according to the proximity and frequency of common ancestors, or eventually perhaps by quantitative genetic analysis. Quine (1969) gives an elucidating example from psychology. We may no longer need to measure and theorize about intelligence in the primitive terms of natural kinds either, but we will be able to provide set-theoretic analyses in terms of proteins, colloids, nerve nets, or quantifiable overt behaviors (138).[9] The problem of biological species, Quine assumes, will be settled when species are defined similarly precisely in terms of specific stimulations. "In this way, on many fronts, man continues his rise from savagery, sloughing off the muddy old notion of kind of similarity piecemeal, a vestige here and a vestige there" (135).

The past may always be accused of savagery, but even current debates in the biology of natural kinds do not bear out Quine's optimistic sense of ongoing progress with the "lusty" logic of quantification theory. Problems in species identification and species formation have not dissolved. If anything, problems surrounding natural kinds are more complex, perplexing, and momentous than they were in the nineteenth century. Competing ways of thinking about species continue to suggest different answers to new and pressing questions in bioethics currently related to genetic therapies, cloning, and techniques of animal and plant husbandry. How we conceptualize natural kinds affects our sense of what it is to be animate and alive, what is the relation between humans and other organisms. If organic individuals have not settled into sets that render them clearly useful to human interests, it is not only because human interests can be variously theorized. More important are the questions generated about the meaning and purpose of life when biologists grapple with the original predications that are the propositional substance of science.

Nevertheless among nonfeminist philosophers of science, problems surrounding natural kinds continue to be posed in terms of the prevailing mathematical logic. Natural kinds are either individual things or they are sets of individual things; the problem is to decide which. One defender of the view that they are sets is Philip Kitcher (1984). In mathematical logic, argues Kitcher, sets of the same numbers can be composed in an endless variety of ways. In the same way, individual organisms can be grouped in different ways depending on the kind of explanation one wants to give of biological phenomenon. As he puts it, "Natural kinds are the sets that one picks out in giving explanations. They are the sets corresponding to predicates that figure in explanatory schemes" (315, n. 10). If one wants to theorize about interbreeding populations, then a biological species concept based on reproductive isolation is useful; if one wants to study biological lineages, then a species concept based on descent is useful. If one wants to study certain problems in paleontology where descent and reproductive isolation are unknown, then a morphological concept works better. Set pluralism is beneficial. It diffuses disputes. If, for example, a fossil record without intermediate forms between species that would support gradual evolution seems to be a problem, one can argue that external form is only one way to sort out natural kinds. Kitcher, consistent with Quine's ontological relativity, acknowledges "that our objective interests may be diverse, that we may be objectively correct in pursuing biological inquiries which demand different forms of explanation, so that the patterning of nature generated in different areas of biology may cross-classify the constituents of nature" (330). What there are in the world are objects over which the variables of a theory range. There is no way to test theory at the level of ontology; the question must be whether or not it serves our purposes.

Pluralists are not all so accepting. The eliminative set-theoretic pluralism of Marc Ereshefsky (1992) draws the line at certain "illegitimate" sets. The sorting of objects into sets must, he argued, be done according to some principle, and that principle must be properly "motivated." Species concepts that are based on the idea of a species as a "lineage," whether that lineage is defined by interbreeding, ecological niche, or common descent, are properly motivated.[10] Species based on "idealist morphology" criteria are not.

Ereshefsky's reasoning brings out some of the inherent problems in the set-theoretic analysis of predication. Regardless of the usefulness of set theory in mathematics, a significant scientific category cannot be understood as a random assortment of objects; not only would the extension of the predicate (a random list of objects) be impossible to remember, but there would be no reason to think that such a predicate could figure in useful theory. Sets must be formed on the basis of a principle, claims Ereshefsky, and it must be a principle that is consistent with current theory, the theory for which taxonomy is devised. On this reasoning, inclusion of a structural classification, based on internal body plan, developmental program, or some other feature independent of evolutionary lineage, is illegitimate; it is not motivated by "currently proposed" theory. As he puts it:

> Since the inception of evolutionary theory, species taxa have been considered evolutionary units: that is groups of organisms capable of evolving. The evolution of such groups requires that the organisms of a species taxon be connected by hereditary relations. Heredity relations, whether they be genetic or not,

> require that the generations of a taxon be historically connected; otherwise information will not be transmitted. The upshot is that if species taxa, or any taxa, are to evolve, they must form historically connected entities. By allowing nonhistorical species concepts, Kitcher's pluralism falls outside the domain of evolutionary theory and should be rejected. (365)

For Ereshefsky, consistent with Quine's ontological relativity, the objects of biological research are the objects over which theory ranges, not just any theory consistent with the evidence, but accepted current theory. There are no legitimate objects outside of that theory. Although there may be groupings consistent with evidence, the proper choice is between groupings according to accepted theory. Given the history of the term *species*, Ereshefsky suggests, perhaps the word itself should be jettisoned because it "has outlived its usefulness and should be replaced by terms that more accurately describe the different types of lineages that biologists refer to as 'species'" (357). Then any temptation to allow the word *species* to posit groupings inconsistent with current evolutionary theory would be averted, and a tighter fit would be obtained between a predicate like *interbreeding* and interbreeding individuals that satisfy those predicates.

Worries about the indeterminacy in how a species set is formed have driven some philosophers to the other set-theoretic alternative. Species are not sets of individuals but individuals. A species is not a set that can be formed in different ways but an identifiable and rigidly designated individual whose place in predication is not as predicate but as subject. Species themselves can then be gathered into sets, sets of species individuals, the objects over which the variables of evolutionary theory range. Elliott Sober's (1984) version of this argument is in specific opposition to Kitcher's set-theoretic pluralism. To allow pluralism, Sober argues is to ignore that those on the winning side in science with an "active" research program should get the "prize at stake," in this case the right to define key words such as *species*. What scientific winners say is a species is what really is a species. A species word—whatever it may have been in the past—is no longer a predicate term indicating a natural kind, but a name for an existing spatiotemporal entity: an "incredibly heterogeneous but integrated breeding population, shaped by the fortuitous whims of natural selection," "putty in the hands of a tinkering Mother Nature" (336). "Natural kind" terms such as "predator," or "asexual" can figure as sets with species as members (e.g., Hull 1978; Holsinger 1984). Such classes complement evolutionary theory by supplying predicates which subject species satisfy. Because species are individuals, similarity in form between groups without a common ancestor can be disregarded.

The result is that the failure to find common characteristics among parts of a species object does not matter but only its ordained internal organization, which is theoretically dictated to be relations of heredity. Once a hereditary line dies out, like an individual organism, a species is extinct and cannot be revived, no matter how similar an organism may reappear elsewhere. If members of the same interbreeding species are different in form, this point can be disregarded, just as a single organism can be expected to have different internal organs. Biologists can find and baptize new species; they can change their descriptions of old species to suit new purposes. As Holsinger (1984, 297) puts the advantage, if you treat species as sets, then you must deal separately with the question of descent. If you treat species as individuals on the basis of common descent, then evolutionary theorizing is facilitated. Even though different ways of determining descent may yield different individual taxa, this poses no problem. "Taxa participate in a variety of processes and no unique characterization of those entities is possible with respect to all of the processes in which they participate" (305). Evolutionary processes and the groupings on which they operate are what evolutionary theory says biologists study, and these are what exist, no matter how they happened to be individuated or named.[11] In set-theoretic analyses—whether individualistic, set-pluralistic, or set-eliminative—the logic of science demands a certain circularity. Objects are the objects theory requires; theory is the theory of theory's objects. From the standpoint of mathematical logic, this is the necessary structure of truth. Basic predications are true if the subjects in those predication satisfy the predicates or, alternately, if the individual named by the subject term yields the value true for the function indicated by the predicate term.

A current example of the limitations of set-theoretic logic in science might be found in current genetic research. Many nonfeminist philosophers of biology assumed that, as Quine predicted, genes would be the rigidly defined objects that would secure the logic and scientific respectability of biology. Substituted for the still-messy "lineages" or "reproductive groups," genes would be the hard fact that would constitute biological truth. Biologists might then, as Evelyn Fox Keller (1983) puts it, "prune down the luxuriant variety of biology to a few elementary cases that might show the way to a simple explanatory model" (164). As explained by Keller, the microbiologist Barbara McClintock, however, bypassed studies of bacteria where quantifying over genetic objects was a growth industry and continued work on more complex organisms like corn in the natural history tradition of researchers like D'Arcy Thompson.[12] Correlating observed patterns on leaves and kernels with microscopic chromosomal changes, she observed that the supposed objects of microbiology that control production of the proteins that regulate growth are not, in fact, on fixed places on chromosomes, as genes were supposed to be. Instead, DNA rearranges itself in response to changes in the organism or in the environment in a process McClintock called "transposition." These findings do not fit the logic that defines genes as individuals located at fixed places on chromosomes, directing organic processes with no feedback from the rest of the organism. McClintock's work was ignored and sometimes ridiculed until eventually gross discrepancies in bacteria genetics appeared. Genes are not rigid objects or sets of objects but part of a complex regulatory system, but McClintock's finding that genes are deleted, inserted, translocated, turned off and on, did not fit the rigidly defined logic of biology and so was neglected.

The full implications of the discovery that the genome is not a numbered series of objects but a system in responsive dynamic equilibrium have still to be assimilated.[13] If there is any logic that might clear the way for such an advance in biological understanding, it is not the logic of set theory. Genetic theory posited the objects over which its quantifiers were to range. Findings were construed accordingly. McClintock returned to original predications, predication that may have committed Aristotle's original sin of interchanging subjects and predicates as well as Quine's savagery of natural kinds. In McClintock's practice, corn was an organism whose nature had to be observed and described, abstracted from a mass of evidence. Corn was both subject and predicate, an object whose characteristics and identity were in question, a predicate that defined the nature of an interrelated group of organisms.

The moral that can be drawn from this briefly sketched example is modest. Philosophy of biology and philosophical logic, set-theoretic or other, has less influence on science, no doubt, than old-boy networks or vested research interests. On the other hand, alternate feminist approaches to the logic of biology might be useful in undermining any rationalizing support logic gives to vested research interests and weakened professional resistance to the work of women scientists such as McClintock. To go further, feminist versions of the logic of science might provide conceptual tools with which to dismantle misconceptions of science's message and mission, misconceptions that hold in place practices and attitudes harmful to women and other oppressed groups. Should the objects of biological theorizing, as Quine suggests, be objects of a particular theory and subject to change whenever scientific experts decide that theory should be replaced? Should theory be a net cast on a confusion of sensory "stimulations" so that men can better predict and manipulate pleasurable sensations? Should we welcome the time when predication, as Quine (1969) argues, is a sign of "primitive," "savage" thinking and when Western science has succeeded in describing all phenomena as part of a vast "cosmic mechanism" (136–138)?

In fact, in the past and present, other logics operate in science not expressible in set-theoretic terms, and other resources exist in technical language, as evidenced by the work of McClintock, that can be brought to bear on issues surrounding feminist concerns about the environment or medical practice. Should we view the health of the human body, male or female, as a function to be adjusted in mathematical formulae that link drug or surgical input to specified output? Should we relate to plant life as manipulators of cosmic mechanisms? Although it may suit the human interests of some funders of biological research to prove that the input of particular therapies affects genetic mechanisms or that herbicides are a necessary part of agricultural management, a logic that takes such interests as determinative of meaning and truth may in fact impede our grasp of what things are. More fruitful might be research rooted in original predications that are the fruit of intuitive and careful observation of the natural world.

Notes

1. *Sophist*, 261c6–264b3 (my translation from the Greek text in *Loeb Classical Library*, Cambridge, Mass.: Harvard University Press, 1921).

2. See "Concept and Object," Frege (1970); for further discussion, see Nye (1992, Part III, "Reading Frege").

3. See Marcus (1974) where she notes and regrets the common practice among logicians of conflating mathematical sets and logical classes and limiting talk of classes to truth-functional contexts.

4. See, for example, Quine (1960, 96).

5. The Goodman puzzle is directed to the problem of induction as posed by Hume in the eighteenth century: How can we know that the future is like the past?

6. Strawson's solution to the problem of universals is the following: Types or kinds can themselves be put in subject position giving fuel to nominalism, but the relation between higher and lower types requires an analogy with predication proper where something is said of "a spatiotemporal particular." Understanding this as an analogy makes it possible to avoid nominalism and at the same time not be guilty of regression to Platonism. Strawson (1967) concludes:

> And now, surely, we are in a position to understand the nominalist prejudice, and to discount it—without flattering the fantasies of Platonism. If by accepting as entities, on this logical test, things other than spatio-temporal particulars, we were claiming for them any other, any further likeness to such particulars than the logical analogy

itself contains, we should indeed be running into danger of committing the characteristic category-confusion of Platonist mythology. (88)

7. Kant's "Critique of Teleological Judgement"—the second part of his "third" *Critique of Judgement*—did not depend on essences, fixed species, or divine creationism. His point was that processes of self-regulation and self-production characterize living organisms and cannot be completely explained by external or internal mechanisms. Although he did not rule out a priori the possibility that unknown mechanisms could be found working in tandem with self-regulation, biological science still must begin and end with the self-produced unity of an organism. Evolutionists might posit physical mechanisms that account for the emergence of life and the evolution of species, but given the result of determinate living forms, some purpose to the mechanisms is still necessary. In particular, the end for man, the only organism with a "capacity for setting before himself ends of his deliberate choice" (94), cannot be either bare physical survival or the prediction and manipulation of pleasurable sensation but purposeful elements of culture such as civil society, art, and science (97).

8. Actually, theories of evolution were debated before Darwin, and many were more sophisticated than Darwin's. The Aristotelian Linnaeus studied the constant formation of varieties and decided that species might not in fact be fixed. Buffon saw a constant stream of individuals merging and changing without fixed divisions between the species. St. Hilaire's homologies blurred the line between species and even genera, suggesting links between dissimilar organisms. Cuvier saw infinite adaptive variations on basic body plans.

9. For a discussion of Tarski's use of the same example to show the possible advantages of truth-functional logic in the sciences, see Nye (1998, 278–282).

10. One of the requirements Ereshefsky (1992) lists for a legitimate grouping is that the taxonomy be consistent, but, Ereshefsky argues, different self-consistent taxonomies based on interbreeding, descent, or ecological niche are all be consistent with evolutionary theory. Evolutionary theory posits a tree with different branches, but various evolutionary forces can be at work in the branching (358).

11. One embarrassment for evolutionary theory is that individuating criteria for lineages cannot be directly established in practice. Human history records family histories; whether a plant or an animal organism interbreeds or has a common ancestor must be a matter of inference from geographical continuity, fossil evidence, or more commonly by way of "illegitimate" groupings based on similarity of form. Nor has genetic analysis saved the day and provided rigid designation for lineages because genetic similarities do not line up very neatly with interbreeding or common descent, either. Nor are genes themselves identified without reference to observable traits. Quine's (1969) conviction, therefore, in "Natural Kinds" that evolution allows the logically unambiguous definition of species in terms of "proximity and frequency of common ancestors" and eventually in terms of genes is unfounded.

12. A long tradition of researchers, among them Aristotle, Geoffrey St. Hilaire, D'Arcy Thompson, Joseph Needham, and current developmental biologists and em-

bryologists (see Amundson 1994; Depew and Weber 1994; Webster and Goodwin 1996), have productively studied the structural and dynamic features of living organisms apart from assumptions of common descent or neo-Darwinian adaptation. A classic example of such work is Thompson's (1961) *On Growth and Form.*

13. Much of the work of the microbiologist and philosopher of science Evelyn Fox Keller (1985, 1992) has been an attempt to explore what such a change in logical and epistemological paradigm might entail.

References

Amundson, Ron. "Two Concepts of Constraint: Adaptationism and the Challenge from Developmental Biology." *Philosophy of Science* 61 (1994): 556–578.

Davidson, Donald. *Inquiries into Truth and Interpretation.* Oxford: Clarendon, 1984.

Depew, David, and Bruce Weber. *Darwinism Evolving: Systems Dynamics and the Genealogy of Natural Selection.* Cambridge, Mass.: MIT Press, 1994.

Ereshefsky, Marc. "Eliminative Pluralism." *Philosophy of Science* 59 (1992): 671–690.

Frege, Gottlob. "Concept and Object"; "Sense and Reference." *Translations from the Philosophical Works of Gottlob Frege*, ed. Max Black and Peter Geach. Oxford: Blackwell, 1970.

Geach, Peter T. "History of the Corruptions of Logic." Reprinted in *Logic Matters.* Berkeley: University of California Press, 1972. (Originally published 1968.)

———. *Reference and Generality.* Ithaca, N.Y.: Cornell, 1962.

Glass, Bentley, Owsei Temkin, and William Straus, eds. *Forerunners of Darwinism: 1745–1859.* Baltimore, Md.: Johns Hopkins University Press, 1959.

Hintikka, Merrill, and Jaakko Hintikka. "How Can Language Be Sexist?" In *Discovering Reality: Feminist Perspectives on Epistemology, Metaphysics Methodology, and Philosophy of Science*, ed. Sandra Harding and Merrill Hintikka. Dordrecht: Reidel, 1983.

Ho, Mae-Wan, and Peter Saunders, eds. *Beyond Neo-Darwinism.* London: Academic Press, 1984.

Holsinger, Kent. "The Nature of Biological Species." *Philosophy of Science* 51, no. 2 (1984): 293–307.

Hull, David. "A Matter of Individuality." *Philosophy of Science* 45, no. 3 (1978): 335–360.

Kant, Immanuel. *Critique of Judgement.* Oxford: Clarendon, 1952. (Originally published 1790.)

Keller, Evelyn Fox. *A Feeling for the Organism: The Life and Work of Barbara McClintock.* New York: Freeman, 1983.

———. *Reflections on Gender and Science.* New Haven, Conn.: Yale University Press, 1985.

———. *Secrets of Life/Secrets of Death.* New York: Routledge, 1992.

Kitcher, Philip. "Species." *Philosophy of Science* 51 (1984): 308–333.

Kourany, Janet A., ed. *Philosophy in a Feminist Voice.* Princeton, N.J.: Princeton University Press, 1998.

Kripke, Saul. *Naming and Necessity*. Cambridge, Mass.: Harvard University Press, 1980.

Larson, James. *Reason and Experience*. Berkeley: University of California Press, 1971.

Marcus, Ruth. "Classes, Collections, and Individuals." *American Philosophical Quarterly* 11, no. 3 (1974): 227–232.

Needham, Joseph. *Order and Life*. Cambridge, Mass.: MIT Press, 1936.

Nye, Andrea. "Frege's Metaphors." *Hypatia* 7, no. 2 (Spring 1992): 18–39.

———. "Semantics in a New Key." In *Philosophy in a Feminist Voice*, ed. Janet A. Kourany. Princeton, N.J.: Princeton University Press, 1998.

———. *Words of Power: A Feminist Reading of the History of Logic*. New York: Routledge, 1990.

Otte, Daniel, and John Endler, eds. *Speciation and Its Consequences*. Sunderland, Mass.: Sinauer, 1989.

Quine, Willard Van Orman. *Ontological Relativity*. New York: Columbia University Press, 1969.

———. *Word and Object*. Cambridge, Mass.: MIT Press, 1960.

Raby, Peter. *Bright Paradise: Victorian Scientific Travelers*. Princeton, N.J.: Princeton University Press, 1996.

Sober, Elliott. "Sets, Species, and Evolution: Comments on Philip Kitcher's 'Species.'" *Philosophy of Science* 51 (1984): 334–341.

Stafleu, Frans. *Linnaeus and the Linnaeans*. Utrecht: Oosthoek, 1971.

Strawson, P. F. *Individuals*. London: Methuen, 1959.

———. "Singular Terms and Predication." In *Philosophical Logic*, ed. P. F. Strawson. Oxford: Oxford University Press, 1967. (Originally published in *Journal of Philosophy* 58, no. 15 [1961]: 393–412.)

Rosenberg, Alexander. *Instrumental Biology or the Disunity of Science*. Chicago: University of Chicago Press, 1994.

Tarski, Alfred. "The Semantic Conception of Truth and the Foundations of Semantics." *Philosophy and Phenomenological Research* 4 (1944): 341–375.

Thompson, D'Arcy. *On Growth and Form*. Cambridge: Cambridge University Press, 1961. (First edition 1917.)

Webster, Gerry, and Brian Goodwin. *Form and Transformation: Generative and Relational Principles in Biology*. Cambridge: Cambridge University Press, 1996.

CHAPTER NINE

~

"What Do Girls Know Anyway?": Rationality, Gender, and Social Control

PAM OLIVER

In the last quarter-century, as a result of the women's movement, progress toward equalizing the positions of women and men has included equal opportunities and equal-pay legislation, affirmative action programs, and other efforts to emphasize the value of women's particular contributions to the well being of societies. Nonetheless women in all contemporary societies remain significantly underrepresented in managerial and other leadership positions in every sphere of public life, and conversely overrepresented in service and subordinate positions (Lengermann and Wallace, 1985; Lipman-Blumen, 1984). Part of the reason for this lies arguably in the continuing stereotypic views of the genders, where men typically are seen as dominant, objective, cool, controlled, decisive, and rational, whereas women are characterized as more passive, emotional, temperamental, subjective, and nonrational in their thinking (Broverman et al., 1970; Keller, 1985; Middleton, 1984; Rosenkrantz et al., 1985). Given these characterizations, it is hardly surprising that women are seen as less suited to managerial and leadership positions, since these are deemed to require the kinds of traits seen commonly as belonging primarily or exclusively to males. The equation of rationality with objectivity and with masculinity has a very long history, and has been apparently confirmed by psychological research as well as being a part of ordinary folk wisdom.

In the following discussion I examine what I term the "rationality equation," that is, the established links among rationality, logic, objectivity, and masculinity, and show how these links are neither essential nor immutable.

In particular I argue that rationality hitherto has been defined and understood too narrowly, and because of this has become rationalism and rationalization in the dual causes of, first, maintaining a set of stereotypic beliefs about gender which have not so much become outmoded as simply recognized now as having never been entirely valid, and, second, justifying an existing, unequal power base which operates to exclude women from positions of power and control in our society. Part of this process has been exacerbated by the contribution of psychological research and theory which is itself androcentric.

The Rationality Equation

Rationality and Logic

The equation of rationality with the rules of logic can be traced back to the eighteenth-century philosophers of the Enlightenment, whose values of secularity and humanism were a then liberal reaction against the restrictive dictates of the dual tyrannies of church and monarchy. Spirituality and subjectivity were associated with supremely egocentric regimes of oppression, so that rationalist humanism was seen as a liberating force and these new values were the means of a new self-determination for the bourgeoisie. By the end of the nineteenth century they were entrenched ideology, the philosophic basis for the growing anti-imperialism of the epoch, and the springboard for the movements of modernism and structuralism in the pursuit of secular or objective knowledge. Science was the new religion, and the reasoning of science was that of logic, ergo objectivity.

Out of this tradition, rationality had come to be regarded by philosophers and psychologists alike as equated with the rules of Aristotelian logic. The most authoritative nineteenth-century writers on logic believed that their discipline was the science of thought and that logic was the basis of all mental processes. Kant, for example, claimed that "logic is a science of the *necessary* laws of thought, without which no employment of the understanding and the reason takes place" (Kant, 1885, cited in Henle, 1962: 366; emphasis added), and John Stuart Mill also thought that it was logic which constituted the "science of reasoning" (Mill, 1874).

By the 1930s, however, there had been a change in the intellectual climate as psychology developed as a separate discipline from philosophy, and writers were suggesting that everyday thinking was not based on pure logical forms. Schiller (1930: 282) claimed that the rules of syllogistic reasoning had "nothing whatever to do with actual reasoning, and can make nothing of it," and psychologists studying reasoning processes had begun to conclude that logical principles were often largely irrelevant to people's ordinary thinking. Bruner, Goodnow, and Austin, for example, concluded that:

> much of human reasoning is supported by a kind of thematic process rather than by an abstract logic. The principal feature of this thematic process is its pragmatic rather than its logical structure. (Bruner et al., 1956: 104)

and the general consensus of psychologists working in this area at that time was that, in their ordinary thinking, people tended to prefer empirically reasonable propositions to logical ones (Henle, 1962).

This conclusion did not, however, detract from an apparent belief that people ought to be able to think logically. It remained implicit in psychological discourse about human reasoning that logical, analytical thinking was intrinsically superior to and different from "intuitive" thinking, and there was no suggestion that logic might not be the most desirable basis for rational thinking. For example, Lefford (1946) wrote that the principles of logical inference were "not the common property of the *unsophisticated* subject" (p. 144; emphasis added). Dollard and Miller (1950) theorized that logic was a learned drive, and that children were selectively reinforced for logical thinking and punished for illogical contradictions and absurdities. It was even argued from analyses of errors in the reasoning of schizophrenic patients that their reasoning was not unrelated to logic, but rather that it conformed to rules of logic which were not the same as those of Aristotelian logic (e.g., Brown, 1976; Von Domarus, 1944; and Arieti, 1955, cited in Henle, 1962). Logical thinking as an *ideology* as the right or best way of reasoning, was established firmly in the theorizing of psychologists; the intrinsic superiority of logical thinking was not being questioned. In spite of clear demonstrations by more recent philosophers (e.g., Gould, 1971) and social anthropologists (e.g., Scribner, 1978) of the distinction between rational and logical processes of thought, the acceptance of logical thinking as superior remained relatively unquestioned within psychology as a discipline.

This ideology of rationality was affirmed with the development of social cognition as a subdiscipline in psychology which investigated people's thinking processes in relation to their ordinary social interactions. Nisbett and Ross (1980) produced a model, drawing heavily on Fritz Heider's theorizing about attribution and based almost exclusively on laboratory experimental research on attribution processes and social inference, which posited man (*sic*) as a "lav scientist" in his thinking. Nisbett and Ross's theory supposed that "lay" people (by which they presumably meant non-scientists), in their everyday efforts to problem-solve and understand their social world, attempt to think things through in the same way as do professional scientists—that is, that we engage in the same kinds of thinking tasks as does the professional scientist—looking for covariation, analysing causality, trying to predict possible outcomes, testing hypotheses about our social world, and so on. In going about this, according to Nisbett and Ross, we try to use the same kinds of knowledge structures and judgmental processes as do real scientists: the difference is that "lay" people just don't do it as well.

Apart from its evident elitist and patronizing overtones, the main problem with this theory, of course, is its implicit assumption that people actually *want* to be logical, want to follow the rules of science, and want to achieve clear outcomes, an assumption which is not supported empirically or anecdotally. The language which Nisbett and Ross used to describe their theory manifests a strong androcentric bias, and the theory is based on research which, like much psychological research of the era, must be criticized for having drawn disproportionately on male subject samples (see Wallston and Grady, 1985).

A more recent model of rationality proposed by White (1984) reflects the conclusions of psychologists in the 1940s and 1950s (e.g., Bruner et al., 1956; Morgan and Morton, 1944) that pragmatist considerations are more important than logical ones in everyday thinking. White proposes a model of the "layperson (*sic*) as pragmatic," whose "primary orientation is to the practicalities of living" (p. 333). Thus he argues that we focus on concrete and everyday information, and although we retain a "desire to make correct, accurate inferences," that desire is "invariably subservient to practical concerns" (p. 334). In a very thorough critique, White argues against the lay scientist model of rationality on several grounds which have to do firstly with the inappropriateness of applying the rules of pure logic or scientific method as criteria for the effectiveness of everyday judgments, and secondly with the equally inappropriate laboratory tasks which had been used to assess the competence of "lay" judgments. However, White does not question the underlying assumption that rationality is ultimately desirable, and universally desired. Although he questions both the connection between rationality and Aristotelian logic, and the idea that "lay people" attempt to use scientific methods, he does so on the basis that the necessary skills and information are not available for most of us to use those methods in our everyday thinking; he does not confront the assumption that people would prefer to be logical and rational in their thinking if they only could. Even though White claims that his pragmatist model opposes an idealized view of science, it remains implicit in his continued use of the word "layperson," and in his conclusion that professional scientists also are "*potential victims* of concrete and practical considerations" (p. 344; emphasis added), that scientific, logical thinking remains thc ideal, and that we ordinary folk are still not quite up to the professional scientist when it comes to achieving accurate inferences.

It is clear also that the notion of rationality, for people in general, continues to be equated with logic. When I recently asked a current third-year psychology class to give a definition of rationality, before ever discussing the concept with them, more than 80 percent included the words "logic" or "logical" in their answers. There is no shortage of anecdotal evidence in our everyday encounters with other people that thinking and behaving logically ate considered signs of maturity. Flights of fantasy, indulged and even encouraged in preschoolers, are actively discouraged after that magic age, and continued imaginativeness, except in certain approved forms such as drama or wit, is taken as a sign of silliness and failure to mature. The line which separates the tolerable and even amusing eccentricity of the rich, famous, or elderly, or the desirable "lateral" thinking of writers and other artists (de Bono, 1953), from the intolerable and irrational craziness of other divergent thinkers, is easily transgressed, and the consequences of overstepping the boundary are often extremely punishing.

Rationality, Objectivity, and Emotionality

The ideology of rational thinking assumes further that rationality and emotionality are, if not mutually exclusive, certainly incompatible. Emotionality is seen as a personal, subjective, passionate expression and therefore, it follows, not compatible with "objective" logical thought. This notion can be traced back to Plato's belief that passion was inimical to rationality, that emotions were dangerous forces which could overcome all reason in both thought and behavior, so that they must be suppressed and held in check before we can think rationally.

The modern continuance of this belief can be found readily in the writings of contemporary psychologists. In a recent reevaluation of Cartesian dualism, the philosopher Oliver Letwin (1987) has described how the re-emergence of a cognitive trend in mainstream psychology has promoted theories which see thought and feeling as separate processes, each disrupting the other. Letwin presents cogent philosophical arguments which show how rationality has two distinct but interactive senses—one based on cognitive or logical judgments, and the other on the individual's subjective sense of what is "right" for them. Since rational judgment or decision making involves using both of these senses. Letwin sees no "struggle between reason and desire," since they are essentially interdependent and both intrinsically rational in the personal/pragmatic sense. Due to the powerful influence of modern

Anglo-Saxon philosophy, Letwin (1987: 96) believes that "everyone ought to have been persuaded that the passions, whether in the form of emotions or in the form of sheer desire, intrinsically involve rational judgments and rational capacities." Nonetheless, he argues, psychological theories consistently present an understanding of "emotion . . . [as] irrational in the sense that it disrupts or qualifies normal 'rational' business-like activity, because it involves the expression of a judgment" (p. 103). The implicit suggestion is that truly reasonable behavior is instrumental and objective, and involves no personal judgment or bias.

Although the ideology of rationality as superior thinking has continued to underlie most of psychology, it is rarely made explicit. In formulating his very influential rational-emotive therapy, for example, Ellis (1959) wrote that:

> the rational belief is that emotions and motivations of humans raised in a civilised community consist of attitudes, perceptual biases, beliefs, assumptions and ideas which are acquired by social learning *and can therefore be reviewed, questioned, challenged, reconstructed and changed with sufficient effort and practice* on the part of the emoting individual (1959: 55: emphasis added).

Thus, in Ellis's view, even if emotionality and rationality can be allowed to coexist, rationality is to be imposed over the emotions, which are seen as an impediment to clear, rational thinking. (Other examples of this view follow in later sections of this chapter.) It is largely through the connection of emotionality with irrationality, together with the traditional association of women with expressivity, that rationality has come to be equated with the thinking of men, and irrationality with that of women.

Rationality and Masculinity

The notion that rational thinking is the province of men is ancient. Aristotle's viewpoint on this part of the rationality equation was of the

> female as an incomplete male, psychologically incomplete in possession of deliberative reason, not wholly without it as is the slave, her reason is not firm, and lacks authority. (cited in Edel, 1982: 103)

Examples abound throughout history, past and recent, of the dichotomized stereotypes of men as rational, and women as irrational and therefore inferior. The construction of women as expressive, emotional, elemental, volatile and therefore nonrational has continued across centuries and cultures, and has been used in myriad suppressive and oppressive ways to indict women's practices, from witchcraft to midwifery (French, 1985). These practices could thus be usurped by men and turned into more scientific, rational activities such as medicine and obstetrics, from which women were then effectively excluded (Fee, 1983), further reducing their power.

The contemporary popularity of the perceived gender dichotomy in rationality is demonstrated in the studies of Broverman and colleagues (Broverman et al., 1970; Rosenkrantz et al., 1968). Repeated investigations showed that males were seen as unemotional, objective and logical, and that these traits were equated also with self-confidence, trustworthiness, higher general intelligence, good decision-making ability, and dominance. Women, on the other hand, were seen as prone to emotional outbursts and having poor reasoning ability, traits which were matched also with quietness, tactfulness, and a strong need for security. The connections between rational thinking ability and who ought to be in control were very clear. Perhaps the greatest indictment in the Broverman team's findings was that these views were held also by a wide range of mental health professionals, psychologists, psychiatrists and others, who believed moreover that the characteristics seen as masculine were more indicative of good psychological adjustment and mental well-being than were those designated feminine. The message again was very clear—logical (male) thinking was seen as healthy and normal, emotionality (female) as inferior and indicative of dysfunction, maladjustment, incomplete maturity. Although some aspects of these gender stereotypes have changed in the past twenty-five years, women continue to be seen as more emotional and less rational than men (Middleton, 1984; Rosenkrantz et al., 1985; cf. Widiger and Settle, 1987).

Hare-Mustin and Maracek (1988) have shown how this "long-standing association of women with nature and emotion, and men with their opposites, reason, technology, and civilization" is just one example of a consensually constructed bias which has perpetuated the notion of the sexes as essentially and invariably different, as having mutually opposite and exclusive traits. Moreover, the traits historically associated with women tend to have been those which portrayed them as passionate, expressive, and volatile, while those associated with men depicted them as stable, instrumental, and sane. These characterizations, of course, have permitted women to be seen as lacking the skills and characteristics which might allow them to become adequate leaders, and as therefore properly suited only, but ideally, to subordinate societal roles.

The "liberal ideology of rational man" (Fee, 1983), then, is based on a constructed sexual dichotomy which sees as inherent sex opposites emotionality and rationality, objectivity and subjectivity, beauty and truth, art and science. The historical construction of this dichotomization has been traced by Elizabeth Fee in a structuralist critique of the sociobiological explanation of sex difference, where she shows how capitalist, patriarchal structures designed to control female labor and rationalize the subordinate status of women have been the impetus for the continued promulgation of theories which depict females as innately emotional, nonlogical, and therefore nonrational. The construction of women as passive, nurturing, expressive, emotional, has often taken the form of flattery, incorporated in laudatory litanies of these quintessential female qualities as an intrinsic pan of women's attractiveness and fascination to men (Lipman-Blumen, 1984), or even as vital to the maintenance of societies and of humanity itself (Theriot, 1988). The same kind of adulatory propaganda was used in World War II to inspire German women to stay at home and breed strong sons, and has played a central part in creating the mythical "feminine mystique" which has kept women on such precarious pedestals (Friedan. 1963). As Erica Jong has pointed out acerbically, women are "the only exploited group who have been idealized into powerlessness" (Brown and O'Connor, 1984).

The basic fallacy in this gendered notion of rationality is the belief that objectivity is innate. Keller (1985) has pointed out that, even though the cognitive potential for objectivity may be innate, the capacity for objective analysis is not born in us, but learned through the ordinary process of socialization by which concepts of self and other are acquired. This process is subject to the same gender differentiation as is all socialization, and indeed is part of accurately learning one's gender role identity—a process hitherto considered essential to "normal" development. For example, Chodorow (1982) has argued that the greater emotional detachment which is part of being masculine is a consequence of the development of differentiated gender role identity. Because of their stronger infantile attachment to mothers rather than fathers as primary caregivers, boys' gender identification requires a greater differentiation than does that of girls. Boys have to distance themselves from identification with their mothers in order to achieve their gender identity, and this involves effectively rejecting the characteristics of femininity. Becoming male, then, according to Chodorow's argument, means that boys:

> come to define themselves as more separate and distinct . . . (whereas) the basic feminine sense of self is connected to the world, the basic masculine sense of self is separate. . . . Masculine personality, then, comes to be defined more in terms of denial of relation and connection. . . . Thus relational ability and

> preoccupations have been extended in women's development and curtailed in men's. . . . This points to boys' preparation for participation in non-relational spheres and to girls' greater potential for participation in relational spheres (1982: 169–170).

Like objectivity, rationality and emotionality are also learned. Thus the continued socialization process sees boys, but not girls, encouraged to keep their emotionality under strict control, to play games which are orientated toward logical problem-solving, to follow science subjects at school, to aim for careers in areas where they can exercise their best masculine abilities of clear thinking and detachment, and so on. Moreover, this process does not stop in adulthood. The socialization continues into learning the accepted roles and paradigms within particular occupations and disciplines, which are also gendered (Keller, 1985).

The masculine equating of non-emotionality and objectivity can be understood, then, as a part of learning to distinguish one's own from others' perspectives, which is seen by men, and by scientists, as necessitating divorce from emotional attachment to one's own perspective in order to understand the other person's. This conceptualization of the prerequisites to "real" understanding is completely discrepant with the notion of empathic understanding which characterizes the female role as relational.

Mainstream psychology has been far from neutral in the process of constructing this image of women as emotional, non-objective and therefore interior. Freud's view of females as incomplete and would-be males, and of hysteria as emanating from the womb; the theories of Bowlby and Winnicott which described the emotional bond as an intrinsic part of the mothering "instinct" of women, and as essential to the normal development of children; even very recent views of women's "irrationality," "neuroticism," and "diminished responsibility" as resulting from raging hormones (Dalton, 1978); these theories, as much as the more explicit claims of sociobiologists such as E. O. Wilson (e.g., Wilson, 1975) that women are by their nature less rational, have all served to support, and in some opinions confirm, the image of women as inferior in reasoning ability. The irony is that these theories themselves are nonrational, since, by applying too narrowly the syllogistic reasoning of hypothetico-deductive method, they have all made the fundamental error of confusing correlation with causality, or at least have ignored the possibility that causality may lie in the opposite direction from that assumed, or even may be circular. And they have erred also in believing that consensual validation produces some objective truth. Nevertheless they have established the belief that women are less able than men to operate effectively within rational/objective systems where the systematic application of the rules and principles of logic are deemed to be necessary. This interpretation ignores the operation of social forces which shape women to other more pragmatic reasoning styles, and the possibility that, as Hare-Mustin and Maracek (1988: 459) point out, "Man's propensity to reason from principles may stem from the fact that the principles were formulated to promote their interests."

The inaccuracies and invalidity of these earlier psychological theories and interpretations have been exposed for their inherent male bias (e.g., Chesler, 1972; Ehrenreich and English, 1979; Hare-Mustin, 1983). But trying to repair a belief decades old and apparently confirmed repeatedly by otherwise reputable psychologists, and especially to challenge it from a defensive base, is a difficult task, to say the least. Carol Gilligan's (1982) research on women's and girls' modes of reasoning in relation to moral issues has helped to dispel some of the beliefs that women were incapable, or less capable than men, of reasoning logically. Like Keller (1985), Gilligan has shown that women are perfectly capable of thinking logically and objectively, and that their use of alternative reasoning modes is based on an active *choice* to include in their reasoning, on moral issues at least, an ethic of care—that is, women do not attempt in the same ways, or to the same degree, as men, to separate out thinking and feeling, but include emotionality in their reasoning.

However, there is a danger, ironically, that the task of demonstrating the validity of women's ways of thinking may be exacerbated rather than helped by some of the writings of feminist psychologists. As Hare-Mustin and Maracek (1988) note,

> by construing rationality as an essential male quality and relatedness as an essential female quality, theories like those of Gilligan and Parsons conceal the possibility that those qualities arise from social inequities and power differences. (1988: 459)

Even Sandra Bem's (1974) pioneering work on the concept of androgyny reinforced ideological legitimacy of traditional gender differentiation (Eichler, 1980). That is, by affirming the differences between men and women, albeit for reason of gender rather than sex, feminist theorists are in danger of perpetuating further the notion of women as lacking logical/rational capacity. The implication, as always, is that these gender differences, although environmentally caused, are nonetheless fixed, universal, and immutable.

Rationality and Social Control

It can be seen, then, that the equating of rationality with objectivity, and masculinity, has been at the expense of women's status, both at the societal level and in interpersonal relations. In *For Her Own Good: 150 Year of Experts' Advice to Women*, Ehrenreich and English (1979) have described the myriad arguments which have been put forward to show that women's thinking is nonrational, so that they are not suited to positions of responsibility which, men insist, require cool, detached, impersonal decision-making ability. Such arguments have been used to exclude women from positions of power and relegate them instead to roles which are seen as most suited to their more emotional, expressive nature. Invariably these roles have been characterized as less vital or productive, and useful only in that they are necessary supports to the more important business undertaken by men.

While the relegation to subordinate roles can be interpreted simply as an unfortunate consequence of women's characterization as nonrational, an alternate interpretation is possible—that characterizing women as overly emotional and lacking in objective reasoning capacity means that they can be excluded deliberately and with apparent justification from positions of authority and power. The arguments which have been used to rationalize women's subordination in this way are so familiar as to be cliches—he controls the family financial and legal affairs because she's given to impulsive spending, doesn't understand the complexities of the business world, or "isn't good with figures"; females are denied access to highly paid occupations such as aerospace engineering or flying aircraft (but considered nonetheless capable of the equally stressful jobs necessary to support men in those occupations) because of their emotional liability when menstruating; women are not suited to positions of political or managerial authority, or in the public arena generally, because of their inability to remain cool and emotionally detached in situations of stress or conflict; and so on. The equating of femininity with nonrationality has achieved the status of a universal truth which is constantly reinforced in popular language and media images, and typically in derogatory ways—the "woman's prerogative" to be unpredictably changeable and inconsistent; the dizzy blonde in situation comedies; the cartoons which depict men as bemused and frustrated by women's lateral reasoning; "women's intuition," seen sometimes as a kind of magical insightfulness, is more often regarded as insubstantial or even mildly menacing (Lipman-Blumen, 1984). Jean Lipman-Blumen (1984) sees the equating of women with nonrational thinking as one of several complexly linked "control myths"—contrived social truths which self-perpetuate. In this case, women are portrayed as "intuitive, holistic, contextual, but men are analytical, abstract, field independent, *and therefore smarter than women*" (p. 79, emphasis added). Similarly, in a careful analysis of the consequences of stereotyping, Carmen Huici (1985) has shown the functional aspects for men of characterizing women in ways which demonstrate their deficits. The acceptance of such gender differences as universal and inevitable ignores the self-fulfilling prophecy in them—that females are selectively and actively discouraged from learning and activities which would develop those "masculine" abilities. This results in what Lipman-Blumen refers to as a "structured ignorance" of the information and abilities which are essential to holding or gaining power.

The incorporation of these beliefs into even relatively modern psychological and social theories such as those of Parsons, Kohlberg, and the sociobiologists has served to entrench a social construction of women as inherently unsuited to positions seen as requiring discipline, control, rational decision making or authority, and thus has sustained the power inequality between the sexes. Some theorists (e.g., Nahem, 1980) have used a Marxist interpretation to show how these theories have contributed to the maintenance of Western capitalism, by justifying the social control of women as an unpaid domestic labor force or exploited servant class. Although there are clear connections between capitalism and the economic subjugation of women, feminist analyses show that the same arguments against women's abilities have been used with equal effect in socialist states, where women are no less disadvantaged (Eichler, 1980; Hubbard, 1983).

While the power inequality of the sexes has begun to ameliorate in some societies, any real change will continue to be impeded by a sustained equation of rationality with the detached, rule-based, empirical, instrumental mode of thinking and reasoning which is associated with men but seen generally as outside of women's capacity, and an insistence that this kind of thinking is both intrinsically superior and essential to positions of power. The connection of a rule-based rationality to power becomes clearer in considering Hare-Mustin and Maracek's (1988: 459) point that "typically those in power advocate rules, discipline, control, and rationality, whereas those without power espouse relatedness and compassion." For those with power, the rules they impose ensure its maintenance; for those without power, relatedness and compassion are essential to their social survival. This differentiation of roles and beliefs, of course, is perfectly self-perpetuating, and sustains the power inequality. Recent reconstructions of the place of women in history shows that the apparently liberating milestones for "mankind"—Greek civilizations, the Renaissance, the French Revolution—invariably rendered women more oppressed. According to Harding (1982: 229–230), "the reduction of women's human progress now appears to have been a necessary condition for, or outcome of . . . the progress of men." The development of the liberal ideology of rational man has played a major part in the deliberate (if not always conscious) disempowerment and control of women, as of other social groups, through the establishment of scientific rationality as orthodox thinking (Deconchy, 1985).

Deconstructing the Rationality Equation

The liberal ideology which equates rationality with logic, objectivity, detachment, and masculinity, rather than with pragma, subjectivity, connectedness and femininity, exemplifies the hitherto accepted hierarchical valorizations and rationalizations which neo-Marxist and postmodern critics have taken it upon themselves to interrupt. The theoretical and philosophical substance of poststructuralism and deconstructivism, and their application to contemporary science and psychology, have been argued soundly elsewhere (e.g., Derrida, 1978; Gergen, 1985: Lather, 1989), and I do not find it necessary to review them here. Rather, I apply them systematically to the associations which constitute what I have called the rationality question.

As a process of critique, deconstruction forces us to self-examine, to uncover ideologies and challenge the bases of their imposition, "to discover what it is we have been incorporated into and what it is we have been unable to ask" (Sholle, 1988: 38, cited in Lather, 1989). The process of deconstructing is not so much a matter of pointing out that the emperor has no clothes on, as it is of systematically stripping him of his outer garments so that we can see the real color of his underpants and how well they fit, and that is what I propose to do with each aspect of the rationality equation. Derrida's approach to the deconstruction exercise involves identifying the binaries or oppositions which are valorized hierarchically in a particular belief or system, reversing the valorization, and observing the effects of that displacement or disordering. A variation of that technique for deconstruction which I introduce here, is to interrupt accepted or taken-for-granted associations and equations, and substitute instead associations which have been perceived hitherto as opposite, contradictory, or inconsistent. The goal, as with all deconstruction, is not to resolve or replace, but simply to explore the effects of disrupting an ideology, to change the perspective from "either/or" to "both/and," and observe the shifts in meaning.

Questioning Rationality as Logical, Analytic, and Objective

The continued assumption that rationality is based ideally and essentially on firm rules of logic, even if its exercise may become polluted or distorted by rationalization or everyday pragmatic consideration of more or less irrelevant information, derives from two arbitrary premises: first, that syllogistic reasoning is based on perfect rules; and second, that adhering to those rules is a purer form of reasoning than taking into account pragmatic associations.

The equation of rationality with logic is authorized by reference to the early Greek philosophers' apparent preference for syllogistic over pragmatic reasoning. However, this perception also is selective, a construction of later philosophers and other interpreters of these ideas. In a recent analysis of the relationship between rationality beliefs, justice, and power, MacIntyre (1988) has pointed out that rationality, itself . . . is a concept with a history; . . . there are *rationalities* . . . rather than rationality" (p. 9, emphasis added), and that while Aristotle's preference as a theorist may have been for syllogistic reasoning, he drew a distinction between theoretical and practical rationality and acknowledged explicitly that practical rationality was superior in personal adaptive terms. Practical rationality, according to Aristotle, required a person to be able both to recognize and to take into account multiple aspects of one's personal and social world, including especially a sound subjective understanding of what is for one's own good within one's own particular social situation. The ability to reason this way required the complex skill of being able to consider all the relevant facets of one's situation, distinguish between one's own good and the common good, and sort through the sundry factors in search of the best personal solution. While it required some syllogistic reasoning ability, it relied primarily on relational thought—an ability to integrate personal, social, and moral factors. Rational facility in these terms was judged by its outcome, by the subjective and social adaptiveness of the person's reasoned solution.

There is nothing intrinsically superior in syllogistic reasoning. Indeed, its own weakness lies in the inevitability of subjective bias in the construction of initial premises, as demonstrated in the ultimately arbitrary equation of rationality with logic. In this sense the concept of rationality is prone to infinite regress, and not capable of final definition. In using the rules of logic it is first necessary to form premises which are adaptive and relevant to the reasoning person, so that subjectivity cannot be avoided entirely, and exclusively syllogistic reasoning is impossible. Rational thinking, then, whether in everyday behavior or in science, not only requires but cannot avoid using several types of reasoning, including relational. Nor should it want to, as it is essentially through inductive rather than deductive reasoning that novel ideas, interpretations, and solutions are spawned (Dreyfus and Dreyfus, 1986). However, the power of the ideology of rationality is such that people feel obliged to demonstrate it in order for their reasoning to be accepted as valid. One of the clearest examples of this is in "psych-speak" (Harré, 1985)—the contrived rhetoric which uses a language of impersonality, detachment, objectification, and implied causality and is employed within academic psychology, as in science generally, so that rationalized hunches can masquerade as logical hypothetico-deduction. Analyses from Rom Harré and others (e.g., Latour and Woolgar, 1979) have shown how "retrospective accounts of scientific discoveries are constructed . . . [which] transform formally invalid logical structures (e.g., syllogisms) into formally correct forms by the modification of initial premises" (Harré, 1985: 181). Women also recognize how objectified, unemotional language is used in this way by men when they attempt to prove their points and win disagreements, especially in interpersonal contexts by defining the woman's position as emotional ergo irrational, but their own position as calm objective and therefore rational.

The ultimate impossibility of objectivity in human reasoning or knowledge, whether in scientific endeavor or everyday thought, and the fallacy in adhering to the belief that objectivity is possible, have been so thoroughly substantiated by the sociophilosophical analyses of Polanyi Popper, Kuhn, Feyerabend, Knorr-Cetina, Mulkay, and now dozens of other writers in the area known as the social sciences (see Campbell, 1988, for a full review of these arguments), that I feel no need to add to their demonstrations of the myth of objectivity. Instead I find myself perplexed and disappointed that educators from primary to tertiary levels, including researchers and teachers in psychology, remain either unaware or so unaccepting of the demythologizing of objectivity that it is still being held up as the ideal, and subjectivity disparaged and disapproved. Perhaps the most pertinent example, in psychology as a discipline, of the almost pathological scepticism with which subjectivity is regarded and objectivity idealized, is seen in the sustained rejection, or at best suspicion, which continues to be directed toward feminist research methods by those whom Ken Gergen (1988, personal communication) has called the "card-carrying empiricists" within academic and university psychology. Research which incorporates and even embraces objectivity within its method frequently is criticized by thesis supervisors, external examiners, journal reviewers, and even colleagues, as insufficiently objective and therefore unscientific and of dubious validity. Thus, as Maria Mies (1983) has pointed out, feminist researchers are faced constantly with the dilemma of either conforming to the required standards of the discipline so that their work can be recognized within their field through the usual process of publication, and in doing so compromising their subjective realities, or retaining their integrity at the expense of undertaking or describing research in ways which are meaningful to them. This issue has been dealt with now by many other feminist psychologists (e.g., Fee, 1983; Wilkinson, 1986) and is probably personally familiar in the experience many people reading this chapter!

Questioning Rationality as Masculine

By removing the constraining equation of rationality with "pure" objective logic, and seeing rationality instead as essentially pragmatic, it is possible to consider what comprises rational thinking and behavior if we interpret them as incorporating any response which is aimed at personally and socially functional problem-solving. If we look at pragmatic behavior within the context of power inequality between the sexes, rational responses become those which allow women to maximize both self-protection and whatever power they do legitimately have available within their subordinated situation. Thus rational behavior for women as a less powerful social group means, for example, internalizing the greater sensitivity to nonverbal behavior and other contextual cues (Henley, 1977) which they have developed as a necessary part of avoiding antagonizing those with power, and using it with a high degree of efficiency and automaticity—that is, being "intuitive." It means continuing to adopt a nurturing role toward men as their economic providers, while at the same time using their ascribed attributes as sources of power to optimize their personal status—that is, being "expressive" and "manipulative." It also means sometimes expressing the inevitable frustrations of being denied advantages automatically accorded to men—that is, being "emotional," or "given to irrational outbursts." And as the primary nurturers of both men and children, and of themselves, it means having to consider a multiplicity of perspectives and trying to make fair allocations where that is realistically impossible—that is, being "changeable" and "inconsistent."

All of these characteristics, stereotypically applied to women, are also those which have been used to disparage other oppressed minorities, rationalize their inferiority, and justify their subordination. For example, the messianic and revolutionary movements of minority ethnic groups such as the Maori in New Zealand and the Mau Mau in Africa were attributed to their innate characteristics of spirituality, emotionality, "native cunning" and deficits in logical analytical ability, rather than being understood as an adaptive response to oppressive colonization. Similar victim-blaming interpretations have disparaged homosexuals and transsexuals as given to effeminate temperamentality and hysterical behavior (Stoltenberg, 1989) and it is only in relatively recent years that psychotic behavior has been interpreted as a functional response to a personally intolerable social context (e.g., Chesler, 1972; Nahem, 1980). Reinterpreted in the context of power inequality, then, women's ways of knowing, reasoning, and acting can be seen as entirely rational/adaptive responses to their disempowerment.

Rationality, Relationality, and Subjectivity

Sandra Harding (1982), in her cogent argument for a reconstruction of rationality to incorporate relationality, points out that logics are norms. Like all standards, these norms are ultimately arbitrary, and their idealness is imposed. Neither logic nor rationality can be assumed always to provide the most adaptive solutions to particular situations. Sylvia Scribner's (1978) research with so-called primitive peoples shows quite clearly that people very often *choose* not to think logically, because to do so would be irrational and could even produce wrong answers and bad solutions; that is, it is not that some people lack the ability to reason syllogistically, but that it is not pragmatic to do so in terms of outcomes. This same motive for rejecting both logic and rationality has been recognized in the pragmatic and adaptive reactions of psychiatrically distressed people attempting to cope with oppressive psychiatric treatment (e.g., Brown, 1976). However, we have to look no further than our own day-to-day decisions and rationalizations, for example, in relation to our decisions about food, personal spending, or whom we choose to live with and why, to see that pragma, rather than logic, is an important part of the reasoning and problem-solving of our so-called civilized selves as well.

There is an evident analogy from pragmatic versus syllogistic rationalities to the distinction between social intelligence (pragmatic, adaptive), which we use for much or even most of our ordinary reasoning and intellectual capacity (logical, analytic), which we tend to use only for novel or especially difficult decisions (Langer, 1978). What I am arguing here is that human behavior and thought cannot be judged as rational or otherwise by considering it out of its entire sociocultural context. Because of the apparently infinite human capacity for both creativity and perversity, our social, economic, and political relations are inevitably complex, even messy. However, these complexities are ignored at our peril, and it is in fact irrational to *not* take both subjective and contextual factors into account in our social reasoning. The attractiveness of a rule-based logic lies in its simplicity—logical deduction is orderly, tidy, clean. But it results too easily in simplistic decisions which can be disastrous in their consequences, witness the rationalized decision making which spawned catastrophes such as the Jewish genocide during World War II (Sabini and Silver, 1982), the Bay of Pigs invasion (Janis, 1982), the infamous syphilis studies (Brandt, 1978), and a now rampant technology which has long since outstripped the ability of men to use it wisely in the interests of humanity today, let alone in our world's very uncertain future. The reframing of rationality is not merely a gender issue; it has consequences for our global future.

At the level of personal and interpersonal gender behavior, it is becoming vital that rationality be recognized as incorporating rationality and subjectivity. For example, the changing economic status of women is allowing more of us the freedom to reject traditional heterosexual relationships, either temporarily or permanently, when men refuse to give recognition to women's ways of thinking and knowing. This in turn leaves men confused and perplexed about what is expected of them, and more generally dissatisfied with their own inability to think subjectively and relationally when they suddenly need to in order to form non-heterosexual social supports or come to terms with their anger or grief at being left (Marriott, 1988; Miller, 1983). Denied the opportunity in childhood and adulthood to develop subjective and connected ways of thinking, men are being forced in the 1980s to develop those skills not only in their private relations, but also in their public and business lives as moral/ethical accountability becomes a major social issue of the era (Steinem, 1985). An overly rigid gender differentiation, together with the masculine imperative of separating thought and feeling, has served both women and men badly because of a compulsory gender identification which is functional for neither sex in contemporary society (e.g., Kimmel, 1987; Pleck, 1987).

Some feminists believe that it is not possible for the social status of women to improve without necessarily detracting from that of men (e.g., French, 1985). However, I would argue that one change from which both sexes may benefit is the reframing of rationality to include multiple understandings of what constitutes rational thinking, so that in both scientific and social realms it is not confined to the instrumental, analytic reasoning characterized as masculine, but also recognizes contextuality, pragma, culture and the artificiality of separating thought from feeling.

Reframing Rationality

My main objective in this chapter has been to show the need for a reframing of what we understand as rationality so as to include diverse styles of reasoning which are variously functional within particular cultures (in the broadest sense of that word, and including, for example, the worlds of women and of scientists as cultures) or for particular purposes. An alternative to reframing rationality per se would be to look for a different term altogether to describe women's ways of reasoning. For example, Harding talks about "female" rationality; other writers have referred to "women's intuition" and "women's ways of knowing" (Belenky et al., 1986; Lipman-Blumen, 1984). However, I do not believe that this approach is useful or viable, for several related reasons. First, rationality has the status of ideology, entrenched over centuries; the word as a part of our everyday language connoting the superior way of thinking would be strongly resistant to change or competition. Second, as I have argued throughout this chapter, it is plainly counterproductive to perpetuate the notion of either a gender dichotomy or a female deficit in rationality, as would certainly happen if we were to label differently what is seen currently as women's preferred style of thinking. Third, it is inaccurate and likewise counterproductive to suggest in any way that women all, only, or always reason in subjective and relational ways. Women are perfectly capable of using logical forms of reasoning when they see it as the most suitable mode for problem-solving (Gilligan, 1982; Keller, 1985). And finally, history has shown repeatedly that when anything is labeled as female or associated with women it is almost invariably dismissed or considered in some way inferior or second-rate, often by both sexes (Cline and Spender, 1987; Lipman-Blumen, 1984). For example, Lipman-Blumen (1984) argues that the reason why women have not tried to capitalize more on the value of women's intuition as a weapon in their struggle for social power is simply that, along with men, we still acknowledge the preferred status of rational, analytical, scientific thought and see intuitive understanding as only a secondary source of knowledge. If we are not to remain "subjugated knowers" (Foucault, 1980, cited in Todd and Fisher, 1988), it is essential that women work actively to reshape conceptualizations of rational thinking. Inevitably there is going to be resistance to this change process from people whose positive social identity rests on their belief that they are privy to ways of thinking and knowing which are superior to those of other groups in society (Tajfel and Turner, 1979).

Harding (1982: 235) has argued that women and men have very different rationalities: for women, the rational person "values highly her abilities to emphasize and 'connect' with particular others and wants to learn more complex and satisfying ways to take the role of the particular other in relationships"; for men, the rational person "values highly his ability to separate himself from others and to make decisions independent of what others think . . [and] to take the role of the generalized other." Harding believes that this causes men and women to feel alienated from each other's ways of thinking, and thus the antipathy self-perpetuates. While I agree with

Harding that the gender differences she describes exist, I see them as a tendency rather than a dichotomy, and as closely linked to traditional gender role differentiation. As these roles are beginning to change and merge in our societies, so the sexes are learning that different ways of reasoning are appropriate to different roles, contexts, and decisions. Perhaps as part of this blending of roles, there is an apparent movement toward the recognition among men also that relational thinking and "human intuition" are essential to human progress and survival, and to the avoidance of mindless errors in an era where simplistic, inhuman computer logic is too often given credence over ordinary common sense (Dreyfus and Dreyfus, 1986).

Ironically it may only be as men themselves begin to criticize overly rational and analytical approaches to problem-solving and decision making, to recognize the absence of absolutes and the real "fuzziness" of logic (e.g., Zadeh, 1975), and to acknowledge openly the value of connected, subjective thinking (e.g., de Bono, 1953; Dreyfus and Dreyfus, 1986), that these latter styles will become accepted finally as credible and valid. Nonetheless the progress is welcome, and it is important now for psychologists to assist this progress.

An implicit objective of psychological research and theory is the betterment of the human condition, and many psychologists are now recognizing explicitly the part our discipline has played in the shaping of dominant and oppressive ideologies and social structures through the promulgation of particular theories (e.g., Eichler, 1980; Murphy et al., 1984; Sampson, 1986; Wexler, 1983). It is incumbent now on academic psychologists to recognize the myths, values, and social norms which have shaped the ideology of rationality as objective logic, both within our discipline and beyond, and to defuse those which are destructive and oppressive. This means reexamining previous research and theory, especially in areas of social and general cognition, for inherent gender bias, acknowledging the social and political consequences of such theories and interpretations, and being more honest about declaring publicly the invalidity or limitations of those theories which have achieved public popularity and influence (see Murphy et al., 1984). We also need to formulate new theories which will help to promote a truly liberal comprehension of rationality to include subjective and common sense reasoning as well as cultural diversity, and which will also reduce the trivialization and ridicule of women's ways of knowing.

Personal Note

For me, perhaps the most poignant demonstration of my arguments in this chapter has emerged through the process of composing them. Socialized into a need to give "objective" credibility to my reasoning—to justify ideas which, as a person, I "know" from my own experiences over four decades, and from those of other people who have been part of my life—I have felt it necessary in this text to refer to women impersonally as "they" rather than use the subjective "we"; to meticulously cite others' arguments as "authority" in support of my points; to use tight, rationally structured arguments; and to refer for ultimate authority and support to the male philosophers of ancient (and androcentric) regimes, rather than to rely simply on the brilliant and sensible arguments for contemporary women philosophers and theorist.

I wish to express my thanks to my friend and colleague Kathryn McPhillips for her valuable criticism of an earlier draft and for her support.

References

Belenky, M. F., Clinchy, B. M. Goldberger, N. R. and Tarule, J. M. (1986) *Women's Ways of Knowing: Development of Self, Voice and Mind.* New York: Basic Books.

Bem, S. (1974) "The Measurement of Psychological Androgyny," *Journal of Clinical and Counselling Psychology* 422: 155–162.

Brandt, A. (1978) "Racism and Research: The Case of the Tuskegee Syphilis Study," *The Hasting Center Report* (Dec.): 21–29.

Broverman, I. K., Broverman, D. M., Clarkson, F. E., Rosenkrantz, P. and Vogel, S. R. (1970) "Sex Role Sterotypes and Clinical Judgments of Mental Health," *Journal of Consulting Psychology* 34: 1–7.

Brown, R. (1976) "Psychosis and Irrationality," in S. I. Benn and G. W. Mortimore (eds.) *Rationality and the Social Sciences*. London: Routledge & Kegan Paul.

Brown, M. and O'Connor, A. (1984) *Woman Talk: A Woman's Book of Quotes*. London: Macdonald.

Bruner, J. S., Goodnow, J. and Austin, G. A. (1956) *A Study of Thinking*. New York: Wiley.

Campbell, D. T. (1988) *Methodology and Epistemology for Social Science*. Chicago: University of Chicago Press.

Chesler, P. (1972) *Women and Madness*. New York: Doubleday.

Chodorow, N. (1982) *The Reproduction of Mothering*. Berkeley: University of California Press.

Cline, S. and Spender, D. (1987) *Reflecting Men at Twice Their Natural Size*. London: Andre Deutsch.

Dalton, K. (1978) *Once a Month*. Glasgow: Fontana Paperbacks.

de Bono, E. (1953) *Lateral Thinking: A Textbook of Creativity*. Harmondsworth: Penguin.

Deconchy, J-P. (1985) "Rationality and Social Control in Orthodox Systems," in H. Tajfel (ed.) *The Social Dimension*, chapter 21. Cambridge: Cambride University Press.

Derrida, J. (1978) "Structure, Sign and Play in the Discourse of the Human Sciences," in J. Derrida (ed.) *Writing and Difference*. Translated by A. Bass. Chicago: University of Chicago Press.

Dollard J. and Miller, N. E. (1950) *Personality and Psychotherapy*. New York: McGraw-Hill.

Dreyfus, H. L. and Dreyfus, S. E. (1986) *Mind over Machine: The Power of Human Intuition and Expertise in the Era of the Computer*. New York: Free Press.

Edel, A. (1982) *Aristotle and His Philosophy*. Chapel Hill: University of North Carolina Press.

Ehrenreich, B. and English, D. (1979) *For Her Own Good: 150 Years of Experts' Advice to Women*. Garden City, NY: Anchor Books.

Eichler, M. (1980) *The Double Standard*. London: Croom Helm.

Ellis, A. (1959) "Rationalism and Its Therapeutic Applications," *Annual Psychotherapy*, 1: 55–64.

Fee, E. (1983) "Women's Nature and Scientific Objectivity," in M. Lower and R. Hubbard (eds.) *Woman's Nature: Rationlizations of Inequality*. New York: Pergamon Press.

Foucault, M. (1984) "What Is Enlightenment?" in P. Rabinow (ed.) *The Foucault Reader*. New York: Pantheon.

French, M. (1985) *Beyond Power: Women, Men and Morals*. New York: Ballantyne.

Freidan, B. (1963) *The Feminine Mystique*. Harmondsworth: Penguin.

Gergen, K. (1985) "The Social Constructionist Movement in Modern Psychology," *American Psychologist* 40: 166–175.

Gilligan, C. (1982) *In a Different Voice: Psychological Theory and Women's Development*. Cambridge, MA: Harvard University Press.

Gould, S. J. (1971) *The Rational Society*. London: Athlone Press.

Harding, S. (1982) "Is Gender a Variable in Conceptions of Rationality? A Survey of Issues," *Dialectica* 36: 225–242.

Hare-Mustin, R. (1983) "An Appraisal of the Relationship between Women and Psychotherapy: 80 Years after the Case of Dora," *American Psychologist* 38: 593–601.

Hare-Mustin, R. and Maracek, J. (1988) "The Meaning of Difference: Gender Theory, Postmodernism, and Psychology," *American Pyschologist* 43: 455–464.

Harré, R. (1985) "Situational Rhetoric and Self-presentation," in J. Forgas (ed.) *Language and Social Situations*, chapter 10. New York: Springer-Verlag.

Henle, M. (1962) "On the Relation between Logic and Thinking," *Psychological Review* 69: 366–378.

Henley, N. M. (1977) *Body Politics: Power, Sex, and Non-verbal Communication*. Englewood Cliffs, NJ: Prentice-Hall.

Hubbard, R. (1983) "Social Effects of Some Contemporary Myths about Women," in M. Lowe and R. Hubbard (eds.) *Women's Nature*. New York: Pergamon.

Huici, C. (1985) "The Individual and Social Functions of Sex-role Stereotypes," in H. Tajfel (ed.) *The Social Dimension*, chapter 28. Cambridge: Cambridge University Press.

Janis, I. L. (1982) *Groupthink: Psychological Studies of Policy Decisions and Fiascoes.* Boston: Houghton Mifflin.

Keller, E. F. (1985) *Reflections on Gender and Science.* New Haven, CT: Yale University Press.

Kimmel, M. S. (1987) "Rethinking 'Masculinity': New Directions in Research," in M. S. Kimmel (ed.) *Changing Men.* Newbury Park, CA: Sage.

Langer, E. (1978) "Rethinking the Role of Thought in Social Interaction," in J. Harvey, W. Ickes and R. Kidd (eds.) *New Directions in Attribution Research,* Volume 20, Hillsdale, NJ: Erlbaum.

Lather, P. (1989) "Deconstructing/Deconstructive Inquiry: The Politics of Knowing and Being Known," Paper presented at the American Educational Research Association Annual Conference, San Francisco, California, March 1989.

Latour, B. and Woolgar, S. (1979) *Laboratory Life.* Newbury Park, CA: Sage.

Lefford, A. (1946) "The Influence of Emotional Subject Matter on Logical Reasoning," *Journal of General Psychology* 34: 127–151.

Lengermann, P. M. and Wallace, R. A. (1985) *Gender in America: Social Control and Social Change.* Englewood Cliffs, NJ: Prentice-Hall.

Letwin, O. (1987) *Ethics, Emotion, and the Unity of the Self.* New York: Croom Helm.

Lipman-Blumen, J. (1984) *Gender Roles and Power.* Englewood Cliffs, NJ: Prentice-Hall.

MacIntyre, A. D. (1988) *Whose Justice? Which Rationality?* Notre Dame, IN: University of Notre Dame Press.

Marriott, A. (1988) *The Prance of Men . . . and a Process for Change.* Christchurch, NZ: Hazard Press.

Middleton, S. (1984) "Sex Role Stereotyping: A Critique," *New Zealand Journal of Women's Studies* 1: 65–74.

Mies, M. (1983) "Towards a Methodology for Feminist Research," in G. Bowles and R. Duelli Klein (eds.) *Theories of Women's Studies.* London: Routledge & Kegan Paul.

Mill, J. S. (1874) *A System of Logic,* 8th edition. New York: Harper.

Miller, S. (1983) *Men and Friendship.* London: Gateway Books.

Morgan, J. J. B. and Morton, J. T. (1944) "The Distortion of Syllogistic Reasoning Produced by Personal Conviction," *Journal of Social Psychiatry* 20: 39–59.

Murphy, J., John, M. and Brown, H. (1984) *Dialogues and Debates in Social Psychology.* London: Erlbaum.

Nahem, J. (1980) *Psychology and Psychiatry Today: A Marxist View.* New York: International Publishers.

Nisbett, R. E. and Ross, L. (1980) *Human Inference: Strategies and Shortcomings of Social Judgment.* Englewood Cliff, NJ: Prentice-Hall.

Pleck, J. (1987) "The Theory of Male Sex-Role Identity: Its Rise and Fall, 1936 to the Present," in H. Brod (ed.) *The Making of Masculinities.* Boston, MA: Allen & Unwin.

Rosenkrantz, P., DeLorey, C. and Broverman, I. (1985) "One Half a Generation Later: Sex Role Stereotypes Revisited." Paper presented at the Annual Convention of the American Psychological Association, Los Angeles, August 1985.

Rosenkrantz, P., Vogel, S., Bee, H., Broverman, I. and Broverman, D. (1968) "Sex-role Stereotypes and Self-concepts in College Students." *Journal of Consulting and Clinical Psychology* 32: 287–295.

Sabini, J. and Silver, M. (1982) "On Destroying the Innocent with a Clear Conscience: A Soci-Psychology of the Holocaust," in J. Sabini and M. Silver (eds.) *Moralities of Everyday Life*. Oxford: Oxford University Press.

Sampson, E. E. (1986) "Justice Ideology and Social Legitimation," in H. W. Bierhoff, R. L. Cohen and J. Greenberg (eds.) *Justice in Social Relations*. New York: Plenum.

Schiller. F. C. S. (1930) *Logic for Use*. New York: Harcourt, Brace.

Scribner, S. (1978) "Modes of Thinking and Ways of Speaking: Culture and Logic Reconsidered," in P. N. Johnson-Laird and P. C. Wason (eds.) *Thinking: Readings in Cognitive Science*. Cambridge: Cambridge University Press.

Steinem, G. (1985) "Is a Feminist Ethic the Answer?" Ms. *Magazine* (May): 35–38.

Stoltenberg, J. (1989) *Refusing to be a Man: Essays on Sex and Justice*. Harmondsworth: Penguin.

Tajfel, H. and Turner, J. (1979) "An Integrative Theory of Intergroup Conflict," in W. G. Austin and S. Worchel (eds.) *The Social Psychology of Intergroup Relations*. Monterey, CA: Brooks/Cole.

Theriot, N. M. (1988) *The Biosocial Construction of Femininity*. New York: Greenwood.

Todd, A. D. and Fisher, S. (1988) *Gender and Discourse: The Power of Talk*. Norwood, NJ: Ablex Publishing.

Wallston, B. S. and Grady, K. E. (1985) "Interating the Feminist Critique and the Crisis in Social Psychology: Another Look at Research Methods," in V. E. O'Leary, R. K. Unger and B. S. Walston (eds.) *Women, Gender and Social Psychology*. Hillsdale, NJ: Erlbaum.

Wexler, P. (1983) *Critical Social Psychology*. Boston: Routledge & Kegan Paul.

White, P. (1984) "A Model of the Layperson as Pragmatist," *Personality and Social Psychology Bulletin* 10: 333–348.

Widiger, T. A. and Settle, S. A. (1987) "Broverman et al. Revisited: An Artifactual Sex Bias," *Journal of Personality and Social Sychology* 53: 463–469.

Wilkinson, S. (1986) "Sighting Possibilities: Diversity and Commonality in Feminist Research," in S. Wilkinson (ed.) *Feminist Social Psychology*. Milton Keynes: Open University Press.

Wilson, E. O. (1975) Sociobiology: *The New Synthesis*. Cambridge, MA: Harvard University Press.

Zadeh, L. A., ed. (1975) *Fuzzy Sets and Their Applications to Cognition and Decision Processes*. New York: Academic.

Index

~

About the Contributors

Rachel Joffe Falmagne is professor of psychology and former director of Women's Studies at Clark University. Her interests draw from feminist theory, critical psychology, and epistemology and have been informed also by philosophy of logic. Her recent publications include *Mind and Social Practice: Selected Writings by Sylvia Scribner* (Cambridge University Press, 1997) and articles and chapters on the gendered foundations of culture; the dialectic of discursive, material, and agentic constituents of subjectivity and thought; feminist approaches to reasoning; critical epistemological and methodological issues for the social sciences.

Carroll Guen Hart has, for many years been fascinated by the connections between John Dewey's logic and his commitment to the making of wise public judgments. She is currently adapting this interest to her involvement in the structuring of public dispute resolution and fostering active citizenship. She lives in Toronto where she is involved with a social housing agency.

Marjorie Hass is associate professor of philosophy at Muhlenberg College. She has published articles on topics in philosophy of language and philosophy of logic. Hass has won awards for her teaching at the University of Illinois and Muhlenberg College.

Marie-Geneviève Iselin is a Ph.D. candidate in clinical psychology at Clark University. She obtained her master's degree in psychology at the New School for Social Research in New York after receiving a master's degree in philosophy at the University of Geneva, Switzerland. Her research interests include laypeople's beliefs about causes and treatments for depression, deductive reasoning in everyday situations, male bariatric patients' discursive identity constructions, and qualitative methodological issues.

Jack Nelson is vice chancellor for academic affairs at the University of Washington, Tacoma. He is the author (with Lynn Hankinson Nelson) of *On Quine* (Wadsworth, 1999) and (with Merrie Bergman and James Moor) of *The Logic Book* (McGraw-Hill, 1980). He is currently working on *Reconstituting Empiricism: The Project and Legacy of W. V. Quine* with Lynn Hankinson Nelson.

Lynn Hankinson Nelson is professor of philosophy at the University of Missouri, St. Louis, and visiting professor at the University of Puget Sound. She is the author of *Who Knows: From Quine to a Feminist Empiricism* (Temple University Press, 1992) and (with Jack Nelson) *On Quine* (Wadsworth, 1999). She is currently working with Jack Nelson on *Reconstituting Empiricism: The Project and Legacy of W. V. Quine.*

Andrea Nye is professor emeritus of philosophy at the University of Wisconsin–Whitewater. She is currently lecturer at the University of Massachusetts–Boston. Her published books include *Words of Power: A Feminist Reading of the History of Logic* (Routledge, 1990) and, as editor, *Philosophy of Language: The Big Questions* (Blackwell, 1998), a reader for use in philosophy of language courses that includes multicultural and feminist selections as well as historical and analytic perspectives.

Pam Oliver was raised in rural and provincial New Zealand in the 1950s and has lived much of her adult life in Australia and other Pacific nations. She spends most of her time between New Zealand and the Solomon Islands. She has worked variously in grassroots social services, university teaching, and, most recently, social services evaluation, specializing in work concerning the Maori (New Zealand's indigenous people).

Dorothea E. Olkowski is professor and cochair in the Department of Philosophy at the University of Colorado, Colorado Springs, where she was formerly director of women's studies. Her recent publications include *Resistance,*

Flight, Creation: Feminist Enactments of French Philosophy (Cornell University Press, 2000) and *Gilles Deleuze and the Ruin of Representation* (University of California Press, 1999). She is coeditor with Gail Weiss of *Feminist Interpretations of Merleau-Ponty* (Penn State Press, forthcoming).

Val Plumwood is Australian Research Council Fellow at the University of Sydney. Her books and other publications include *Feminism and the Mastery of Nature* (Routledge, 1993) and *Environmental Culture: The Ecological Crisis of Reason* (Routledge, 2001). She was trained initially in logic and analytical philosophy, developing her interests in feminist and ecological philosophy in the 1970s. Plumwood believes in integrating logical insights into her social and ecological philosophy but warns that logic (and analytical philosophy) is a good servant but a poor master.